AQA Spanish

GCSE

John Halksworth
Ana Kolkowska
Libby Mitchell
Fiona Wilson

Nelson Thornes

Published in 2009 by:
Nelson Thornes Ltd
Delta Place
27 Bath Road
CHELTENHAM
GL53 7TH
United Kingdom

13 14 15 16 / 10 9 8 7 6

A catalogue record for this book is available from the British Library

ISBN 978 1 4085 0430 7

Cover photograph Photolibrary / Digital Vision
Illustrations by Kathy Baxendale, Dylan Gibson, Mark Draisey and Celia Hart
Page make-up by eMC Design, www.emcdesign.org

Printed in China

Contents

Context 2 – Leisure

Context 3 – Home and environment

Context 4 – Work and education

Nelson Thornes has worked hard to ensure this book and the accompanying online resources offer you support for your GCSE course. You can feel assured that they match the specification for this subject.

These print and online resources together **unlock blended learning**; this means that the links between the activities in the book and the activities online blend together to maximise your understanding of a topic and help you achieve your potential.

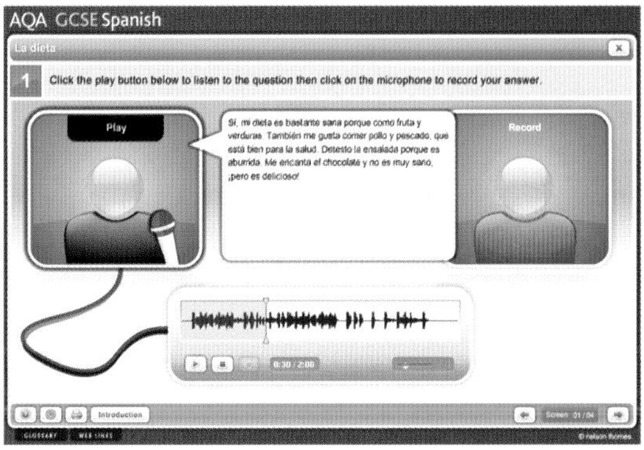

These online resources are available on kerboodle which can be accessed via the internet at www.kerboodle.com/live, anytime, anywhere. If your school or college subscribes to kerboodle you will be provided with your own personal login details. Once logged in, access your course and locate the required activity.

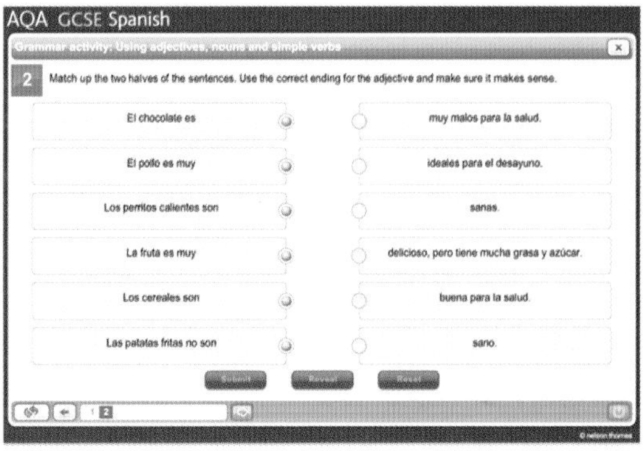

For more information and help on how to use kerboodle visit www.kerboodle.com

How to use this book

Objetivos

Look for the list of **Objetivos** based on the requirements of this course.

Study tip

Don't forget to read the **Study tips** which accompany the Controlled Assessment sample tasks. **Practice questions** are also available online.

Visit www.nelsonthornes.com for more information.

GCSE Spanish

How to use this book

- The book is split into four sections, one for each Context of the specification.
- Each Context is split into two Topics.
- The Topics are divided into sub-topics which fit the Purposes of the specification.

At the beginning of each Context you will find the sub-topics, grammar and communication strategies listed, so you can see how the content you are learning matches the GCSE specifications.

The features in this book include:

Reading icon – you can listen to the reading texts in your book on kerboodle, so you can hear the language spoken by native speakers as you read it. Interactive reading activities are also available.

Listening icon – audio material for listening and/or reading activities is online. Interactive listening activities are available on kerboodle.

Video icon – videos can be found online to support listening activities, with further interactive activities also available on kerboodle.

Speaking icon – an activity designed to practise speaking skills. Worksheets for further practice are also available on kerboodle.

Writing icon – an activity designed to practise writing skills. Worksheets for further practice are available on kerboodle.

Estrategia – outlines different strategies you can employ to help you communicate effectively. The strategy box includes the icon of the activity it supports: Listening, Reading, Speaking or Writing.

Strategy icon – When this icon appears next to an activity, you should use the communication strategy introduced in the strategy box on that page to complete the task.

Consejo – provides handy hints which you can use to help you with your language learning.

Gramática – provides a summary of the main grammar point. Further grammar points are also provided here. Go to the pages listed to find activities to practise them.

G Grammar icon – an activity designed to help you practise the grammar point introduced on the page. You will also find interactive grammar practice on kerboodle.

V Vocabulary icon – a vocabulary learning activity. The essential vocabulary used within each Topic is listed on Vocabulary pages. Here you can learn key words for each Topic. You can also go to kerboodle to hear how they sound. Some words are in light grey. This is to indicate that while you do not need to learn them for your Listening and Reading exams, you may still want to use them in your Speaking and Writing Controlled Assessments and to build your overall vocabulary.

Language structure – boxes show you how to construct key sentences designed to help you carry out the Speaking and Writing tasks.

Controlled Assessment – Controlled Assessment tasks are designed to help you learn language which is relevant to the GCSE Topics and Purposes.

These tasks are not designed to test you and you cannot use them as your own Controlled Assessment tasks and submit them to AQA. Although the tasks you complete and submit to AQA may look similar to the tasks in this book, your teacher will not be able to give you as much help with them as we have given with the tasks in this book.

Go to kerboodle to see sample answers.

Study tip

These provide advice to help you with your study and exam preparation.

Resumen – a summary quiz at the end of each Context tests key language and grammar learnt in that Context. This is also available as a multiple-choice quiz, with feedback, on kerboodle.

¿Lo sabes? – an anecdotal insight into facts/figures relating to the Context.

Numbers, ages and days of the week

1 Match up each person with the correct photo.

1 Tengo quince años.
2 Tengo veinte años.
3 Tengo tres años.
4 Tengo ocho años.

A

B

C

D

E

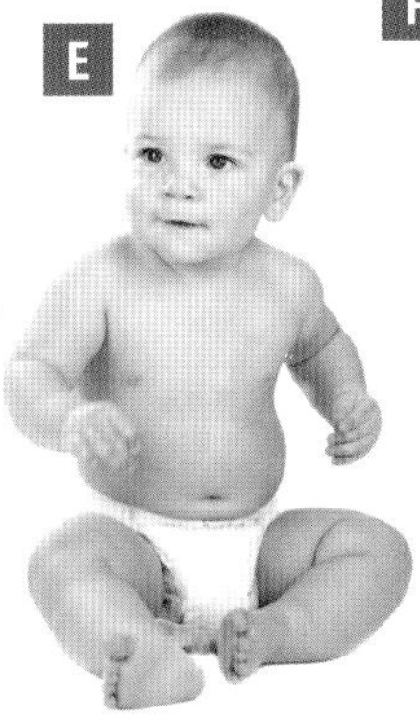

F

Vocabulario

0	*cero*	*11*	*once*
1	*uno*	*12*	*doce*
2	*dos*	*13*	*trece*
3	*tres*	*14*	*catorce*
4	*cuatro*	*15*	*quince*
5	*cinco*	*16*	*dieciséis*
6	*seis*	*17*	*diecisiete*
7	*siete*	*18*	*dieciocho*
8	*ocho*	*19*	*diecinueve*
9	*nueve*	*20*	*veinte*
10	*diez*		

2 Read out the following telephone numbers in Spanish.

Ejemplo: 6–17–10–02–20

seis–diecisiete–diez–cero dos–veinte

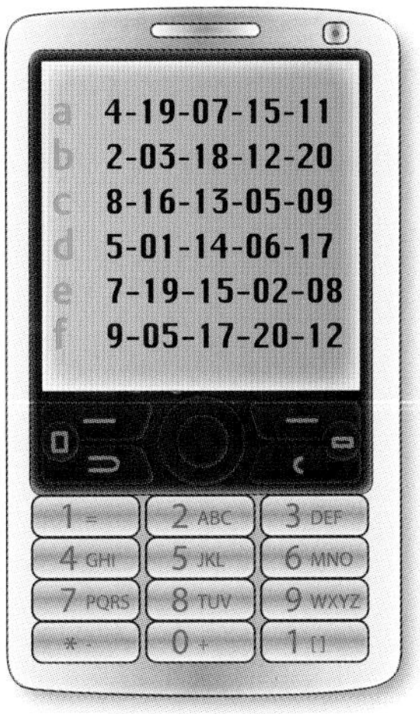

Notice that for telephone numbers you group the numbers into pairs (six–seventeen–ten–zero two–twenty).

3 Put the days of the week into the correct order, starting with Monday.

miércoles sábado lunes
jueves domingo viernes martes

4 Design a programme for a week of activities for a Spanish exchange visit, writing the days (and activities if you can) in Spanish.

Ejemplo: lunes – (excursión a) York … sábado – discoteca

Pronunciation

ce / ci / z = th (as in 'three')
e.g. *cero, diez*

ch = ch (as in 'chair') e.g. *ocho*

h = silent e.g. *hola*

ge / gi / j = sounds like spitting!!
e.g. *junio*

ll = y (as in 'yet') e.g. *me llamo*

qu = k e.g. *quince*

r at beginning of word
or rr = rolled (if you can!)
e.g. *Roberto, perro*

v at beginning of word = b
e.g. *veinte*

Vowels

Keep them short.

a = apple

e = egg

i = feet

o = orange

u = like 'oo'

Gramática

página 194

See page 194 ➡

Months, dates and time

Fechas y celebraciones en Gran Bretaña
El primero de **enero** es un día festivo y una oportunidad para celebrar con la familia.
El catorce de **febrero** es el Día de San Valentín para los novios y parejas enamoradas.
Un domingo en **marzo** es el Día de la Madre.
El primero de **abril** es el Día de los Inocentes.
El primero de **mayo** es el Día del Trabajo.
En **junio** hay el Día del Padre.
En **julio** y **agosto** hay vacaciones escolares.
El cinco de **noviembre** hay fuegos artificiales y una fogata.
Los niños reciben sus regalos de Navidad el veinticinco de **diciembre**.

Vocabulario

el + number + *de* + month
e.g. *el 12 de noviembre*
BUT *el uno / primero de marzo* – the first of March

1 Read the information in the table above and answer the following questions.

1 Which special days that we celebrate in the UK are mentioned?
2 What happens in July and August?
3 Which months are missing?

2 Write a list of birthdays that are important to you. You can write the numbers in figures.

Ejemplo: *Mi cumpleaños es el 22 de abril.*
My birthday is on the 22nd of April.
El cumpleaños de mi (madre) es el 13 de septiembre.
My (mother's) birthday is on the 13th of September.

3 Match up each time mentioned with the correct clock face.

1 Nos vemos a las cinco.

2 La película empieza a la una y media.

3 ¿Qué hora es? Son las seis y cuarto.

4 ¡Rápido! Son las ocho menos cuarto.

5 El tren sale a las diecisiete diez.

6 Nos encontramos a las tres y cinco.

Gramática *página 189*

La hora

las doce

menos cinco  y cinco 

menos diez  y diez 

menos cuarto  y cuarto 

menos veinte  y veinte 

menos veinticinco  y veinticinco 

y media 

son *las (doce)* = it is (12) o'clock
a *las (doce)* = at (12) o'clock
BUT ***es la*** *una* = it is 1 o'clock
a la *una* = at 1 o'clock

24-hour times

13.10 = *a las trece diez*
18.20 = *a las dieciocho veinte*
20.15 = *a las veinte quince*

See page 189

Weather and the seasons

1a Match up each picture with the correct expression in the box.

A B C D E F G H I J

1 hace mal tiempo	3 hay tormenta	6 llueve / está lloviendo	8 hace viento
2 nieva / está nevando	4 hace calor	7 hace frío	9 hace buen tiempo
	5 está nublado		10 hace sol

1b Read sentences a–d and answer questions 1–4 that follow, in English.

a Quería salir a montar en bicicleta pero esta mañana está lloviendo y por eso no puedo ir.

b Íbamos a la costa a practicar la vela pero hay niebla y es peligroso. No vamos a ir.

c Está nevando. Me encanta la nieve. Hace frío pero no me importa.

d Estoy viendo la tele y no pienso salir. Hay tormenta y prefiero quedarme en casa.

1 Why can't Joaquín go cycling this morning?

2 Why is it dangerous for him to go sailing?

3 Why is it cold?

4 Why doesn't he want to go out?

2 Look at the pictures. For each one, write a sentence in the present continuous tense describing the weather and what is happening.

Ejemplo: Está nevando así que estoy viendo la tele.

ver la tele

Vocabulario

la primavera	spring
el verano	summer
el otoño	autumn
el invierno	winter

1 comer un helado

2 tomar el sol

3 comprar un paraguas

4 jugar al tenis

5 hacer un muñeco de nieve

3 Working in pairs, look at the table below. Partner A asks a question about the information in it and Partner B gives the answer. Then swap roles.

¿Qué tiempo hace en Edimburgo en primavera?

Hace viento.

	en primavera	en verano	en otoño	en invierno
en Edimburgo				
en Sevilla		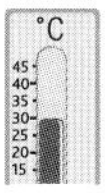		

Gramática página 181

The present continuous tense

The present continuous tense describes something that is happening at the time of speaking.

It is formed by adding the gerund to the present tense of *estar*:

estoy *-ar* habl**ando** (talking)
-er com**iendo** (eating)
-ir sal**iendo** (going out)

¿Qué estás haciendo? What are you doing?

See page 120

kerboodle

Classroom equipment, colours

1a Copy the sentences and fill in the gaps with *el, la, los* or *las*.

1 Cierra ______ puerta, por favor.
2 Abrid el libro y mirad ______ páginas 12 y 13.
3 Primero hay que leer ______ texto.
4 No os olvidéis de hacer ______ deberes.

1b Match up the Spanish sentences 1–4 in Activity 1a with their English translations below.

a First you have to read the text.
b Open the book and look at pages 12 and 13.
c Don't forget to do your homework.
d Close the door, please.

2 Match up each sentence with the correct picture.

1 ¿Puedo ir al lavabo?
2 Siento llegar tarde. Perdí el autobús.
3 No entiendo la pregunta. ¿Podría repetirla, por favor?

3 Look at the pictures. Which box, A or B, does each item 1–8 appear in?

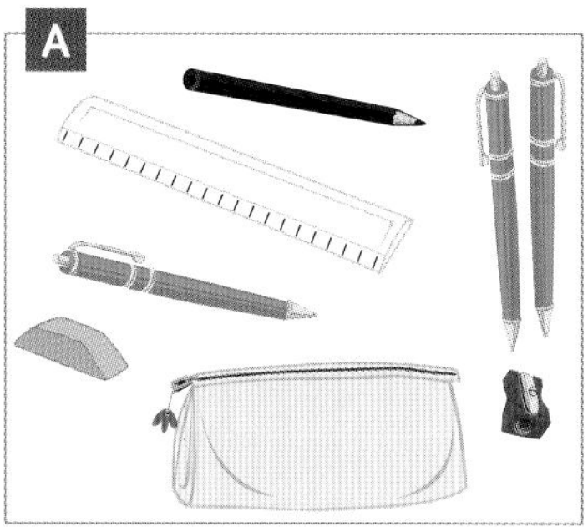

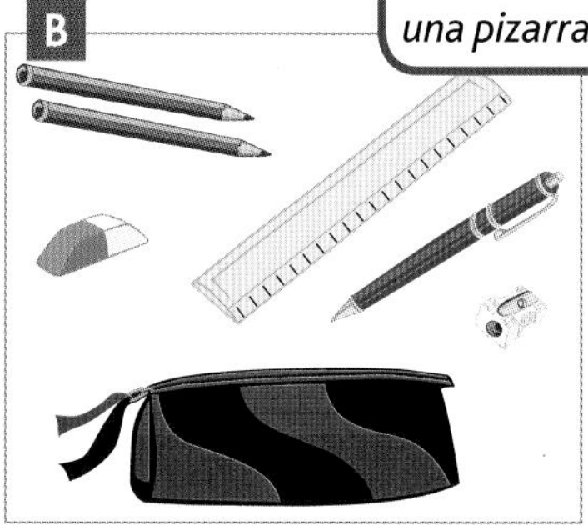

Ejemplo: 1 B

1 un bolígrafo rojo
2 un sacapuntas rojo
3 un estuche negro y rojo
4 una goma verde
5 un estuche amarillo
6 una goma blanca y azul
7 unos lápices grises
8 una regla amarilla

Vocabulario

el aula (f)	classroom
la carpeta	folder
el chicle	chewing gum
el cubo de la basura	rubbish bin
los deberes	homework
el estuche	pencil case
el libro	book
la ficha de trabajo	worksheet
la goma	eraser
la hoja de papel	sheet of paper
los lápices de colores	coloured pencils
el lápiz	pencil
la prueba	test
la regla	rule, ruler
el sacapuntas	pencil sharpener

Articles: *el, la, los, las*

The Spanish word for 'the' agrees with the noun that follows:

el libro – the book | *los libros* – the books
la pizarra – the board | *las pizarras* – the boards

Articles: *un, una, unos, unas*

The words for 'a / an' (singular) and 'some' (plural) also agree with the noun that follows:

un libro – a book | *unos libros* – some books
una pizarra – a board | *unas pizarras* – some boards

Gramática página 174

Colours and agreement of adjectives

Colours are adjectives. They agree with the word they describe: *un estuche amarillo, unos bolígrafos azules, una carpeta negra.*

Learn more about agreement of adjectives.

See page 28

Gramática página 174

All numbers, dates

1 Work in pairs. Partner A writes down six numbers and reads them out. Partner B writes them down. Check the numbers together, then swap roles.

2 Match up the dates.

1 1/11
2 20/8
3 31/12

a el veinte de agosto
b el treinta y uno de diciembre
c el primero de noviembre

Carlota: Mi hermano Sebastián y yo somos gemelos. Yo nací primero, a las 23h52 el siete de julio y él nació a las 00h06 del día siguiente, el día ocho.

Gerardo: La fiesta de mi pueblo se celebra el primer domingo del mes de agosto. Este año cae el día dos pero el año pasado cayó el día uno.

José Carlos: El último día de curso es el 24 de junio. Las clases no empezarán otra vez hasta el tres de septiembre. Me voy de viaje casi todo el mes de agosto, desde el día dos hasta el veintinueve.

3 Read the bubbles and answer the questions in English.

1 a When is Sebastián's birthday?
  b When is Carlota's birthday?
2 a What date is the village festival this year?
  b What date was the village festival last year?
3 a What date does the new school term start?
  b When does José Carlos get back from holiday?

4 Look at the following pictures and dates. Use the words under each picture to write a description of what happens on each date.

Ejemplo: El 22 de septiembre es el cumpleaños de María. Lo celebramos con una tarta.

22/9 celebrar – cumpleaños – tarta

8/4 restaurante – abrir – cena

17/8 vacaciones – avión – Mallorca

Vocabulario

20	*veinte*
21	*veintiuno (veintiuna)*
30	*treinta*
31	*treinta y uno (treinta y una)*
40	*cuarenta*
50	*cincuenta*
60	*sesenta*
70	*setenta*
80	*ochenta*
90	*noventa*
100	*cien, ciento*
101	*ciento uno (ciento una)*
200	*doscientos (doscientas)*
300	*trescientos/as*
400	*cuatrocientos/as*
500	*quinientos/as*
600	*seiscientos/as*
700	*setecientos/as*
800	*ochocientos/as*
900	*novecientos/as*
1000	*mil*
1002	*mil dos*
2000	*dos mil*
5000	*cinco mil*
10,000	*diez mil*
1,000,000	*un millón*
2,000,000	*dos millones*

Gramática

Numbers

Numbers 16 to 29 are written as one word, e.g. *diecisiete.*

For compounds of *ciento* note the spelling of *quinientos*, *setecientos* and *novecientos.*

y is used between the tens and unit digits: 146 *ciento cuarenta y seis.*

The word *mil* is never pluralised in a specific number and is never preceded by *un*: 2012 *dos mil doce.*

But: *Había miles de personas en la plaza de toros.*

The word *millón* is pluralised and is used with *un* in the singular: *un millón, cinco millones.*

Dates

***el** primero / uno **de** agosto*	1st August
***el** dos **de** abril **del** dos mil once*	2nd April 2011

See page 188

página 188

kerboodle

Parts of the body, frequently-used words

1a Read the instructions and match up each set with the correct picture.

1
Movimiento:
Levanta los talones y estira las piernas.
Repite 10 veces.
Atención:
Mantén los brazos y el cuello relajados.

2
Movimiento:
Levanta la pierna derecha flexionada hacia arriba, empujando la pierna hacia atrás.
Repite 6 veces.
Al final de las repeticiones, repite el ejercicio con la otra pierna.
Atención:
No dobles la espalda.

3
Movimiento:
Levanta la cabeza un poco y gira el brazo izquierdo hacia la rodilla derecha.
Repite 5 veces.
Luego repite el ejercicio, girando el brazo derecho hacia la rodilla izquierda.
Atención:
No cruces los dedos detrás de la cabeza. No levantes demasiado la cabeza y la espalda porque es importante evitar tensión en la espalda.

A
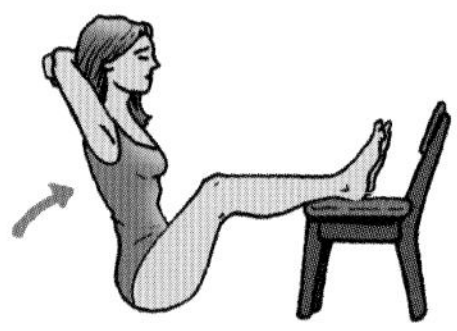

B
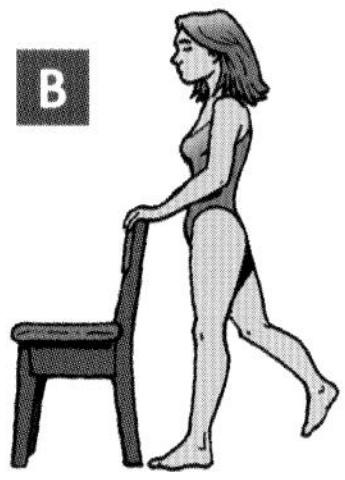

C
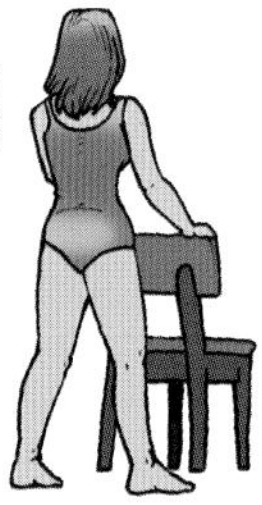

1b Work in pairs. Write down some instructions, using words from the box below. Take turns to give and carry out the instructions. Make up some longer instructions using the joining words in the box.

Dobla / Estira	el brazo	derecho
Levanta / Mueve	el pie	izquierdo
No dobles / No estires	la mano	derecha
No levantes / No muevas	la pierna	izquierda
	la rodilla	
luego / pero / y		

Vocabulario

el cuerpo	body
los brazos	arms
la cabeza	head
el cuello	neck
los dedos	fingers, toes
la espalda	back
las manos	hands
los pies	feet
las rodillas	knees
los talones	heels
los tobillos	ankles
arriba	up
atrás	back
fuera	away
hacia	towards
ponerse de pie	to stand up
luego	then
pero	but
porque	because
y	and

Gramática *página 184*

Imperatives

The activity instructions in the texts on this page use imperatives (commands) in the *tú* form.

Regular verbs:

Levanta *los talones.*
Lift your heels.

No dobles *la espalda.*
Don't bend your back.

To learn more about imperatives

See page 85

1 Lifestyle

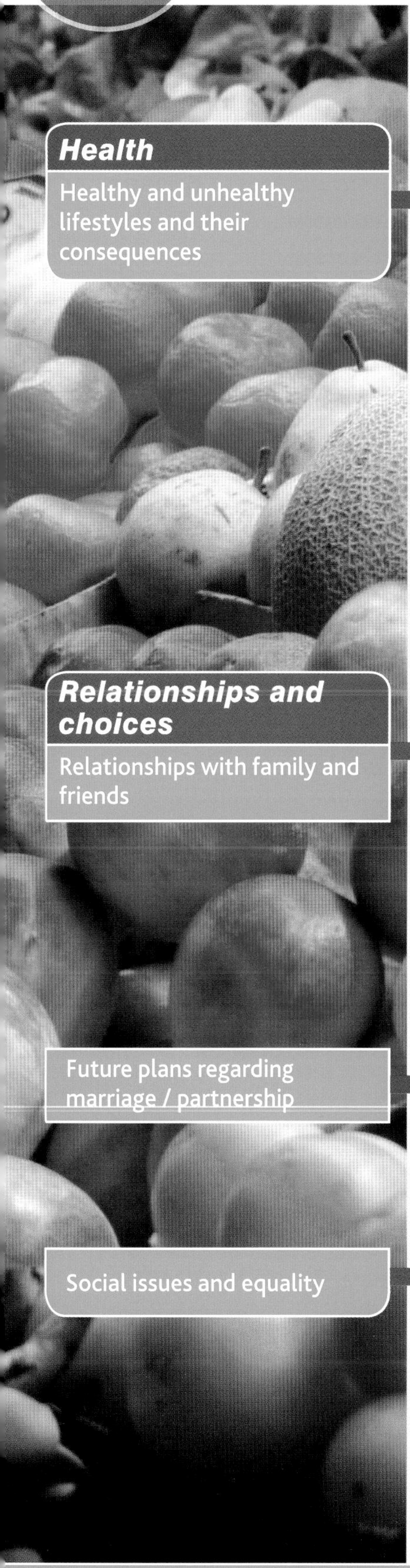

Key Stage 3 Revision

Health
Healthy and unhealthy lifestyles and their consequences

1.1 La dieta
- Making adjectives agree
- Picking out the key words when reading and listening

1.2 El bienestar
- Using verbs with the infinitive
- Testing yourself on meanings of words

1.3 El tabaco
- Using regular *-ar* verbs in the present tense
- Giving opinions

1.4 El alcohol y las drogas
- Making comparisons
- Asking and answering questions in written work

Relationships and choices
Relationships with family and friends

1.5 Las descripciones personales
- Saying 'my, your, his / her, our, their'
- Avoiding being caught out by false friends

1.6 La situación familiar
- Using *estar* + past participle
- Working out the meaning of new words from the context

1.7 Las relaciones personales
- Using reflexive verbs
- Extending phrases in speaking and writing tasks

Future plans regarding marriage / partnership

1.8 Los planes del futuro
- Talking about what you are going to do
- Keeping your conversation going

Social issues and equality

1.9 La igualdad para todos
- Using reflexive phrases like *se puede*
- Checking pronunciation

1.10 La pobreza
- Saying what you have to do or must do
- Ignoring words you don't need to understand

Family, pets

1a Look at the family tree and fill in each gap a–f with the name of the correct family member.

hermanastro **abuelo** **tío** **madre**

primo **prima**

1b Work in pairs. You both make up an imaginary family and write a description of it following this example:

Student A: Mi abuelo se llama Bert, mi abuela se llama Dorothy, mi madre se llama Barbara, mi tío se llama Nigel …

Try to include as many relatives as possible. Student B now has 30 seconds to repeat as much of Student A's description as they can remember. Award a point for each correct piece of information. Then swap roles.

2a Read the poems and work out which three unusual pets are mentioned.

2b Write a description of some real or imaginary pets, including colours, size and character. You could write it as a poem.

2c Read out your description and get a partner to draw it.

Tengo un pez,
Es aburrido.
Quiero un delfín.

Tengo un perro,
Es muy ruidoso.
Quiero un conejo.

Tengo una tortuga,
Es muy lenta.
Quiero una pantera.

Tengo dos gatos,
Son antipáticos.
Quiero periquitos.

Tengo una cobaya,
Es muy nerviosa.
Quiero una leona.

Tengo un pájaro,
No es muy activo.
Quiero un caballo.

Vocabulario

la abuela	grandmother
el abuelo	grandfather
aburrido/a	boring
antipático/a	unpleasant
el caballo	horse
la cobaya	guinea pig
el conejo	rabbit
es	is
el gato	cat
la hermana	sister
la hermanastra	stepsister
el hermano	brother
el hermanastro	stepbrother
lento/a	slow
la madre	mother
el padre	father
el pájaro	bird
el periquito	parakeet
el primo	(male) cousin
la prima	(female) cousin
quiero	I want
son	are
tengo	I have
el tío	uncle
la tía	aunt
la tortuga	tortoise

Food, drink and adverbs

Lucía: Para el desayuno me gustan los cereales y me gusta beber té y café. También me encanta la fruta, por ejemplo me gustan las naranjas. No me gustan mucho las verduras y detesto el pescado.

Eduardo: Para el almuerzo me gusta beber agua mineral y me encantan las patatas fritas y los helados. No me gusta el queso y detesto la ensalada.

Margarita: Para la cena me encanta tomar pollo y perritos calientes. No me gusta nada la sopa.

1 Read what Lucía, Eduardo and Margarita say they like to eat and choose the letters of the correct pictures from the box below. Then find what they don't like to eat.

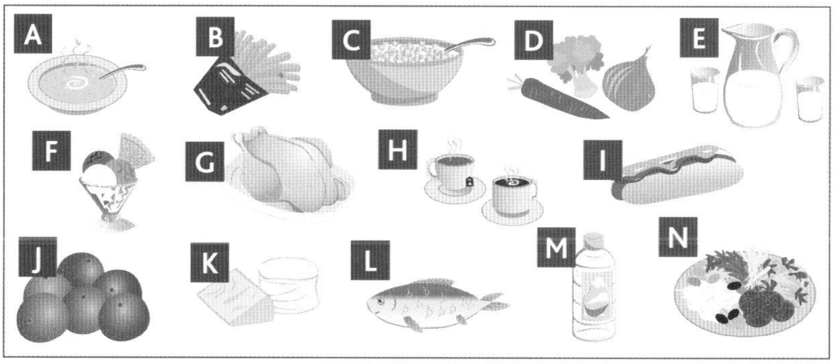

2 Write two lists, saying what you do and don't like to eat and drink.

3 Make up some sentences of your own containing adverbs. Use the suggestions in the grammar box and the list of verbs and adverbs below.

Verbs	Adverbs
hablo – I talk	*rápidamente* – quickly
bailo – I dance	*lentamente* – slowly
canto – I sing	*ruidosamente* – noisily
corro – I run	*bien* – well
como – I eat	*mal* – badly

Vocabulario

el agua (f) mineral	mineral water
el almuerzo	lunch
el bocadillo	sandwich
la cena	evening meal
el desayuno	breakfast
la ensalada	salad
la fruta	fruit
la hamburguesa	hamburger
el helado	ice cream
el jamón	ham
la naranja	orange
el perrito caliente	hot dog
el pescado	fish
el pollo	chicken
el queso	cheese
la sopa	soup
las verduras	green vegetables

Me gusta = I like

Gramática – página 186

me gusta el café I like coffee (literally 'the coffee pleases me')

For something plural, change to *me gustan*

e.g. *me gustan las patatas fritas* I like chips

Adverbs

Gramática – página 177

Adverbs describe **how** you do something.

In English they often end in '-ly', e.g. quickly, slowly, normally.

In Spanish they are often formed by adding *-mente* onto the end of the feminine form of the adjective,

e.g. *rápido* – quick	*rápidamente* – quickly
lento – slow	*lentamente* – slowly

But note:

bueno – good	*bien* – well
malo – bad	*mal* – badly

Objetivos

- Discussing different types of diet
- Making adjectives agree
- Picking out the key words when reading and listening

1.1 La dieta

A Normalmente como hamburguesas, perritos calientes, patatas fritas y pizza todos los días. Me gusta mucho la comida rápida. Mi dieta no es muy sana, pero es barata y deliciosa. También es muy fácil de seguir. Detesto la ensalada, las verduras y todo tipo de fruta. En mi opinión, los vegetarianos son muy raros. Javier

B Mi dieta es muy sana. Como mucho pescado normalmente porque soy vegetariana. El pescado es importante en mi dieta porque contiene proteínas. España es ideal, porque el pescado es muy bueno y hay muchos mariscos. Los mariscos son deliciosos, pero muy caros. Como muchas verduras también – ¡son muy ricas y baratas! Luisa

C Mi dieta es limitada porque no hay supermercados en la selva. Como mucho pescado y mucha fruta. Claro, ¡el pescado y la fruta son muy frescos! Mi plato favorito es el plátano frito y es muy típico aquí. También bebo 'chicha'. La chicha es una bebida alcohólica preparada con yuca (un tipo de patata) y saliva. Para los turistas, la idea es horrible. En mi opinión, es una bebida deliciosa. Elena

D Mi nueva dieta es muy difícil para mí. Para el desayuno tomo cereales con fruta y bebo un zumo de naranja. Para el almuerzo como pescado o pollo con ensalada porque no contienen mucha grasa y son saludables. Bebo agua mineral. Finalmente, para la cena tomo sopa y un yogur. La dieta es aburrida y no me gusta nada. Prefiero comer chorizo, tortilla y tapas, pero contienen mucha grasa y no son saludables. Antonio

1

2

3

4
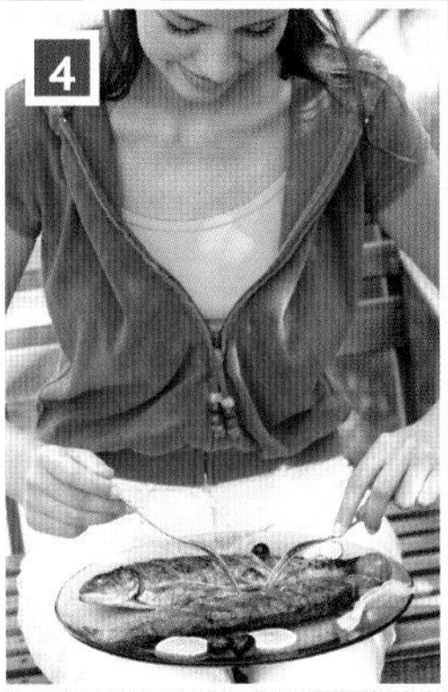

1a Match up each photo with the correct speech bubble. Write the name of the person and 1, 2, 3 or 4.

1b Write the name of the person who …

1. eats salad.
2. eats cheap, unhealthy food.
3. drinks something strange.
4. loves seafood.
5. doesn't like their diet.
6. catches their own fish.
7. likes typical Spanish, non-vegetarian food.

Estrategia

Picking out key words

With a partner, write down as many positive and negative adjectives as you can think of, related to healthy eating, e.g.

bueno …

malo …

But watch out for other words which can change a positive into a negative like: *poco* – not very; *demasiado* – too (much).

El chocolate es poco saludable. – Chocolate is **not very** healthy.

La comida basura es demasiado barata. – Junk food is **too** cheap.

2 Listen to some people talking about their diet. Decide if they eat a healthy diet, an unhealthy diet or both. Write notes in English to back up your answer.

Write H = healthy diet U = unhealthy diet
or H + U = healthy and unhealthy diet.

Ejemplo: Ana U Loves fast food.
Goes to pizza / hamburger places a lot.

1 Carolina 2 Juan 3 María 4 José

3 Ⓖ Copy the sentences and fill in the gaps with the appropriate adjective and ending from the list below.

1 El pescado es _______.
2 Los cereales son _______ para el desayuno.
3 El chorizo es ________, pero tiene mucha grasa.
4 Las patatas fritas son muy _______ para la salud.
5 En México hay muchos platos _______ como chile con carne.
6 La sangría es una bebida muy _______ de España.

delicioso **ideales** **típica** **sano**
picantes **deliciosas** **sanas** **malas**

4 Work in pairs. Take turns to be A and B. It is healthy-eating week at school.

Change the underlined parts to fit the pictures and try to add reasons as to why what is eaten is healthy. Award up to 10 points for being healthy.

A Para el desayuno tomo cereales.

B Los cereales son sanos. ¡Muy bien! ¡Ocho puntos!

A Para la cena como pollo y patatas fritas. No como fruta.

B Las patatas fritas son malas. ¡Un desastre! ¡Tres puntos!

(No) Como	cereales / tostadas / huevos / pollo / pescado / sopa / verduras / patatas fritas	para	el desayuno / el almuerzo / la cena.
(No) Bebo	café / té / leche / agua		
El pollo / El pescado La fruta / La sopa	es contiene / tiene	sano / rico / picante / ideal. sana / rica / picante / ideal. mucha grasa / mucha proteína / mucho azúcar.	
Los cereales / Los huevos Las hamburguesas / Las patatas fritas / Las verduras	son contienen / tienen	sanos / ricos / picantes / ideales. sanas / ricas / picantes / ideales. muchas proteínas / muchas vitaminas.	

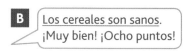

Gramática *página 174*

Making adjectives agree

Adjectives ending in '*o*':

el pescado es sano (masculine)

los cereales son sanos (masculine plural)

la fruta es sana (feminine)

las verduras son sanas (feminine plural)

Other adjectives stay the same for the singular and add '*s*' or '*es*' for the plural.

Some adjectives are irregular, e.g. nationalities. *See page 175* ➡

Also learn more parts of the verb *ser* (to be). *See page 28* ➡

Consejo

Mucho (a lot of) + noun also has to agree:

mucho chocolate (masculine)
mucha tarta (feminine)
muchos pasteles (masculine plural)
muchas galletas (feminine plural)

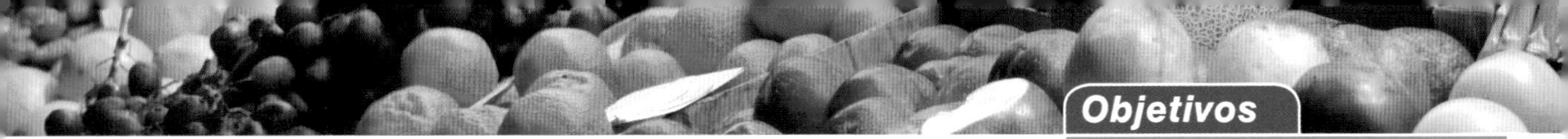

1.2 El bienestar

Objetivos

- Discussing well-being and what can prevent it
- Using verbs with the infinitive
- Testing yourself on meanings of words

1 Ⓥ Choose which statement you agree with most and write down **a**, **b** or **c**.

1	Prefiero comer	a	fruta	b	pasteles	c	chocolate.
2	Detesto beber	a	gaseosas	b	agua	c	café.
3	Prefiero acostarme	a	antes de las 10	b	después de medianoche	c	antes de las 11.
4	Es necesario evitar	a	el tabaco	b	el ejercicio	c	la comida basura.
5	Es importante	a	estar en forma	b	comer mucho	c	relajarme.
6	Me gusta más	a	hacer ciclismo	b	ir al cine	c	ir a la discoteca.

Si la a es tu respuesta favorita, eres como Gabriela:

Para mí es importante comer y beber cosas sanas y quiero mantenerme en forma. Me gusta dormir bien, pero no demasiado porque así es posible estar aun más cansada. Odio los malos hábitos como el tabaco.

Conclusión: ¡Enhorabuena! La alimentación buena es necesaria. Sabes lo que es bueno y malo para tu cuerpo. Quieres llevar una vida sana y activa.

Si la b es tu respuesta favorita, eres como Marta:

Me encanta comer y tomo bastante comida rápida y gaseosas. Soy joven y necesito energía, ¿no? No soy muy deportista y creo que hacer ejercicio es realmente aburrido y difícil. Prefiero salir con mis amigos o jugar en el ordenador hasta medianoche.

Conclusión: ¿Quieres morir joven? Tu rutina es un desastre para el cuerpo. Tienes que comer más sano y dormir más. Otra cosa: el ejercicio es necesario para tener energía – las gaseosas, no. Se pueden hacer muchos deportes divertidos con tus amigos. Es importante cambiar tus hábitos AHORA.

Si la c es tu respuesta favorita, eres como Juan:

Quiero llevar una vida sana, pero es difícil. No tengo hábitos muy malos como el fumar. Tengo que estudiar mucho y no tengo tiempo para practicar deportes. Además el chocolate es necesario para motivarme.

Conclusión: Tienes buenas intenciones, pero es necesario hacer más para estar en forma. Se pueden hacer muchas actividades activas como parte de tu rutina normal. Comer un poco de chocolate no es un problema, pero es importante también comer frutas y verduras. ¡Tienes que hacer un esfuerzo, hombre!

2a Read the article and decide if the following statements are true (T), false (F) or not mentioned (?).

1 Gabriela eats a healthy diet.
2 Marta needs more sleep.
3 Marta is a very energetic person.
4 Juan has stopped smoking.
5 Juan doesn't have enough time to exercise.

2b What three pieces of advice are given to Marta and Juan?

3a Ⓖ Make a list of all the infinitives used in the magazine article.

Ejemplo: comer

3b **G** Match up these key Spanish verbs with their English equivalent.

1 Odio / Detesto …
2 Me gusta …
3 Quiero …
4 Tengo que …
5 Se puede …

a You can …
b I want …
c I like …
d I hate …
e I have to …

3c **G** Translate these sentences into Spanish.

1 I hate eating fruit, but I like drinking water.
2 It's important to sleep well and to be fit.
3 I have to do more sport.
4 You can avoid bad habits.

4a People call *el médico Miguel* on his radio show. What are they worried about? Choose one option from this list for each of the four people.

sleeping **drinking** **diet** **smoking**
not being fit **feeling ill** **feeling stressed**

4b Listen again. What advice does Miguel give to each person?

5a Pick a team: the 'Superfits' or the 'Sofa Slobs'.

'Superfits' team:
- Write a list of things you do to lead a healthy lifestyle.
- Now write some negative comments about the 'Sofa Slobs' team and also write some advice for them.

'Sofa Slobs' team:
- Write a list of things you do to lead an unhealthy lifestyle.
- Now write some negative comments about the 'Superfits' team and give them some advice.

5b Use your lists to argue with the other team and prove that your lifestyle is the best. You can do this in pairs or groups.

(No) Me gusta / Prefiero / Tengo que Detesto / Odio Puedo	fumar mantenerme en forma acostarme (temprano)	para llevar una vida sana.	
(¿) (No) Te gusta (?) / (¿) Quieres (?) Tienes que / Puedes	comer (más fruta) hacer (más ejercicio)		
Es importante / necesario / difícil / fácil / horrible Se puede	evitar (el tabaco) dormir (8 horas) practicar deporte	porque	es bueno / malo para la salud. (no) es sano.

Gramática — página 180

Using verbs with the infinitive

1st verb +	**infinitive** (end in *-ar*, *-er* or *-ir*)
quiero (I want)	*jugar* (to play / playing)
prefiero (I prefer)	*comer* (to eat / eating)
tienes que (you have to)	*hacer* (to do / doing)
¿quieres …? (do you want?)	*dormir* (to sleep / sleeping)

Reflexive verbs end in *se*:

e.g. *Es importante mantenerse en forma.*

But if you talk about yourself:

*Quiero mantener**me** en forma.*

Also learn the verb *tener* (to have) and phrases to use it with. *See page 28* ➡

Estrategia

Testing yourself on meanings of words

- Look for any connections e.g. *muerto* – dead (links in meaning to 'post mortem').
- Copy out the words in diagrams, on the computer, colour-coded.
- Make cards with Spanish on one side, English or pictures on the other to play word games.
- Record the Spanish word and its English translation to listen to.

Consejo

Verbs in the informal 'you' form usually end in '*s*':
tienes **you have**
quieres **you want**

Except *gustar*:
te gusta you like

For questions, just add: ¿ ?
e.g. *¿Quieres comer?*
Do you want to eat?

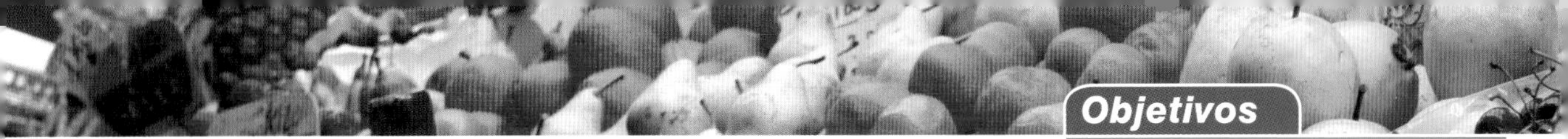

1.3 El tabaco

Objetivos

- Discussing who smokes and the consequences
- Using regular *-ar* verbs in the present tense
- Giving opinions

1 Ⓥ Look at the two texts and write down all the words you can find that relate directly to smoking.

El tabaco en España

- Entre 8–10 millones de españoles son fumadores (sobre una población de 44 millones).
- El tabaco causa la muerte de 50.000 españoles cada año.
- El número de mujeres que fuman es el doble que hace 25 años (31,3%).
- El 30% de las mujeres embarazadas fuman.
- A los 13 años hay más chicas fumadoras que chicos.

La Ley Anti-tabaco: 1 enero 2006

Está prohibido fumar en ...

- los lugares de trabajo.
- los lugares públicos.
- los bares y restaurantes de más de $100m^2$.

Los bares y restaurantes pequeños tienen la opción de fumador o no fumador.

2 Read the two texts again and answer the following questions in English.

1 How many Spanish people smoke?
2 What happens to 50,000 Spanish people every year?
3 What is said about female smokers? (mention two things)
4 Where can you now **not** smoke in Spain? (mention three places)

En España hay más fumadores que en toda Europa (a excepción de Grecia). Tradicionalmente el tabaco forma una parte importante de la vida social en los bares y cafeterías. Los adolescentes observan a los adultos y quieren imitarles.

Pero ahora existe mucha información sobre los peligros del tabaco. Además, es más difícil fumar con las restricciones de la Ley Anti-Tabaco porque no se puede fumar en los sitios públicos.

Los jóvenes dan su opinión sobre el uso del tabaco:

Ana

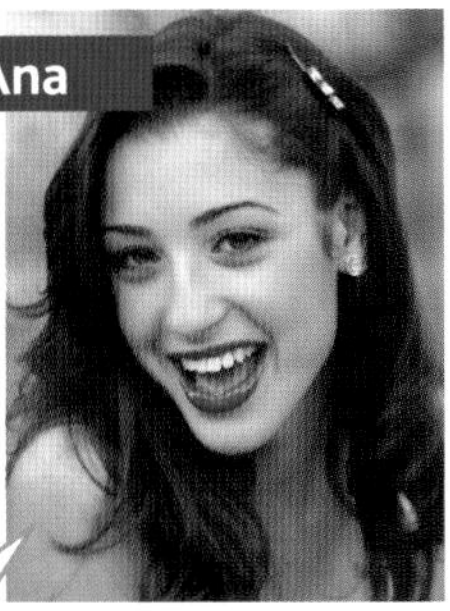

No fumo y no me gusta el tabaco. Creo que es un hábito muy malo y el olor es asqueroso. Los cigarrillos causan muchos problemas de salud: cáncer, enfermedades cardíacas y problemas respiratorios. Además el fumar pasivo nos afecta a todos. Es muy preocupante.

Javier

Mi padre fuma 20 cigarrillos al día. Sé que es difícil dejar de fumar y en mi opinión el tabaco es demasiado barato. También necesitamos una prohibición total – en el 90% de los bares todavía se puede fumar.

Nuria

En el instituto mis profesores hablan mucho del tabaco y las consecuencias para el corazón y los pulmones. No es saludable, claro, pero mis amigas fuman en la discoteca y quiero hacer lo mismo. Sólo fumamos dos o tres cigarrillos los sábados por la noche. No causan mucho daño.

3 Match up each person with the correct statement. Write A (Ana), J (Javier) or N (Nuria).

1 "It's a worrying health issue."
2 "I want to be the same as the others."
3 "There should be more practical help."
4 "We are given plenty of information about smoking."
5 "Giving up smoking is not easy."

4 Listen to announcements 1–4. Match up each one with one of the summaries below.

a Pregnant women should not smoke.
b Say 'no' to your friends.
c We can help you to stop smoking.
d Passive smoking can be just as harmful as smoking.
e Smoking doesn't make you thin.
f You cannot smoke here.

5 Ⓖ Choose the appropriate verb form in each sentence.

Ejemplo: 1 No fumo.

1 No fuma / fumas / fumo porque no me gusta el olor. (*I*)
2 ¿Fumamos / Fumas / Fuma? – Yo, no. (*You singular*)
3 El tabaco afecta / afecto / afectan a muchas personas. (*Smoking*)
4 Los cigarrillos causáis / causan / causa cáncer. (*Cigarettes*)
5 Necesito / Necesitan / Necesitamos una prohibición total. (*We*)
6 ¿Evito / Evitamos / Evitáis todos los cigarrillos? ¡Muy bien! (*You plural*)

6 You are conducting a survey with sixth-form students from your Spanish-speaking link school. Interview your partner about smoking.

A ¿Fumas?
B No, no fumo.
A ¿Y tus padres o tus amigos fuman?
B Mis amigos no fuman, pero mi padre fuma veinte cigarrillos al día.
A ¿Cuál es tu opinión sobre el tabaco?
B Creo que es horrible porque los cigarrillos causan muchos problemas de salud.

¿Fumas?

Mi padre / madre Mi amigo/a	(no) fuma	porque y	el olor el tabaco	es	asqueroso. un hábito malo.
Mis padres / amigos	(no) fuman		los cigarrillos	son	nocivos. malos para la salud.
Creo que / Pienso que / En mi opinión			el tabaco	causa	cáncer. problemas del corazón / de pulmones.
			los cigarrillos	causan	

Gramática *página 180*

Using regular *-ar* verbs in the present tense

Fumar – *to smoke*

SINGULAR		PLURAL	
fumo	I smoke	*fumamos*	**we** smoke
fumas	**you** smoke	*fumáis*	**you (plural)** smoke
fuma	**he / she / it** smokes	*fuman*	**they** smoke
mi padre fuma	my father smokes	*mis amigos fuman*	my friends smoke

Also:

***usted** fuma*	**you (formal)** smoke
***ustedes** fuman*	**you (formal, plural)** smoke

N.B. Some *-ar* verbs do not follow this pattern – always check! *See page 181* ➡

Also learn more about how to ask questions. *See page 28* ➡

Estrategia

Giving opinions

Try to add some of these to your dialogue:

- Creo que / Pienso que / Opino que / Me parece – I think that
- En mi opinión – In my opinion
- Me da igual – I don't care
- Estoy de acuerdo – I agree
- Estoy a favor (de) – I am in favour (of)
- Estoy en contra (de) – I am against

Consejo

Making questions easy:
Say something about yourself, then add *¿Y tú?* at the end.
No fumo. ¿Y tú?

1.4 El alcohol y las drogas

Objetivos
- Talking about drugs and alcohol
- Making comparisons
- Asking and answering questions in written work

1a Work in pairs. Take turns to read the following statements from a web debate. Decide if you agree or not.

1 El alcohol es más adictivo que las drogas.
2 El vino es menos alcohólico que la sidra.
3 La rehabilitación es mejor para los drogadictos que la cárcel.
4 El canabis es peor para la salud que el alcohol.
5 La droga blanda es tan peligrosa como la droga dura.
6 Las drogas causan tantos accidentes como el alcohol.
7 El éxtasis causa más problemas mentales que el alcohol.
8 Las drogas causan más problemas sociales que el alcohol.

1b Read the blogs and decide if the following statements are true (T), false (F) or not mentioned in the text (?).

Felipe says that …
1 Now more young people get drunk in Spain.
2 There are strict laws about under-age drinking.
3 Alcohol is more expensive in Spain than in the UK.

Graciela thinks that …
4 There is a serious drug problem in her town.
5 Drugs cause violence and crime.

Buscar

Inicio | Índice | Sitemap | Ayuda | Versión texto

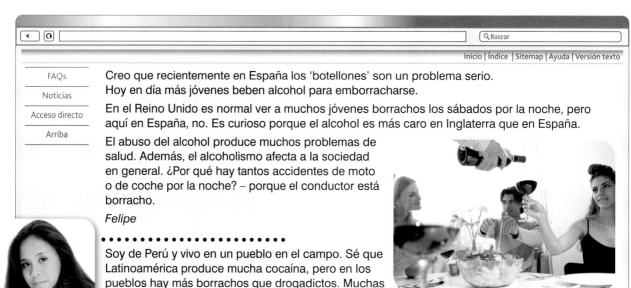

FAQs
Noticias
Acceso directo
Arriba

Creo que recientemente en España los 'botellones' son un problema serio. Hoy en día más jóvenes beben alcohol para emborracharse.

En el Reino Unido es normal ver a muchos jóvenes borrachos los sábados por la noche, pero aquí en España, no. Es curioso porque el alcohol es más caro en Inglaterra que en España.

El abuso del alcohol produce muchos problemas de salud. Además, el alcoholismo afecta a la sociedad en general. ¿Por qué hay tantos accidentes de moto o de coche por la noche? – porque el conductor está borracho.

Felipe

Soy de Perú y vivo en un pueblo en el campo. Sé que Latinoamérica produce mucha cocaína, pero en los pueblos hay más borrachos que drogadictos. Muchas personas llevan una vida difícil y el alcohol barato es una manera de olvidar sus problemas. Y, ¿por qué cultivamos la coca? Porque paga mejor que cultivar otros alimentos.

En las grandes ciudades la vida es distinta. Hay más dinero y más oportunidades para comprar las drogas, lo que provoca mucha violencia y más crimen.

Graciela

2 **G** Copy the sentences and fill in the gaps with *más, menos, mejor, peor, tan, tanto(s)* or *tanta(s)*.

1 El alcohol es _______ caro en Inglaterra que en España.
2 La droga blanda es _______ adictiva que la droga dura.
3 Las drogas causan _______ problemas para la sociedad como para el individuo.
4 El agua es _______ que el alcohol para la salud.
5 El alcohol es _______ peligroso como el tabaco.
6 La violencia de drogas en Colombia es _______ que en España.

3 You are going to hear four parts (a–d) of a TV debate about drugs and alcohol. Match up each part with one of the summaries 1–6.

1 Drug rehabilitation isn't working.
2 Alcohol abuse is getting worse.
3 Soft drugs should be legalized.
4 A lot of crime is drug-related.
5 Alcohol abuse can cause depression.
6 Drugs are too easily available.

4 You are taking part in a web debate about alcohol and drugs with some Spanish-speaking young people. Include:

- your opinion.
- some facts about alcohol and drugs in the UK.
- comparisons between dangers of drugs and alcohol.
- some questions.

DRUGS AND ALCOHOL JUST AREN'T COOL

Gramática — página 175

Making comparisons

When making comparisons you can use:

más + adjective or noun + *que* – more … than
menos + adjective or noun + *que* – less … than
mejor que – better than
peor que – worse than
tan + adjective + *como* – as … as
tanto(a) + singular noun + *como* – as much … as
tantos(as) + plural noun + *como* – as many … as

e.g. *El agua es más sana que el alcohol* – Water is more healthy / healthier than alcohol.

Also learn how to form *-er* and *-ir* verbs in the present tense.

See page 29 ➡

Consejo

Use vocabulary and structures you have learnt already to add extra detail and opinion to your writing and speaking.

e.g.
creo que (see page 23)
es + adjective + infinitive (see page 21)
Creo que es importante evitar las drogas.

Estrategia

Asking and answering questions in written work

Include some questions in your written work and try to answer them.

e.g.
¿Por qué? Why? *porque …* because …
¿La rehabilitación es mejor para los drogadictos?

Notice that you can use the same word order for a question as for a statement.

Look for examples in Felipe's and Graciela's blogs. Now try to ask and answer some questions yourself.

El alcohol La droga blanda / dura La rehabilitación	(no) es	más menos	adictivo/a peligroso/a caro/a barato/a popular / útil	que	el tabaco. la cárcel.
		tan		como	
Las drogas Los drogadictos	(no) causan	más menos	problemas accidentes violencia	que	las bebidas alcohólicas. los borrachos.
		tanto(s) tanta(s)		como	

kerboodle

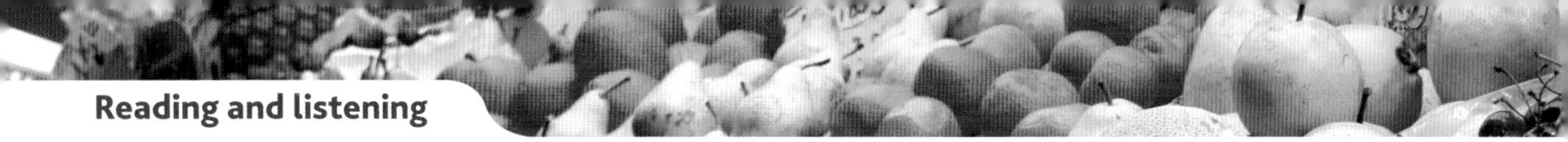

Health

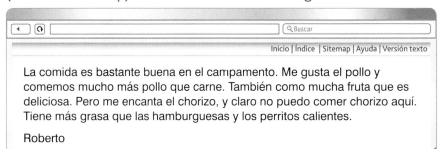

1a Sofía, from Mexico and Roberto, from the Canary Islands are taking part in a worldwide reality TV show *Campamento de salud* (Health boot camp). Read the menu and the blogs on the website.

Buscar

Inicio | Índice | Sitemap | Ayuda | Versión texto

La comida es bastante buena en el campamento. Me gusta el pollo y comemos mucho más pollo que carne. También como mucha fruta que es deliciosa. Pero me encanta el chorizo, y claro no puedo comer chorizo aquí. Tiene más grasa que las hamburguesas y los perritos calientes.

Roberto

Menú

Sopa de verduras

....

Pescado con ensalada

....

Manzanas asadas

1b Look at the menu and name two things that Sofía and Roberto are eating today.

1c Which foods does Roberto say he likes? Write down the letters of three food items.

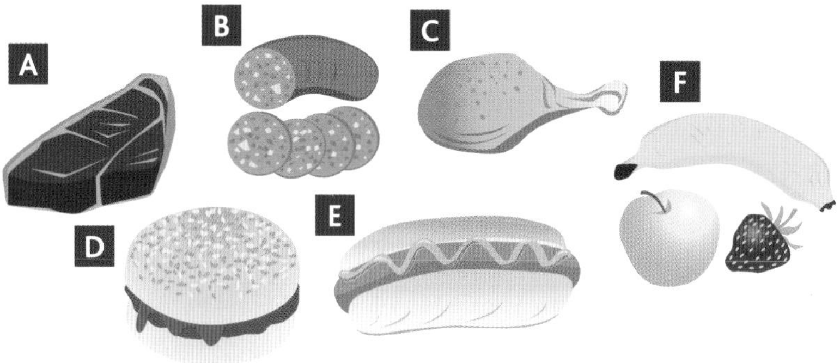

Study tip

Watch out for distractors *(no hay / no es,* etc.):
***no** puedo comer chorizo aquí*:
he can't eat it, but he still loves it.

Gramática

es importante cambiar mis hábitos:
es + adjective + infinitive

See pages 20–21

Comparatives

soy más sano que otras personas:
verb + *más* + adjective + *que*

See page 24

página 175

Buscar

Inicio | Índice | Sitemap | Ayuda | Versión texto

FAQs
Noticias
Acceso directo
Arriba

El campamento es difícil para mí porque no puedo comer lo que quiero. Tengo hambre todo el tiempo y necesito más azúcar. Es como una adicción. Tengo que conversar con el líder del grupo para evitar problemas. Es importante cambiar mis hábitos y es necesario terminar el programa y hacerlo todo bien.

En general, me siento bien porque estoy en forma y practico muchos deportes. Soy mucho más sana que hace dos semanas.

Sofía

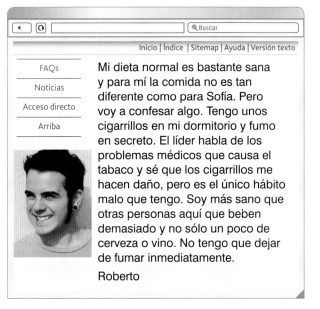

Buscar

Inicio | Índice | Sitemap | Ayuda | Versión texto

FAQs
Noticias
Acceso directo
Arriba

Mi dieta normal es bastante sana y para mí la comida no es tan diferente como para Sofía. Pero voy a confesar algo. Tengo unos cigarrillos en mi dormitorio y fumo en secreto. El líder habla de los problemas médicos que causa el tabaco y sé que los cigarrillos me hacen daño, pero es el único hábito malo que tengo. Soy más sano que otras personas aquí que beben demasiado y no sólo un poco de cerveza o vino. No tengo que dejar de fumar inmediatamente.

Roberto

2a Read the following questions and choose the correct name. Write S (Sofía), R (Roberto) or S + R (Sofía and Roberto).

Who …

1 doesn't want to change his / her habits?
2 is addicted to something?
3 is following the programme properly?
4 is doing damage to himself / herself?
5 is going to get more help?
6 thinks he / she is generally healthy?

2b Read the following questions and choose the correct option, a, b or c for each.

1 How would you describe Sofía's attitude towards the programme?
  a irritated
  b determined
  c unimpressed

2 Roberto is:
  a pleased with his progress.
  b going home early.
  c not taking it seriously.

3a Sofía is talking about a typical day at the health camp. Answer the following questions in English.

1 What does she have for breakfast?
2 What does she drink a lot of?
3 What does she do every day?
4 How many hours sleep does she want to get?
5 What bad habit does she have?

3b What opinion do these other Spanish speakers have of the camp? Write P (positive), N (negative) or P + N (positive and negative).

1 Ana

2 Benjamín

3 Luisa

4 José

Study tip

Don't just go for the obvious answer, e.g. question 2 matched with '*adicción*' (Sofía), especially at Higher Tier. Read all the sentences carefully.

Study tip

In A/A* questions you have to understand the whole text in order to recognise attitudes, summarise and work some things out that are not stated in an obvious way.

Vocabulario

el campamento	camp
conversar	to talk (used in Latin America)
el líder	leader
terminar	to finish
confesar	to confess
algo	something
hace (dos semanas)	(two weeks) ago
único	only

Study tip

Don't just get the answer from the last word you hear. Sometimes it may be correct, but sometimes it could be a distractor. Listen to the whole sentence and listen out for negatives like *no*, e.g. ***no** me gusta*; ***no** fumo*

Study tip

Listen out for positive and negative phrases (*me gusta / me molesta*, etc.) and adjectives (*útil / difícil*, etc.)

G Health

1a Translate the following sentences into English.

Ejemplo: *La fruta es deliciosa.*
Fruit is delicious.
(Notice that in Spanish you say: 'The fruit is delicious'.)

1. Soy inglés.
2. Mi dieta es sana.
3. ¿Eres español?
4. Los perritos calientes son horribles.
5. Somos vegetarianos.
6. Mis amigos son cómicos.
7. Usted es muy inteligente.

1b Now use this box of adjectives to make up your own sentences using different parts of the verb *ser*.

2a Make up conversations for pictures 1 and 2 using the example below. Replace the underlined words with an appropriate expression from the box of *tener* phrases.

2b Now write the dialogues in the plural.

A ¿Tenéis frío?
B No, no tenemos frío.
C Sí, tienen frío.

Ser – *to be*

SINGULAR	PLURAL
soy – I am	***somos*** – we are
eres – you are	***sois*** – you (plural) are
(***¿eres?*** – are you?)	(***¿sois?*** – are you?)
es – he / she / it is	***son*** – they are
mi padre ***es*** – my father is	*mis amigos* ***son*** – my friends are
Also: *usted es* – you (formal) are	*ustedes son* – you (formal, plural) are

There are two verbs meaning 'to be' in Spanish: *ser* and *estar*.

Ser describes a person, place or thing that is permanent and does not change from day to day:
Soy inglés – I am English

Gramática página 187

Adjectives

	SINGULAR	PLURAL
intelligent	*inteligente*	*inteligentes*
important	*importante*	*importantes*
silly	*tonto/a*	*tontos/as*
funny	*cómico/a*	*cómicos/as*
boring	*aburrido/a*	*aburridos/as*

Gramática página 174

Tener – *to have*

Tener can have different meanings when used in certain expressions, e.g.

tener (15) años	to be (15) years old
tener calor	to be hot
tener frío	to be cold
tener hambre	to be hungry
tener sed	to be thirsty
tener miedo	to be frightened
tener sueño	to be tired
tener prisa	to be in a hurry
tener éxito	to be successful
tener suerte	to be lucky

tener dolor de (cabeza / estómago, etc.)
to have a (head)ache / (stomach) ache, etc.

Gramática página 186

3a Write appropriate questions for the following answers.

1 No, no fumo.
2 Sí, hablamos español.
3 Sí, los cigarrillos son adictivos.
4 Sí, el tabaco produce cáncer.
5 No, no como comida basura.
6 Sí, el tabaco afecta a muchas personas.
7 No, no me gusta fumar.
8 Sí, es importante evitar el tabaco.

3b Now make up a survey about health. Make up your own questions.

4a Copy out the following emails and fill in the gaps with the correct part of the regular *-er* and *-ir* verbs in brackets.

Buscar

Me llamo Javier. _______ (comer) mucha fruta y ________ (beber) mucha agua. Mi amigo, Felipe, ______ (comer) demasiadas patatas fritas y mis amigos Juan y Pepe _______ (beber) mucha Coca-Cola, que no es bueno para la salud.

Mi madre _______ (comprender) que una dieta sana es importante y mi familia y yo _________ (comer) mucho pescado y verduras. Y tú, ¿qué _______ (comer) y ________ (beber) normalmente?

Buscar

Me llamo Elena. _____ (vivir) en Chile en América del sur. Mis amigos, Pedro y Gabriela, _______ (vivir) en Argentina ahora. Pedro, Gabriela y yo _______ (escribir) muchos correos electrónicos. También _________ (recibir) tarjetas postales que _______ (escribir) Gabriela. Y tú, ¿dónde_______ (vivir)?

¿Y, tú _______ (recibir) correos electrónicos?

4b Make up some simple sentences of your own using regular *-er* and *-ir* verbs, writing both the Spanish and English. Now work in pairs. Partner A gives the English version and Partner B translates into Spanish. Partner A checks his / her original Spanish sentence.

How to form questions with verbs

Gramática página 186

Asking questions in Spanish is very straightforward.

- add ¿....? when writing a question
- make your voice go up at the end when speaking:

statement: *Tiene un problema.* – He has got a problem.

question: *¿Tiene un problema?* – Has he got a problem?

statement: *Fumas mucho.* – You smoke a lot.

question: *¿Fumas mucho?* – Do you smoke a lot?

(Notice that in English we add 'do' or 'does' to make questions: e.g. Do you like? Does he eat ...?. This does not happen in Spanish.)

Regular *-er* verbs

Gramática página 180

Comer – *to eat*

SINGULAR	PLURAL
como – I eat	*com**emos*** – we eat
*com**es*** – you eat (*¿com**es**?* – do you eat?)	*com**éis*** – you (plural) eat (*¿com**éis**?* – do you eat?)
*com**e*** – he / she / it eats	*com**en*** – they eat
*mi padre com**e*** – my father eats	*mis amigos com**en*** – my friends eat

Also: *usted com**e*** – you (formal) eat
*ustedes com**en*** – you (formal, plural) eat

Regular *-ir* verbs

Gramática página 180

Vivir – *to live*

SINGULAR	PLURAL
*viv**o*** – I live	*viv**imos*** – we live
*viv**es*** – you live (*¿viv**es**?* – do you live ?)	*viv**ís*** – you (plural) live (*¿viv**ís**?* – do you live?)
*viv**e*** – he / she / it lives	*viv**en*** – they live
*mi padre viv**e*** – my father lives	*mis amigos viv**en*** – my friends live

Also: *usted viv**e*** – you (formal) live
*ustedes viv**en*** – you (formal, plural) live

Health

La dieta

pages 18–19

el	*agua (f) mineral*	mineral water
	alcohólico/a	alcoholic
el	*almuerzo*	lunch
el	*azúcar*	sugar
	barato/a	cheap
	beber	to drink
el	*bistec*	steak
la	*carne*	meat
	caro/a	expensive
la	*cena*	evening meal
los	*cereales*	cereal
el	*chorizo*	Spanish sausage
	comer	to eat
la	*comida*	food
la	*comida basura*	junk food
la	*comida rápida*	fast food
la	*cosa*	thing
	delicioso/a	delicious
el	*desayuno*	breakfast
la	*dieta*	diet
la	*ensalada*	salad
	fresco/a	fresh
la	*fruta*	fruit
la	*galleta*	biscuit
la	*grasa*	fat
la	*hamburguesa*	hamburger
el	*helado*	ice-cream
el	*huevo*	egg
la	*leche*	milk
las	*legumbres*	vegetables
los	*mariscos*	seafood
el	*pastel*	cake
el	*perrito caliente*	hot dog
el	*pescado*	fish
	picante	spicy
el	*plátano*	banana
el	*plato*	dish
el	*pollo*	chicken
	raro/a	strange
	rico/a	tasty
	saludable	healthy
	sano/a	healthy
la	*sopa*	soup
las	*tapas*	snacks
la	*tarta*	cake / tart
	típico/a	typical
	tomar	to have (breakfast / food / drink)
la	*tortilla*	omelette
la	*tostada*	toast
	vegetariano/a	vegetarian
las	*verduras*	green vegetables
el	*yogur*	yoghurt
el	*zumo (de naranja)*	(orange) juice

El bienestar

pages 20–21

	acostarse	to go to bed
	adictivo/a	addictive
el	*adicto*	addict
	cambiar	to change
	cansado/a	tired
el	*cuerpo*	body
	deportista	sporty
	después	after(wards)
	dormir	to sleep
el	*ejercicio*	exercise
la	*energía*	energy
el	*esfuerzo*	effort
	estar en forma	to be fit
	evitar	to avoid
	fumar	to smoke
	joven	young
	llevar una vida (sana)	to lead a (healthy) life
	mantenerse en forma	to keep fit
	morir	to die
	necesario/a	necessary
	necesitar	to need

el	*problema*	problem
	relajarse	to relax
la	*respuesta*	reply
la	*rutina*	routine
la	*salud*	health
el	*tabaco*	smoking / tobacco
	tener dolor de (cabeza)	to have a (head)ache
	tener hambre	to be hungry
	tener sed	to be thirsty
	tener sueño	to be tired
la	*vida*	life

El tabaco ➡ *pages 22–23*

el / la	*adolescente*	teenager
	afectar	to affect
	asqueroso/a	disgusting / filthy
	causar	to cause
la	*chica*	girl
el	*chico*	boy
el	*cigarrillo*	cigarette
el	*corazón*	heart
el	*daño*	damage / harm
	dejar de (fumar)	to stop (smoking)
la	*enfermedad*	illness / disease
(no)	*fumador*	(no) smoking area
el / la	*fumador(a)*	smoker
el	*fumar pasivo*	passive smoking
la	*ley*	law
el	*lugar*	place
la	*muerte*	death
la	*mujer*	woman
el	*olor*	smell
el	*peligro*	danger
la	*población*	population
	preocupante	worrying
la	*prohibición*	ban
	prohibido/a	banned
los	*pulmones*	lungs
	respiratorio/a	breathing / respiratory
	se permite (fumar)	(smoking) is allowed
el	*sitio*	place
el	*trabajo*	work

El alcohol y las drogas ➡ *pages 24–25*

el	*alcoholismo*	alcoholism
el	*alimento*	food
la	*ayuda*	help
	borracho/a	drunk
el	*botellón*	binge drinking
la	*calle*	street
el	*canabis*	cannabis
	comprar	to buy
el	*crimen*	crime
el	*dinero*	money
	distinto/a	different
la	*droga*	drug
las	*drogas blandas*	soft drugs
las	*drogas duras*	hard drugs
el / la	*drogadicto/a*	drug addict
	emborracharse	to get drunk
la	*inyección*	injection
los	*jóvenes*	young people
la	*manera*	way
	mejor	better
	mejorar	to improve
	obtener	to get / obtain
	olvidar	to forget
	peor	worse
	preocupar	to worry
	provocar	to cause / provoke
la	*rehabilitación*	rehabilitation
	seropositivo/a	HIV positive
	sin techo	homeless
la	*sociedad*	society
	tener miedo	to be afraid
el	*vino*	wine
la	*violencia*	violence

1.5 Las descripciones personales

Objetivos

- Describing physical appearance and personality
- Saying 'my, your, his / her, our, their'
- Avoiding being caught out by false friends

1 Write down as many words related to someone's physical appearance and personality as you can remember.

Buscar

Inicio | Índice | Sitemap | Ayuda | Versión texto

FAQs | Acceso directo | Arriba

¡Hola! Me llamo Eduardo y tengo 18 años. Tengo el pelo castaño corto y rizado y los ojos azules. Soy simpático, hablador y gracioso. También soy bastante deportivo y mi deporte favorito es el fútbol. ¿Cuál es tu deporte favorito?

Escríbeme. Eduardo

¡Hola amigos!

Me llamo Juanita y tengo 16 años. Soy morena y tengo el pelo largo. Soy sensible y un poco tímida. Normalmente soy bastante callada y por eso me gusta hablar con amigos por Internet. ¿Cuáles son vuestros pasatiempos? ¿Cuáles son vuestras ambiciones?

Juanita

A

¡Hola chicas!

Me llamo Esteban y tengo 17 años. Soy calvo pero tengo un bigote pelirrojo y una barba. Llevo gafas y tengo las orejas enormes. Soy torpe, glotón, vago y muy antipático. ¿Soy vuestro novio ideal?

No, en serio, soy rubio, guapo, y totalmente honesto.

Esteban

B

C

¡Hola! Me llamo Sofía y tengo los ojos azules y el pelo rubio, largo y liso. Tengo pecas en la nariz que detesto. En casa están mis padres Lourdes y Juan Luis, mi hermano Francisco, mi hermana Cristina y yo. Francisco es alto y delgado y muy travieso. Cristina es bastante baja y muy alegre. También tenemos un perro. Se llama Rodrigo y es un poco gordo y muy cómico. Mis amigas me describen como una persona extrovertida, amable y paciente. Nuestro pasatiempo favorito es el baile. ¿Y tú? ¿Cuál es tu pasatiempo favorito? ¿Qué haces con tus amigos?

Sofía

D

E

F

2a Read the web page and answer the following:

1. Match up each description with the correct photo. Write Eduardo, Juanita, Esteban, Sofía and the correct letter.
2. Which person's personality is most like yours? Write your reasons in English.

2b Summarise in English the information Sofía gives about her family. Mention at least eight things.

Estrategia

Looking for words that are similar to English does not always work. There are some 'false friends': words that look like a word in English, but actually mean something different in Spanish.

What English words do these Spanish ones remind you of?
simpático sensible largo vago

Now find out their proper meaning.

3a 🎧 Listen to Nuria talking about herself and her family. Copy the sentences and fill in the gaps.

1. Nuria's eyes are ______ .
2. She has ______ hair.
3. She also describes herself as ______ and ______ .
4. She has ______ sisters.
5. In terms of personality, Nuria describes herself as ______ .

3b 🎧 Answer the following questions in English.

1. Does Nuria get on well with her brother? Yes / No
   Give two reasons for your answer.
2. Why does Nuria like talking?

4a G Find examples of different forms of 'my', 'your' and 'our' in the web page.

4b G Select the appropriate form of the possessive adjective in the following sentences.

1. *Mis / Mi* madre se llama Isabel y mi padre se llama Paco.
2. ¿Cómo se llaman *tu / tus* hermanos?
3. En mi familia tenemos muchos animales. *Su / Nuestros / Nuestro* perro se llama Héctor.
4. Sara y Felipe, ¿ *vuestro / vuestra / vuestros* padres fuman?

Gramática — *página 176*

Possessive adjectives

mi(s)	my
tu(s)	your
su(s)	his / her / your (*usted*)
nuestro(s) / nuestra(s)	our
vuestro(s) / vuestra(s)	your
su(s)	their / your (*ustedes*)

Remember: *mi / nuestro / su,* etc. agree with the noun that follows.

nuestro hermano	our brother (masculine)
nuestra hermana	our sister (feminine)
tus padres	your parents (plural)

Also learn more about subject pronouns (*yo / tú / él / ella*, etc).

See page 46 ➡

5 Imagine you are taking part in a speed-dating event. Talk for 30–60 seconds about yourself and your family.

- Give personal details (name, age).
- Talk about your family / friends.
- Describe yourself (hair, eyes, height).
- Describe your personality.
- Add any other relevant information.

¿Cómo te llamas? ¿Cómo se llama tu hermano/a ¿Cómo se llaman tus padres?	Me llamo Mi hermano/a se llama Mis padres se llaman	Jack. Tom / Hannah. Anne y Chris.
Tengo / Tiene	15 años / los ojos azules. el pelo rubio / castaño / largo / corto.	
Soy / Es	alto/a / bajo/a / gordo/a / simpático/a / hablador(a).	

Consejo

When talking about age do not use *soy* – 'I am' or *es* – 'he / she is'.

Use *tener*:

Tengo 15 años. I am 15.

Literally 'I have 15 years' in Spanish.

Tiene 20 años. He / She is 20.

And remember:

su = 'his / her' not 'he / she'.

kerboodle

1.6 La situación familiar

Objetivos

- Describing different family situations
- Using *estar* + past participle
- Working out the meaning of new words from the context

1 Work in pairs. Partner A chooses one of the people from the photos below and describes them to Partner B, without saying their name. Partner B has to guess who it is. Then swap roles.

Personajes de La Calle de Intriga: una telenovela latinoamericana.

Lucía está casada con Don Marcos desde hace seis meses. Don Marcos es su quinto marido y tienen 12 hijos entre los dos. Lucía es rica, pero no está contenta porque es un matrimonio aburrido y sin amor. Quiere tener más aventuras en la vida, pero no quiere estar separada ni divorciada por quinta vez.

Lucía

Hugo

Hugo es el hijo mayor de Lucía. Vive con su madre y su padrastro porque no tiene trabajo. Está en el paro desde hace dos años y no quiere trabajar. Prefiere dormir, salir en moto y estar con chicas guapas. Su madre, Lucía, busca a una esposa rica para Hugo, pero él no quiere casarse. Prefiere ser soltero. Hay muchos problemas y conflictos entre Hugo, su padrastro y sus hermanastros, pero Hugo no está preocupado por nada. Sólo quiere pasarlo bien.

Mariela es la asistenta de la casa de Don Marcos. Trabaja y vive en la casa desde hace 18 años. Es madre soltera y cuida a su hija sola. Su hija se llama Yolanda y tiene 16 años. Yolanda quiere descubrir quién es su padre. Además, Yolanda está enamorada de Hugo. Es un secreto y sufre mucho porque Hugo no la trata bien.

Mariela y Yolanda

Ramón es el ex-marido de Lucía aunque todavía está enamorado de ella. Vive en la casa de enfrente desde hace tres meses. Está jubilado y ahora que ya no trabaja, puede concentrarse en su obsesión: Lucía. Es muy celoso y está un poco loco. Le gusta espiar a Lucía y a Don Marcos por el telescopio. Tiene una pistola y quiere usarla.

Ramón

Los Señores Menéndez son los vecinos de Don Marcos. Tienen dos niñas de tres años que son gemelas. Parece la familia perfecta. Un día llega Paulina, la nueva niñera y la situación cambia de una manera desastrosa.

La familia Menéndez

2a Read the article and write the name of the person who …

1 is married to Don Marcos.
2 is 16 years old.
3 is Lucía's son.
4 used to be married to Lucía.
5 doesn't want to get married.
6 is a single mother.

Estrategia

When you come across a new word see if you can work out the meaning from other words and phrases you **do** understand.

e.g. *Hugo ... no tiene trabajo.*
Hugo doesn't work.
Está en el paro means he is unemployed.

2b Answer the following questions in English.

1 Why is Lucía unhappy?
2 What is Yolanda's secret?
3 Who is Paulina?
4 Who seems to be the most relaxed character? Why?

3a Listen to the conversations Paulina has with three people (Victor, Rosa and Juan) she meets on the street. Note down their marital status, the number of children they have and how long they have lived in the street.

3b Listen again and answer the following questions.

1 What does Paulina say about herself during the three conversations?
2 What is Rosa's reaction towards Paulina? a friendly. b suspicious. c scared.
3 What is Juan's behaviour towards Paulina like? a helpful. b shy. c flirtatious.

4a G Work in pairs. Partner B pretends to be one of the characters from the article on page 34. Partner A has to work out who it is by asking questions using *estar*. Partner B answers in full sentences. Then swap roles.

Ejemplo: **A** ¿Estás casado/a? **B** No estoy casado/a ...

4b G Now describe a character or pair of characters to the rest of the class for them to guess.

5 Write your own description of a real or imaginary family or group of people. You could make up your own soap-opera characters.

Estoy / Está ¿Estás?	casado/a divorciado/a separado/a enamorado/a jubilado/a	desde hace dos meses / tres años.
Soy / Es ¿Eres?	soltero/a guapo/a inglés / inglesa	

Gramática

Using *estar* + past participle

Estar is used with past participles usually ending in *-ado* or *-ido*.

e.g. *estoy casado*	I am married
está divorciada	she is divorced
están preocupados	they are worried

Notice that the ending of the past participle has to be masculine, feminine or plural, like adjectives.

Also learn how to use *desde hace* + present tense to say how long you have been doing something.

See page 46 ➡

página 187

Consejo

Estar is used for:

- saying where something is (*está en Madrid*).
- describing a situation someone or something is in (*está divorciado*).
- describing a state someone or something is in (*está muerto*).

Estar is also used with some adjectives, usually to describe something that is not permanent, e.g. *loco, contento*.

BUT use *ser* for:

joven (young); *soltero/a* (single); *anciano/a* (old); *feliz* (happy).

1.7 Las relaciones personales

Objetivos

- Discussing relationships with family and friends
- Using reflexive verbs
- Extending phrases in speaking and writing tasks

Buscar

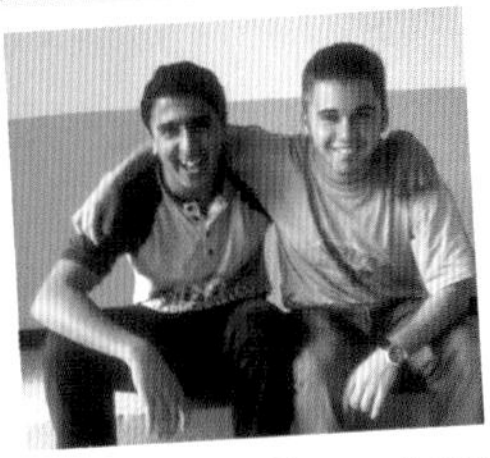

Me llamo María y salgo con Antonio, mi novio, desde hace seis meses. En general somos una pareja feliz y normalmente Antonio es un chico cariñoso, comprensivo y honrado. Sin embargo recientemente no nos llevamos muy bien. Antonio tiene un nuevo amigo que se llama Enrique. Creo que es importante salir con tus amigos y no sólo con tu novia pero, en mi opinión, la influencia de Enrique no es muy positiva. Después de estar con Enrique, Antonio se pone impaciente y se enfada conmigo. Su temperamento cambia totalmente. Al final nos peleamos cuando, en realidad, no hay problema entre nosotros. ¿Qué puedo hacer?

María

Buscar

Ahora mi abuela vive con nosotros porque mi abuelo está muerto y no quiere vivir sola. El problema es que mi hermana mayor, Teresa, no se lleva bien con mi abuela y siempre hay discusiones horribles en casa. Mi abuela critica mucho a los adolescentes: la ropa, los novios, los estudios y las notas del colegio, la dieta, las horas de salir, el dinero ... vamos, todo. Entonces, Teresa se enfada y luego Teresa y mi abuela se pelean. No lo aguanto. Claro que la barrera generacional puede ser difícil. Mi abuela tiene ideas de una generación diferente aunque también pienso que es un poco intolerante. Por otro lado, mi hermana tiene que relacionarse mejor con mi abuela y ser menos egoísta. ¿Cómo puedo ayudar?

Borja

Buscar

Elena es mi novia y estoy muy enamorado de ella. Nos llevamos muy bien, tenemos mucho en común y por eso quiero casarme con ella. Desafortunadamente Elena piensa que el matrimonio sólo causa problemas. Además, tiene una imagen del hombre ideal y, claro, no soy perfecto. Todos tenemos defectos, ¿no? En mi opinión, Elena es cobarde y debe tener más confianza en mí.

¿Qué puedo hacer para convencerla?

Luis

1 Read the emails and answer the following questions in English.

1 What is the relationship between the following people:

	Relationship
María and Antonio	
Antonio and Enrique	
Borja and Teresa	
Luis and Elena	

2 What is the main problem for:
a María b Borja c Luis?
Choose from: different opinions about marriage / age gap / arguments between family members / money / changes of mood / not having friends.

3 Do you think María likes Enrique? Give two reasons.

4 Do you think Borja's grandmother is a positive influence on the family? Give two reasons.

5 Do you think Elena wants to get married? Give a reason for your answer.

2 Watch the video clip and answer the following questions.

1 Which problem with Javier does his mother mention first?
   a bad marks at school   b staying out late
   c not talking
2 Note three things that Javier says his mother criticizes him for.
3 What does Javier want his mother to stop doing?
   a treating him like a little boy
   b being too fussy about tidying the house
   c worrying about him
4 What problem does Javier have with his father?
   a won't give him freedom
   b too busy at work
   c always argues with his mother
5 How would you best describe Elisa's comment?
   a insensitive   b helpful
   c rude

3 **G** Copy the sentences and fill in the gaps with the correct reflexive pronoun: *me / te / se / nos / os*.

1 _______ llevo bien con mi padre.
2 Hay muchos problemas entre mi hermano y mi hermana. Siempre _______ pelean mucho.
3 Estamos muy contentos. No _______ quejamos.
4 ¿_______ llevas bien con tus primos?
5 ¿_______ marcháis ahora?
6 Mi amiga, Rosa, _______ pone roja cuando habla con mi hermano.

Gramática — Using reflexive verbs

página 185

Reflexive verbs have a reflexive pronoun (*me, te, se, nos, os, se*) in front of the verb.

The infinitive of a reflexive verb ends in *-se*, e.g. *lavarse*.

quejarse to complain

SINGULAR		PLURAL	
***me** quejo*	I complain	***nos** quejamos*	we complain
***te** quejas*	you complain	***os** quejáis*	you complain
***se** queja*	he / she complains	***se** quejan*	they complain
*usted **se** queja*	you (formal) complain	*ustedes **se** quejan*	you (formal, plural) complain

Also learn more about conjunctions and how to link phrases together.

See page 46 ➡

Consejo

You may have learnt *me* to mean 'myself' as in:

me lavo I wash myself

But many reflexive verbs cannot be translated as 'myself':

me quejo I complain

4 Work in pairs. Take turns to practise saying the different parts of these verbs. Throw a dice:

⚀ = I   ⚁ = you (singular)   ⚂ = he / she   ⚃ = we   ⚄ = you (plural)   ⚅ = they

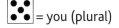

llevarse bien / mal   *quejarse*   *ponerse*   *marcharse*   *pelearse*   *lavarse*

5 Make up your own email to a problem page. Try to extend your sentences using words such as: *pero, también, y, por eso, porque*.

Estrategia

Find words or expressions in the texts opposite and in the language structure box which you can use to link phrases together, e.g.: *y* and *porque* because

En general Desafortunadamente Afortunadamente	me llevo bien / mal mi hermano se pelea mis amigos se relacionan bien / mal	con	mi amigo. mi hermano. mis padres.
luego / por eso pero / además también	(no) hay	problemas con discusiones sobre	los estudios. la ropa / el dinero. los amigos / novios. las horas de salir.

1.8 Los planes del futuro

Objetivos

- Discussing future plans about marriage / partnership and children
- Talking about what you are going to do
- Keeping your conversation going

A los 20 años voy a casarme. Tengo una novia que se llama Rosario y estamos muy enamorados. Para mí el matrimonio será muy importante. Me gustaría tener un niño o dos, pero no quiero una familia muy numerosa. Tengo tres hermanos y cuatro hermanas y es mucho trabajo para mi madre. Además, tienes que considerar el futuro del planeta en general. ¿Habrá suficiente comida para todos? Entonces a los 65 años, ¿qué vamos a hacer Rosario y yo? Pues, no sé exactamente, pero me gustaría estar bien de salud para jugar con mis nietos. ***Raúl***

El año que viene voy a ir a la universidad y por eso a los 20 años voy a vivir con mi familia como ahora. Es demasiado caro vivir sola. Después de la universidad, me gustaría trabajar en Nueva York y será fantástico. Quiero casarme y mi marido ideal sería guapo, inteligente y gracioso. Sin embargo, no tengo mucha paciencia con los bebés. Prefiero ser independiente y por eso no voy a tener niños. ¿Y a los 65 años? Claro, voy a jubilarme, voy a ser rica y voy a aprovechar todas las oportunidades que tengo. Lo importante es pasarlo bien. ***Chelo***

En el futuro quiero ser médico y me gustaría trabajar en Amazonas en América Latina. Hay muchas familias y niños que necesitan ayuda allí. Será necesario dedicarme a la medicina y entonces los pacientes van a ser las personas más importantes para mí. Desafortunadamente creo que no voy a poder casarme porque en la selva la vida sería difícil para una esposa. Es una pena porque me gustaría tener niños. A los 65 años voy a continuar trabajando. Finalmente me imagino que una residencia de ancianos será mi única opción, que me preocupa un poco, pero no quiero ser demasiado pesimista. ***Roberto***

1 Students at your Spanish-speaking link school imagine what their life will be like when they are 25, 35 and 65 years old. Read what they have to say about their future plans. Who …

1. is going to get married when they are 20?
2. is still going to live with their parents in their 20s?
3. is going to be a doctor?
4. doesn't want to have children?
5. doesn't think they will get married?
6. says they will have a comfortable retirement?
7. is a bit worried about old age?
8. wants to spend time with grandchildren?

2 Listen to the extracts from a radio talk show about marriage, partners and children. Choose the correct option for each.

1 Guillermo doesn't want a a wife b children c pets.
2 Salomé would like a to meet a partner b to have children c to leave home.
3 Carolina is a married b going to get married c never going to get married.
4 For Bernardo the idea of marriage is a old-fashioned b unrealistic c important.
5 For Ana the idea of having children is a exciting b horrific c normal.

3 Ⓖ Choose the appropriate verb form for the person named in brackets and copy out the correct sentences.

Ejemplo: No van / voy / va a salir (*they*). No van a salir.

1 Voy / Vas / Va a casarme el año próximo. (*I*)
2 Mi hermana van / va / vamos a trabajar en Australia. (*my sister*)
3 Oye, Cristina, ¿vais / va / vas a tener niños en el futuro? (*you singular*)
4 Mi novio y yo vamos / voy / van a ir a la universidad. (*we*)
5 ¿Van / Vais / Vamos a casaros por la iglesia? (*you plural informal*)
6 Mis padres va / voy / van a visitar a mi abuelo en Argentina. (*my parents*)

Gramática *página 183*

Talking about what you are going to do

To say what people are going to do, use: the correct part of *ir* + *a* + **infinitive**.

e.g. *voy a tener niños*
I am going to have children

Also learn how to say what people **would** like / **would** be, etc. *See page 46* ➡

4 Predict what you will be doing at the ages of 25, 35 and 65. Work in pairs asking and answering the following questions. Use the language structure box to help you.

- ¿Qué vas a hacer a los 25 años?
- ¿Dónde vas a vivir?
- ¿Dónde vas a trabajar?
- ¿Vas a casarte? ¿Por qué?
- ¿Cómo sería tu pareja ideal?
- ¿Te gustaría tener niños? ¿Por qué? / ¿Por qué no?
- ¿Qué te gustaría hacer después de jubilarte?

Estrategia

To keep your conversation going and avoid long pauses, use the following words to create pauses, if you need time to think:

bueno / pues / vamos – well …

vamos a ver – let's see …

Repeat a word: *Mi madre es … es … simpática.*

Consejo

Present	Future
hay – there is, there are	*habrá* – there will be
es – he / she / it is	*será* – he / she / it will be
	e.g. *habrá consecuencias*

(No) Voy a (No) Me gustaría	enamorarme / casarme / tener niños. vivir con mi novio/a / mis padres / mis amigos.	
¿Vas a ...? ¿Te gustaría ...?	ir a la universidad. trabajar en Londres / Nueva York. ser independiente / sano/a / feliz.	
Mi mujer / esposa Mi marido / esposo Mi novio/a Mi pareja ideal	será sería	inteligente. guapo/a. gracioso/a. responsable.

1.9 La igualdad para todos

Objetivos
- Discussing race and gender
- Using reflexive phrases like *se puede*
- Checking pronunciation

1 Work in pairs. Partner A reads out one word from list A below, working out the correct pronunciation. Partner B guesses the meaning. Then swap roles.

A estudiante, violencia, crimen, igualdad

B inmigrante, racismo, discriminación, tolerancia

Estrategia

Checking pronunciation

Remember to follow pronunciation rules (see page 9), especially when the written word is similar to the English. Watch out for the vowels, e.g. 'crime' (long vowel sound in English); *crimen* (always short vowel sounds in Spanish).

Buscar

Inicio | Índice | Sitemap | Ayuda | Versión texto

FAQs
Noticias
Acceso directo
Arriba

El día 8 de marzo se celebra La Noche de la Mujer en Bogotá, Colombia. Los hombres tienen que estar en casa y las mujeres tienen que salir. La mayoría de las mujeres que participan son estudiantes o trabajadoras entre 18 y 25 años. Es interesante porque todos los años durante La Noche de la Mujer hay menos violencia y menos crimen. Según una encuesta, más del 80% de las mujeres piensan que es una buena idea.

Pero, ¿cuál es tu opinión?

Estoy de acuerdo con La Noche de la Mujer porque así se pueden considerar los derechos de las mujeres. Se habla de la igualdad, pero hay mucha discriminación todavía y creo que es necesario hacer más para ayudar.

Marcelo

Estoy en contra de esta idea porque se necesita un programa de acción política y educación más serio. En Colombia la igualdad no existe ni en casa ni en el lugar de trabajo. Y la situación es horrorosa en otros países donde se puede maltratar y matar a las mujeres legalmente. Nunca voy a estar a favor de una noche de diversión cuando hay tantas mujeres que son víctimas de la violencia.

Pilar

2 Read the blogs about Women's Night in Bogotá and decide whether the following statements are true (T), false (F) or not mentioned (?).

1 On 8th March in Bogotá, Colombian women have to stay at home.
2 Most of the people who go out are over 40.
3 Most women think it is a good idea.
4 Originally it was the President's wife who thought of the idea.
5 Marcelo thinks women's rights are important.
6 Pilar thinks that the event helps to promote women's equality.
7 Pilar suffers from domestic violence.

3 Listen to the opinions about gender and race issues (1–6). Which of the following options A–F does each statement refer to?

A Accepting differences
B Changing attitudes through education
C Physical abuse in the home
D Discrimination against gay people
E Immigrant workers
F Women in politics

Using reflexive phrases

Gramática *página 185*

se puede(n) + infinitive	you (in general) can / people can
e.g. Se pueden considerar varias posibilidades.	Various possibilities can be considered.
se debe(n) you must / people must + infinitive	
se habla de + noun	people talk about …
e.g. se habla de la igualdad	people talk about equality
se necesita(n) + noun	… is needed
e.g. se necesita más comprensión	more understanding is needed
se dice que	it is said that … / people say that …

Also learn more about how to make a phrase negative.

See page 47 ➡

4 **G** Put the following words in these phrases into the correct order.

1 más tolerancia necesita se
2 al educar puede público se
3 violencia mucho se doméstica no la habla de
4 racismo que España se hay en dice

5 Write a short speech in Spanish about how to tackle gender and race discrimination. You could look up different nouns and infinitives of verbs. Mention:

- What is said about the issues (facts / details / statistics).
- If you agree or disagree with the situation / issue.
- What is needed to help.
- What people can do to help.
- What people must do.
- You could also talk about other types of discrimination.

(No) Hay Se dice que hay Se habla de	muchos problemas para mucha discriminación / violencia contra (la) igualdad para (la) desigualdad para	las mujeres. los inmigrantes. los extranjeros. los gitanos.
Se necesita (más)	comprensión / educación / tolerancia / trabajo / acción política.	
Se puede(n) Se debe(n)	educar al público / hacer más para ayudar / cambiar las actitudes.	

Consejo

To say that you agree with someone, use:
estoy de acuerdo (con)
estoy a favor (de)
To say that you disagree, use:
no estoy de acuerdo (con)
estoy en contra (de)

1.10 La pobreza

Objetivos

- Discussing and understanding issues relating to poverty
- Saying what you have to do or must do
- Ignoring words you don't need to understand

1 Skim read the following article and pick out as many words as you can that relate directly to poverty, building houses and illness.

Una visita a un pueblo joven

Mi destino es Lima, ciudad capital de Perú. Tiene una población de más de 9 millones y aproximadamente el 50% de los habitantes viven en un pueblo joven. Un 'pueblo joven' es un barrio pobre en las afueras de la ciudad donde las casas son muy básicas y a veces no hay agua corriente ni electricidad.

Las expectativas y la realidad

Muchas personas abandonan sus pueblos en el campo y vienen a los pueblos jóvenes porque buscan colegios mejores para sus niños o trabajo para los adultos. Lo triste es que sus expectativas no son realistas. En muchos pueblos jóvenes las condiciones de vida no son muy sanitarias, por ejemplo no hay agua limpia y hay muchas enfermedades como el cólera. Lo horroroso es que la diarrea causa la mayoría de las muertes entre los niños porque los padres no comprenden o no pueden pagar el tratamiento.

Optimismo y desarrollo

Por otro lado no hay que ser demasiado pesimista. La pobreza no tiene que arruinarles la vida. El nombre 'pueblo joven' es más optimista que los nombres 'shanty town' o 'slums' en inglés. El pueblo es 'joven', es nuevo, es básico, pero en el futuro va a ser mejor. Existe la posibilidad de desarrollo.

Las casas y la comunidad

Al principio las casas están hechas de cartón o de metal, pero, poco a poco, los habitantes pueden construir las casas con piedra o ladrillos, y al final tienen un techo y ventanas de cristal. Lo bueno es que hay una sensación de comunidad. Los habitantes tienen que participar juntos en obras como la construcción de carreteras y alcantarillas. Después, la comunidad puede tener agua limpia y electricidad. Todos están muy orgullosos de los progresos en el pueblo joven.

Los pobres y los ricos

Lo malo es que todavía es difícil para los pobres tener un trabajo bien pagado porque hay muchos prejuicios. El 5% de la población es muy rico y tiene el 95% de la riqueza de Perú. Es una situación muy injusta. Hay ONGs como la Asociación SOLAC para ayudar a los pobres, pero los ricos, los gerentes de la industria y los políticos deben dar más oportunidades de educación, de salud y de trabajo a los pobres.

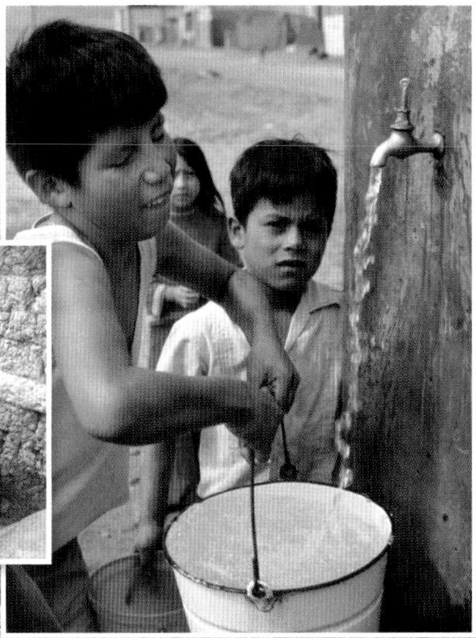

2a Read the article and answer these questions.
Try to work out the meanings of words you don't know before looking them up.
Remember, you do not need to understand every word.

1 Lima is a a capital city b country c village.
2 A 'pueblo joven' is a a country village b shanty town c youth centre.
3 According to the article, in Peru 5% of the population is a very poor b very sick c very rich.

2b Find three positive and three negative things the writer mentions about Peru and the 'pueblos jóvenes'. Note them down in English.

3 Listen to the four people talking about where they live. Decide whether each person's comments are positive (P), negative (N), or both (P + N).

4 G Match up the two halves of these sentences, then translate them into English.

1 Para evitar el cólera hay
2 El gobierno
3 Los pobres deben
4 Tenemos que

a participar en el proceso político.
b considerar el futuro de nuestros niños.
c que tener agua limpia.
d debe crear más oportunidades de educación.

5 Work in pairs. Take turns to ask and answer these questions. Change the underlined parts and add extra details and opinions. Use the language structure box to help you.

A: ¡Hola! ¿De dónde eres?
B: Soy de Venezuela.
A: ¿Hay mucha pobreza en Venezuela?
B: Sí, hay mucha pobreza. Es muy difícil para los pobres.
A: ¿Qué problemas causa la pobreza?
B: Creo que la pobreza causa problemas de salud y de crimen.
A: ¿Qué debemos hacer para ayudar?
B: Debemos buscar soluciones prácticas y los políticos tienen que mejorar la educación.

Estrategia

When reading and listening to these longer texts, remember:

- Read the questions first.
- You will not have to understand all the words, so don't panic.
- When listening, try to predict the kind of answer that might be required.
- When reading, scan the text for clues as to whereabouts the answer is, then read the phrases carefully.

Gramática *página 186*

Saying what you have to do or must do

- Saying '**have to**':

Hay que + infinitive — you / people have to …

Hay que never has a change of ending.

Tener que + infinitive — to have to …

Change *tener* to the correct part of the verb.

Tengo que ayudar. — I have to help.

Tenemos que mejorar. — We have to improve.

- Saying '**must**':

Deber + infinitive

Deber is a regular *-er* verb like *comer*.

Los políticos deben crear trabajos.
The politicians must create jobs.

Also learn more about how to use *lo* + adjective.

See page 47 ➡

(No) Hay ¿Hay …?	mucha pobreza mucha injusticia agua limpia oportunidades de educación oportunidades de trabajo	en Perú / España. en el Reino Unido. en los pueblos jóvenes.
La pobreza causa	problemas de salud / de crimen / de drogas.	
Hay que / Debemos / Tenemos que	mejorar la salud / la educación. crear más trabajos. buscar soluciones prácticas. dar dinero a las obras benéficas.	
Los pobres / Los ricos / Los políticos — deben / tienen que	(as above)	

Consejo

When talking about a more complex topic such as poverty, it is tempting to try to translate literally from the English.

BUT stick to the language structures you know how to use.

Relationships and choices

Nombre:	María
Apellido:	Márquez Ruiz
Nacionalidad:	Guatemalteca
Lugar de nacimiento:	Guatemala
Edad:	20 años
Fecha de nacimiento:	22 de abril 1989
Parientes en España:	tío, tía, primo, abuelo, hermano
Estado civil:	soltera

Reportero: ¿Desde cuándo vives en Madrid, María?

María: Vivo aquí desde hace nueve meses. Mi hermano y yo vivimos con nuestros tíos ahora. También en casa hay nuestro primo y el abuelo.

Reportero: Y, ¿qué haces aquí?

María: Soy estudiante en la universidad. Estudio inglés y francés.

Reportero: ¿Por qué quieres estudiar aquí y no en Guatemala?

María: Bueno, mis tíos me invitaron y es una oportunidad para visitar Europa y conocer culturas diferentes. Voy a viajar a Inglaterra y Francia en agosto. También se puede hacer nuevos amigos.

Reportero: ¿Y piensas que hay muchas diferencias entre los jóvenes españoles y los jóvenes en Guatemala?

María: Creo que depende de la personalidad de cada individuo. No hay que pensar en estereotipos. Por ejemplo, mi mejor amiga en Guatemala se llama Elisa y es muy extrovertida. En cambio, Eduardo, otro amigo, es bastante tímido. Tengo dos amigas españolas, Laura y Juanita. Laura es muy divertida y nos hace reír.
Por otra parte, Juanita es más formal con todos, pero me llevo bien con las dos.

Reportero: Y, ¿tienes amigos de otras nacionalidades?

María: Sí. Yusuf es de Marruecos. Es inmigrante y trabaja en España desde hace tres años. Después del colegio, era muy difícil encontrar trabajo en Marruecos y hay más posibilidades aquí. Debe ser duro estar separado de su familia, pero es una persona muy independiente y madura. Para él, lo más importante es ganar suficiente dinero y así ayuda a sus padres y hermanos en Marruecos porque son pobres. En el futuro le gustaría volver a Marruecos para crear un negocio y así va a dar trabajo a otros jóvenes marroquíes. Es una buena idea. Le admiro mucho.

Reportero: Entonces, ¿los inmigrantes deben volver a su propio país, en tu opinión?

María: No. No digo eso. La tasa de nacimiento en España es muy baja y tiene que acoger a los extranjeros para hacer muchos trabajos importantes. Los inmigrantes son necesarios para la economía. Contribuyen ocho billones de euros en impuestos.

Reportero: Estoy de acuerdo.

1a Read the interview. Which of María's relatives live in Spain? Complete the list in English by adding four more relatives. Brother, ...

1b Match up each of María's friends with the correct description. Copy the grid and fill in the correct letter for each.

Elisa	*Example:* C
Eduardo	
Juanita	
Laura	
Yusuf	

Descriptions

A funny
B chatty
C outgoing
D intelligent
E shy
F independent
G polite

1c Decide whether the following statements are true (T), false (F) or not mentioned (?).

1 María is from Guatemala.
2 María is studying at university in Spain.
3 Yusuf works in a school.
4 Yusuf helps his family financially.
5 In the future Yusuf would like to stay in Spain.
6 María believes that Spain needs people from abroad to come and work there.

2 Listen to the five young people talking about their future plans. Match up each person with the correct summary (A–G) below:

A I want to get married.
B I am not going to still be working when I'm 70.
C I would like to have a good job.
D I would like lots of children.
E I don't want to have children.
F I would like to have a girlfriend.
G I am going to study abroad.

3 Listen to the interview with María and choose the correct answer from the options given.

1 María's relationship with her parents is …
a loving b really bad c up and down.
2 María believes that a true friend must be …
a forgiving b ready to listen c honest.
3 In the future María would like to …
a work with children b have children
c be a nanny in Spain.
4 María thinks that people should …
a help each other more
b be responsible for helping themselves
c demand more help from the government.

Gramática página 187

Desde hace

Trabaja en España desde hace tres años.

Tener que

Tiene que acoger a los extranjeros para hacer muchos trabajos importantes. See page 43

Study tip

In the Listening Examination use the five minutes reading time at the beginning to try to predict the kind of vocabulary and structures you might need to understand. Read the introduction to each question, as it summarises the topic you are going to hear. Don't leave blank answers – write something!

Vocabulario

acoger	to welcome
el apellido	surname
conocer	to (get to) know
la edad	age
el estado civil	marital status
formal	polite
ganar	to earn
el impuesto	tax
el lugar	place
el nacimiento	birth
la nacionalidad	nationality
el negocio	business
el nombre	first name
los parientes	relatives
la tasa	rate
viajar	to travel
volver	to return

G Relationships and choices

1 Copy the sentences and fill in the gaps with the correct subject pronoun.

1 _______ voy al cine y _______ vas al supermercado.
2 _______ es muy simpático, pero _______ es mal educada.
3 _______ tenemos 16 años. ¿Y _______? (*you, informal plural*)
4 Es _______ muy amable. (*you, formal singular*)
5 ¿Son _______ ingleses? (*you, formal plural*)

Subject pronouns

Subject pronouns are usually only used with the verb for the following reasons:

- to emphasise the 'I', 'you', etc.
- to make it clear who is speaking
- to ask questions: *¿Y tú?*

Gramática página 178

2 Imagine that you are a character in a soap opera. Write about how long you have done the things in the box.

estoy ... casado/a / divorciado/a / separado/a / enamorado/a
soy soltero/a
soy feliz / triste
estoy preocupado/a / loco/a / en el paro

Desde hace

Use *desde hace* + present tense to say how long you have been doing something.

Estoy casado desde hace dos años
I have been married for two years.

Gramática página 187

3 Copy the text and fill in the gaps with the most appropriate linking word(s) from the grammar box. There may be more than one option.

Me llamo Ana _______ tengo 17 años. Escribo esta carta _______ tengo un problema. Me llevo muy bien con mi madre _______ es muy estricta. No puedo salir con mis amigos entresemana. _______ no le gusta mi novio, Pedro. _______ quiero ser una hija obediente y _______ sólo salgo con mis amigos los sábados por la noche.
_______ Pedro es mi novio y mi madre no puede controlarme la vida.
_______ necesito ayuda, por favor.

Ana

Linking words

y	and	*luego*	then, next
pero	but	*sin embargo*	however
porque	because	*en cambio*	on the other hand
también	also	*por otro lado*	on the other hand
además	also / moreover	*aunque*	although
por eso	that's why	*después*	afterwards
claro (que)	of course	*al final*	in the end / finally
entonces	so / then		

Gramática página 187

4a Choose the appropriate verb form in each sentence and write out the sentence correctly.

1 Mi novia ideal <u>me gustaría / sería / le gustaría</u> muy inteligente.
2 <u>Me gustaría / Sería / Serías</u> tener muchos niños en el futuro.
3 <u>¿Serías / Nos gustaría / Te gustaría</u> salir conmigo?
4 Mis padres viven en un piso, pero en el futuro <u>les gustaría / le gustaría / serían</u> vivir en una casa.

Saying 'would like'

Use the conditional tense to say 'would like' or 'would be'.

me gustaría	I would like
sería	I would be

Gramática página 184

4b Imagine you are a celebrity. You have been asked to describe your ideal weekend break. Use the conditional tense of *gustar* or *ser* to talk about:

- where you would go and would stay
- who you would go with and why
- what you would do
- what you wouldn't like.

Forming the negative

Gramática *página 186*

- To make a sentence negative put *no* in front of the verb.
  e.g. *No tengo hermanos.*
- You can also use the following negative expressions:

nunca / jamás	never
nadie	no one
nada	nothing
ni … ni	neither … nor
no … ningún(o/a)	no / not any

- There are two ways of using *nunca / nadie / nada:*

1 Put it at the start of the sentence:
e.g. *Nunca voy a Madrid.* I never go to Madrid.

2 Put *no* before the verb, with *nunca / nadie / nada* after the verb.
e.g. *No voy nunca a Madrid.*

5 Write the following sentences in the negative form.

1 Es español.
2 Hay violencia en mi ciudad.
3 Siempre soy paciente.
4 Tenemos muchas oportunidades.
5 Mi amigo tiene todo.
6 Las chicas son inteligentes y divertidas.

siempre always
todo everything

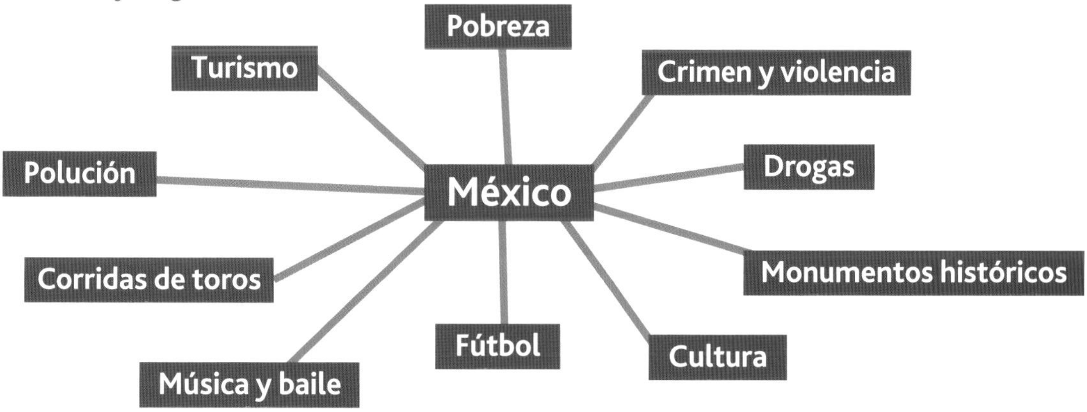

6 Look at the diagram about Mexico. Write some sentences giving your reaction to the information, using the examples in the box below. Try to extend your sentences with more details.

Lo ***bueno***
malo
mejor **(best thing)**
peor **(worst thing)**
importante
necesario
difícil
interesante

Lo + adjective

Gramática *página 174*

- If you put *lo* in front of an adjective it means 'the … thing'. e.g. *lo importante* the important thing
- You can use it with *es que:*
  e.g. *Lo bueno es que hay agua limpia.*
  The good thing is that there is clean water.
- You can also use it followed by an infinitive:
  e.g. *Lo importante es educar al público.*
  The important thing is to educate the public.

V Relationships and choices

Las descripciones personales ➡ *pages 32–33*

	alegre	happy / cheerful
	alto/a	tall
	amable	nice / pleasant
	antipático/a	unpleasant
	bajo/a	short (not tall)
la	*barba*	beard
el	*bigote*	moustache
	calvo/a	bald
	castaño/a	brown
	cómico/a	funny
	corto/a	short (hair)
	delgado/a	thin
	extrovertido/a	extrovert / outgoing
las	*gafas*	glasses
	gracioso/a	funny
	guapo/a	good-looking
	hablador(a)	chatty / talkative
	honesto/a	honest
	largo/a	long
	liso/a	straight
	moreno/a	(dark) brown
la	*nariz*	nose
el	*novio*	boyfriend
las	*orejas*	ears
	paciente	patient
las	*pecas*	freckles
	pelirrojo/a	red-haired
	rizado/a	curly
	rubio/a	blond
	sensible	sensitive
	simpático/a	nice / pleasant
	tímido/a	shy
	torpe	clumsy
	travieso/a	naughty
	vago/a	lazy

La situación familiar ➡ *pages 34–35*

el	*amor*	love
	casado/a	married
	casarse	to get married
	cuidar	to look after
	divorciado/a	divorced
la	*esposa*	wife
el	*esposo*	husband
el / la	*gemelo/a*	twin
los	*hermanastros*	stepbrothers and sisters
la	*hija*	daughter
el	*hijo*	son
los	*hijos*	children
	jubilado/a	retired
	loco/a	mad
la	*madre soltera*	single mother
el	*marido*	husband
el	*matrimonio*	marriage
la	*niñera*	nanny
el	*niño*	child
la	*novia*	girlfriend
el	*padrastro*	stepfather
en el	*paro*	unemployed
	separado/a	separated
	solo/a	alone
	soltero/a	single
el / la	*vecino/a*	neighbour
la	*viuda*	widow
el	*viudo*	widower

Las relaciones personales ➡ *pages 36–37*

	aguantar	to tolerate / put up with
la	*barrera generacional*	generation gap
	cariñoso/a	affectionate
	comprensivo/a	understanding

	comprender	to understand
la	*confianza*	trust
	convencer	to convince
	criticar	to criticize
la	*discusión*	argument
	egoísta	selfish
	enfadarse	to get angry
	feliz	happy
	honrado/a	honest / honourable
	impaciente	impatient
la	*influencia*	influence
	llevarse (bien / mal) con	to get on (well / badly) with
	maleducado/a	rude
la	*pareja*	couple
	pelearse	to fight
	relacionarse	to relate to / get to know
	respetar	to respect

Los planes del futuro ➡ *pages 38–39*

el / la	*compañero/a*	companion / friend
	independiente	independent
	jubilarse	to retire
el / la	*nieto/a*	grandson/daughter
	pesimista	pessimistic
la	*vida familiar*	family life

La igualdad para todos ➡ *pages 40–41*

la	*actitud*	attitude
el	*comentario*	comment
	cometer	to commit
los	*derechos*	rights
la	*desigualdad*	inequality
la	*diferencia*	difference
la	*discriminación*	discrimination
la	*educación*	education
	educar	to educate
la	*encuesta*	survey
	estar a favor	to be in favour
	estar de acuerdo	to agree
	estar en contra	to be against
el / la	*extranjero/a*	foreigner
la	*igualdad*	equality
el / la	*inmigrante*	immigrant
la	*integración*	integration
	maltratar	to abuse
	matar	to kill
la	*mayoría*	the majority
el	*mundo*	world
la	*reacción*	reaction
el	*sentimiento*	feeling
el / la	*trabajador(a)*	worker
la	*víctima*	victim
la	*violencia doméstica*	domestic violence

La pobreza ➡ *pages 42–43*

	acoger	to welcome
el	*agua (f) corriente*	running water
la	*alcantarilla*	drain
	arruinar	to ruin
el	*barrio*	district / area
el	*beneficio*	benefit
la	*carretera*	road
el	*cartón*	cardboard
el	*desarrollo*	development
	encontrar	to find
	estable	stable
las	*expectativas*	expectations
el/la	*gerente*	manager
el/la	*habitante*	inhabitant
	injusto/a	unfair
la	*ONG*	NGO (non-governmental organisation)
el	*país*	country
la	*piedra*	stone
los	*pobres*	poor people
la	*pobreza*	poverty
el	*prejuicio*	prejudice
la	*riqueza*	wealth
el	*techo*	roof
el	*tratamiento*	treatment

1 La vida sana

Your Spanish exchange partner asks you some questions from a survey about healthy living. You have to:

1 Say if your lifestyle is generally healthy or not
2 Talk about your diet
3 Say what activities you can do to be fit and healthy
4 Give your opinion about smoking
5 Talk about alcohol in the UK
6 Say what you will do to be more healthy in future
7 !

! Remember you will have to respond to something that you have not yet prepared.

Study tips

You can use a task planning form to help you remember what you want to say. You are allowed a maximum of 40 words in Spanish, English or both. Any words are allowed as long as they are not conjugated verbs. You cannot use any symbols or codes or any visuals (drawings, etc.) in addition to the 40 words.

1 Say if your lifestyle is generally healthy or not.

- Say if you are healthy or not
- Say if your diet is good or bad for your health
- Say if you are fit or not
- Say if you have any bad habits

Study tips

Start off with *En general, (no) soy muy sano(a)* or *(no) llevo una vida sana*.

Remember to use *estar* for *estoy en forma* and *ser* for *es bueno / malo para la salud*.

Don't go into too much detail at this stage.

Here are some suggested words for the first section: *sano/a, salud, estar en forma, hábito*

2 Talk about your diet.

- Say what you normally eat and drink
- Say which foods are healthy and why
- Say which foods are unhealthy and why
- Give your opinion of eating healthily

Study tips

Suggested words for your notes:
desayuno, contener, verduras, grasa, proteína, odiar

Say what you eat and drink for breakfast, lunch and evening meal. Vary the verbs, e.g. *como / tomo / me gusta comer*. To extend the language you could use a past time frame, e.g. *Ayer comí / bebí* – 'yesterday I ate / drank' … *era / estaba.* – 'it was' … Revise information on past time frames.

3 Say what activities you can do to be fit and healthy.

- Say if you like doing any sports or exercise
- Say if your daily routine helps you to be healthy (sleeping / watching TV, etc.)
- Say what activities you have done recently to be fit and healthy
- Say if you are stressed / relaxed and why

Study tips

Suggested words for your notes:
hacer ejercicio, dormir, estresado/a, necesario

You can use the infinitive of the verb after *me gusta, se puede, es necesario*, etc. To say 'I play' when referring to sports use: *juego al, hago* or *practico*.

Always try to add extra details (e.g. where, who with, when …).

4 Give your opinion about smoking.

- Say if you, your family or friends smoke
- Talk about the dangers of smoking
- Give some facts about smoking (in the UK or a Spanish-speaking country)
- Say if you agree with a smoking ban

Study tips

Suggested words for your notes:
fumar, causar, peligroso, de acuerdo, prohibido
Make sure you link your sentences to extend them using: *porque, pero,* etc.
Check the verb ending agrees with the person you are talking about (I, my mother, my friends, etc.).
See page 180 to revise verb endings.

5 Talk about alcohol in the UK.

- Say if you or your friends drink alcohol
- Mention what kinds of problems alcohol causes in the UK
- Say what the consequences are
- Compare the dangers of alcohol with smoking

Study tips

Suggested words for your notes:
bebidas alcohólicas, adictivo, borracho, violencia, crimen
Always check the pronunciation guide (p.194) when preparing the speaking assessment, especially for more complex vocabulary.

6 Say what you will do to be more healthy in future.

- Say which food or drink you will eat or avoid
- Say what activities you would like to do
- Mention any habits you should change
- Say why you want to be more healthy

Study tips

Suggested words for your notes:
evitar, cambiar, llevar, vida, responsable

Make sure that you use a wide variety of language structures and refer to the past, present and future wherever possible. The simplest ways to refer to the future are using *voy a* + infinitive ('I am going to' ...); *me gustaría* + infinitive ('I would like' ...) ; *se debería* + infinitive ('you / people should'...) See page 183 to revise the future.

7 **!**
At this point, you will be asked another question which you don't know in advance. However, you can try to guess what it might be and prepare various options:

- Does school help you to be fit and healthy
- Your opinion about drugs
- Compare the dangers of drugs, cigarettes and / or alcohol
- Why it is important to be healthy

Study tips

Even if the question is a complete surprise, you will have learnt enough relevant vocabulary and phrases to say something. Use the conversation filler ideas (p.39) to keep your conversation going.

You should now have completed your plan and prepared your answers. Give your plan to your teacher for feedback. Compare your answers to the online sample version – you might find some useful hints to make yours even better.

kerboodle

1 Mi familia, mis amigos y yo

You are writing about yourself on the internet to a Spanish friend, Juan. You could write as yourself or imagine you are a celebrity or a character in a TV programme.
Write about yourself, your family and friends, your opinions and concerns.

1 Say your age and what you look like
2 Describe your personality and interests
3 Talk about your family
4 Say if you get on with members of your family and why / why not
5 Describe your friends
6 Say what you want to do in the future
7 Talk about a social problem you feel strongly about

Study tips

You can use a task planning form to help you remember what you want to write. You are allowed a maximum of 40 words in Spanish, English or both. Any words are allowed as long as they are not conjugated verbs. You cannot use any symbols or codes or any visuals (drawings, etc.) in addition to the 40 words.

1 Say your age and what you look like.

- Give your age
- Describe your hair and eyes
- Describe your height and build
- Give extra physical details (glasses / freckles, etc.)

Study tips

Remember to use *tengo … años* for age. Give a variety of adjectives and link short phrases together. You could compare your present and past appearance: *Antes tenía … era …* (Before, I had … I was …). See page 182 for more information about the imperfect tense.

Here are some suggested words for the first section: *tener, pelo, rubio/a, ojos, alto/a, gafas*

2 Describe your personality and interests.

- Say what you are like as a person
- Compare your personality with your family and / or friends
- Say what your main hobbies are
- Say what doesn't interest you

Study tips

Suggested words for your notes:
simpático/a, gracioso/a, pasatiempo, deporte, interesar

Try to avoid a long list of adjectives after *soy* or *mi amigo es* … Use *bastante, muy, un poco, demasiado* in front of adjectives to vary the language, or use adverbs such as *a veces, mucho*.

3 Talk about your family.

- Say who is in your family
- Say who is married / divorced / single and for how long
- Mention something you have done recently with your family, e.g. a special occasion or celebration
- Ask a question about Juan's family

Study tips

To talk about another person, use *es, está* (he / she is), *tiene* (he / she has). You can mention your extended family as well.

To talk about what you have done use the preterite or perfect tense. See pages 181–182 for more information.

Suggested words for your notes:
hermano, estar casado/a, desde hace, tu

4 Say if you get on with members of your family and why / why not.

- Say who you get on well with and why
- Say who you don't get on well with and why
- Describe a problem you have with your family at home
- Say if it is important to have good family relationships and why

Study tips

Suggested words for your notes:
llevarse, pelearse, discusiones, buenas relaciones

Remember to include the *me* in reflexive verbs, e.g. *me llevo / me peleo con / es importante relacionarme bien con …*

When giving your opinion try to justify it, saying why you like or dislike someone or something and link your ideas with *porque / pero / también*, etc.

5 Describe your friends.

- Say who your friends are
- Say what you like doing with friends
- Describe one friend
- Say what an ideal friend is like

Study tips

Suggested words for your notes:
amigos, ir, jugar, comprensivo/a, pasarlo bien

Here is an opportunity to use the conditional tense: *mi amigo/a ideal sería … / tendría …* (my ideal friend would be … / would have …).

6 Say what you want to do in the future.

- Say what you want to do after leaving school
- Say where you would like to live
- Say if you want to get married
- Give your opinion of having children

Study tips

Suggested words for your notes:
instituto, trabajar, vivir, casarse, niños

To refer to the future use *voy a* + infinitive (I am going to …); *me gustaría* + infinitive (I would like to …)

Try to add reasons to say why you want to do these things.

7 Talk about a social problem you feel strongly about.

- Mention a social problem in the UK or abroad (racism / poverty / drugs / violence / discrimination)
- Give some details about the problem
- Say what you think of the problem
- Say what can be done to help

Study tips

You can keep the language quite simple, using structures such as *se necesita / se puede / se debe* + infinitive.

Suggested words for your notes:
racismo, discriminación, comprensión, ayudar, educar

You should now have completed your plan and prepared your answers. Give your plan to your teacher for feedback. As this is a practice task, your teacher might choose to also give you feedback on your first draft. However, when it comes to a task that is part of your GCSE Spanish, you will get feedback on your plan but **not** on your first draft. Now compare your answers with the online sample version – you might find some useful hints to make yours even better.

kerboodle

Context summary

Resumen

1 Copy and complete the following sentence with one word.

La fruta es muy ______ para la salud.

2 Copy and complete this sentence with a suitable phrase.

Para estar en forma es necesario …

3 Answer the following question.

¿Fumas? ¿Por qué (no)?

4 Translate the following sentence into English.

Las drogas son más peligrosas que el alcohol.

5 Write another sentence which gives the same description as this one, without using *simpática* or *alta*.

Mi amiga, Rosa, es muy simpática, rubia y no es muy alta.

6 Copy and complete the following sentence with one word.

Una persona soltera no está …

7 Copy the sentence and fill in the gap with the most appropriate word.

No hay problemas en casa ______ me llevo bien con mis padres.

8 Answer the following question in a complete sentence.

¿Qué vas a hacer en el futuro?

9 Copy the sentence and fill in the gap with an appropriate infinitive of a verb.

Hay mucha discriminación contra los inmigrantes, que es preocupante. Por eso, se deben ______ las actitudes racistas.

10 Is the following statement true or false?

Para ayudar a los pobres en Perú, se deben crear más oportunidades de educación.

¿Lo sabes?

- Los 'fish and chips' no son británicos. Comer pescado frito es una idea española y la patata tiene su origen en Perú.
- A los 14 años los novios en España normalmente salen en grupos. A los 18 años salen como pareja.
- Muchos jóvenes viven con su familia hasta los 30 años.

2 Leisure

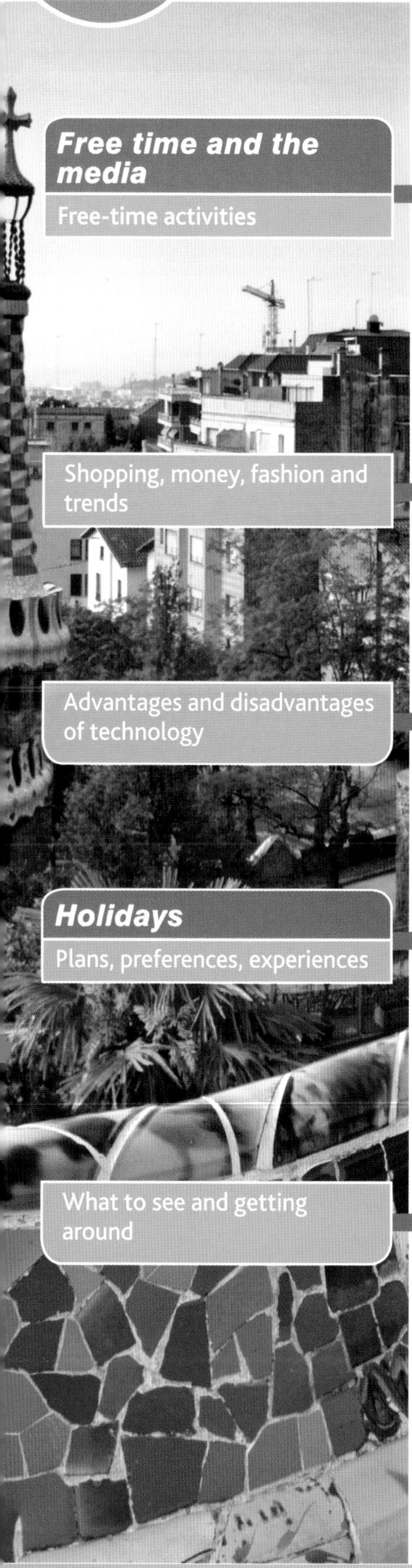

Key Stage 3 Revision

Free time and the media
Free-time activities

2.1 El tiempo libre en casa
- Using the preterite tense of regular verbs
- Improving fluency by learning complete phrases

2.2 Fuera de casa
- Using irregular preterites: *ir, ser*
- Using time expressions to recognise whether a statement is in the past tense or the present

Shopping, money, fashion and trends

2.3 ¿En qué gastas tu dinero?
- Using direct object pronouns
- Learning colloquial expressions

2.4 ¿Te gusta estar de moda?
- Using demonstrative pronouns (*éste, ése, aquél*)
- Using a variety of words and phrases to express preferences

Advantages and disadvantages of technology

2.5 Los jóvenes y la tecnología
- Using indirect object pronouns
- Justifying your opinions and adding extra information

Holidays
Plans, preferences, experiences

2.6 Las vacaciones
- Using irregular preterite verbs
- Showing off the language you know

2.7 ¿Adónde vas?
- Using the immediate future
- Noting prefixes that are the same in Spanish and English

What to see and getting around

2.8 He ido a la fiesta
- Using the perfect tense to talk about what you have done recently
- Using time phrases in your written work

2.9 ¡Vamos de viaje!
- Using imperative verb forms
- Using high numbers and 24-hour time

Sports and other leisure activities, fashion and clothes

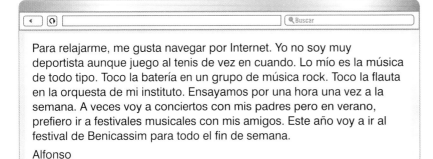

Buscar

Para relajarme, me gusta navegar por Internet. Yo no soy muy deportista aunque juego al tenis de vez en cuando. Lo mío es la música de todo tipo. Toco la batería en un grupo de música rock. Toco la flauta en la orquesta de mi instituto. Ensayamos por una hora una vez a la semana. A veces voy a conciertos con mis padres pero en verano, prefiero ir a festivales musicales con mis amigos. Este año voy a ir al festival de Benicassim para todo el fin de semana.

Alfonso

1 Read Alfonso's blog and answer the following questions in Spanish.

1 ¿Cómo se relaja Alfonso?
2 ¿Qué deporte practica?
3 ¿Qué instrumentos toca?
4 ¿Cuántas veces a la semana toca en la orquesta de su instituto?
5 ¿Con quién va a festivales en el verano?

Cristina, ¿llevas uniforme al instituto?

No, no hay uniforme. Me pongo vaqueros y zapatillas de deporte.

¿Qué te pones para salir con tus amigos?

Depende. Si voy a una fiesta me pongo un vestido.

¿Qué te pones para ir al trabajo?

Tengo un trabajo parcial en una cafetería. Llevo zapatos cómodos, pantalones negros y una blusa blanca.

2a Read the conversation above and answer the following questions in English.

1 When does Cristina wear trainers?
2 When does she wear a dress?
3 What sort of shoes does she wear to work?

2b Work in pairs. Partner A asks the questions in the conversation and Partner B gives their own answers. Then swap roles.

Por and *para* ('for')

- Use *para* to express: a specified future period of time / deadline, e.g. *Voy a ir para tres días.* I'm going to go for three days.
- Use *por* to express: a period of time / timescale, e.g. *Estuve en Gerona por un mes.* I was in Gerona for a month.

Gramática página 187

Vocabulario

escuchar música	to listen to music
jugar …	to play … (a sport)
navegar por Internet	to surf the internet
tocar …	to play … (an instrument)
la batería	drums

Vocabulario

la blusa	blouse
los pantalones	trousers
los vaqueros	jeans
el vestido	dress
las zapatillas de deporte	trainers
los zapatos	shoes
ponerse	to put on
llevar	to wear

Places in town, transport and compass points

Mira, Anita. Este plano es de mi pueblo. Esta plaza es la Plaza Mayor. Aquí está el ayuntamiento.

¿Qué es ese edificio, Paco?

Es la biblioteca y al lado están Correos y la comisaría.

¿Hay un centro comercial?

No, pero esta calle es la calle principal con bancos y unos grandes almacenes.

¿Hay metro?

Todavía no hay. Esa estación es de autobuses. Aquella estación, en las afueras, es la del tren.

¿Qué es aquéllo?

Era una fábrica pero ahora es un hotel. Y aquel hospital es nuevo.

¿Y para diversión?

Hay cines, restaurantes, discotecas ... de todo.

Vocabulario

el ayuntamiento	town hall
la biblioteca	library
el castillo	castle
el centro comercial	shopping centre
el cine	cinema
la comisaría	police station
la estación de autobuses / trenes	bus / railway station
el estadio	stadium
la fábrica	factory
los grandes almacenes	department store
la plaza	square

1 Read the conversation. There is one error in each of the following sentences. Rewrite each sentence correctly.

1 The town hall is on the High Street.
2 The police station, Post Office and bookshop are close to each other.
3 There is no department store.
4 The town has an underground train system.

Demonstrative adjectives

Gramática página 176

Demonstrative adjectives ('this, that'; 'these, those') are used with a noun and must agree with it.

este	*esta*	*estos*	*estas*	this / these
ese	*esa*	*esos*	*esas*	that / those
aquel	*aquella*	*aquellos*	*aquellas*	that / those

Aquel refers to something further away:

Ese polideportivo es viejo pero aquél es nuevo.

The same words are also used as demonstrative pronouns, appearing in place of a noun ('this one' and 'that one', 'these ones' and 'those ones'). Remember that these words have an accent when they are used as pronouns.

2a Read this description and draw a map showing the location of all the places mentioned.

Mi pueblo está en el oeste del país. En el centro de mi pueblo está la plaza. Al norte de la plaza está el río y al sur están el parque y el castillo. Al este del castillo hay una iglesia y al sur hay una fábrica. Al oeste de la fábrica hay un supermercado.

2b Write a description of an imaginary town. Locate four places according to their compass points.

2c Work in pairs. Partner A reads their description and Partner B draws a map to show the places mentioned. Then swap roles.

Vocabulario

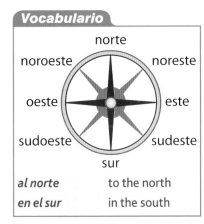

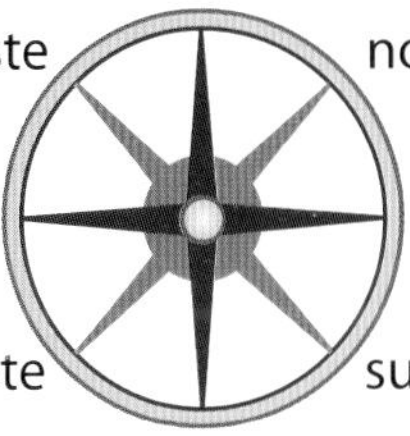

al norte	to the north
en el sur	in the south

2.1 El tiempo libre en casa

Objetivos

- Talking about leisure activities at home
- Using the preterite tense of regular verbs
- Improving fluency by learning complete phrases

El diario de una joven madrileña

sábado, 15 de enero

Por la mañana me despertó un ruido tremendo en casa. Mi hermano empezó a tocar la batería, mi hermana pequeña lloró porque mi padre apagó la tele y justo en el mismo momento, mi madre decidió pasar la aspiradora. ¡Qué jaleo! Invité a mi hermanita a ver dibujos animados en mi ordenador portátil, cerré bien la puerta de mi dormitorio y escuché música en mi MP3. ¡Pura tranquilidad!

Después leí las noticias en el portátil y escribí un correo electrónico. Llamé a unas amigas del insti y hablé un rato con ellas. Luego jugué al ping-pong con mi hermano y gané el partido. Pero luego jugamos un videojuego y ganó él.

Por la tarde recibí un mensaje de mi amiga Alba. Me invitó a ver una película en su casa. Menos mal porque en aquel momento mis hermanos y mis padres se pelearon porque todos querían ver un programa diferente en la tele. A mi hermano le gusta Gran Hermano, a mi madre una telenovela o un documental y a mi padre las noticias o el deporte.

Alba y yo elegimos una película de acción porque no nos gustan nada las películas románticas ni las comedias. Comimos palomitas y bebimos Coca-Cola. Volví a casa a eso de las nueve. Luego cené, leí un rato y me acosté.

Gabriela

1a Read Gabriela's diary, then put the pictures into the correct order.

1b Choose the correct infinitive to complete each phrase and then match up each phrase with the correct picture (A–E).

1 … al ping-pong
2 … la batería
3 … una película
4 … música
5 … mensajes

escuchar | jugar | recibir / enviar | tocar | ver

1c From reading the diary page, what do you know about Gabriela, her family, her personality and what she does in her free time?

2 Ⓖ Copy the sentences and fill in the gaps with the correct verb.

lavó **me desperté** **recibiste** **tocaron**

1 Normalmente me despierto a las 7.30 pero ayer ______ a las 9.00.
2 ¿ ______ mi mensaje ayer? ¿Quieres venir a mi casa a ver una película?
3 Yo corté el césped y mi hermano ______ el coche.
4 Anoche mi hermano y su amigo ______ la guitarra y la batería hasta las diez.

3 Copy the table, then listen to the conversations and tick the boxes to show what each person did at the weekend.

	Alberto	Carla	José Luis
Helped at home			
Listened to music			
Played a sport			
Played a video game			
Played a musical instrument			
Took the dog for a walk			
Watched TV			

4 Write a diary or blog entry about a day at home last weekend. Include the following time expressions:

El sábado / domingo por la mañana
A mediodía
Después de comer
Por la tarde
Antes de cenar

Gramática *página 181*

Using the preterite tense of regular verbs

Regular verbs have the following endings in the preterite:

-ar	**-er**	**-ir**
escuchar	*comer*	*escribir*
*escuch**é***	*com**í***	*escrib**í***
*escuch**aste***	*com**iste***	*escrib**iste***
*escuch**ó***	*com**ió***	*escrib**ió***
*escuch**amos***	*com**imos***	*escrib**imos***
*escuch**asteis***	*com**isteis***	*escrib**isteis***
*escuch**aron***	*com**ieron***	*escrib**ieron***

Also learn about the use of infinitives.

See page 71 ➡

Consejo

Useful time expressions for talking about the past:

a eso de	about, around (of time)
a mediodía	at midday
anoche	last night
antes (de)	before
ayer	yesterday
después	after
(justo) en aquel / ese / este momento	(just, exactly) at that / this moment
luego	then
por la mañana	in the morning
por la noche	at night
por la tarde	in the afternoon / evening
un rato	for a little while
el sábado por la mañana	on Saturday morning
la semana pasada	last week

Escuché	música / la radio / un CD.	
Escribí Envié Recibí	un correo electrónico / un mensaje / una carta.	
Leí	un libro / una revista un periódico / un tebeo	en mi dormitorio / en el salón. en el jardin / en el patio. en la terraza.
Jugué	al fútbol / al ping-pong al baloncesto / un videojuego	
Toqué	la batería / la flauta / la guitarra / el piano.	
Vi	una película / telenovela un documental las noticias	en la tele / en el portátil.

Estrategia

You can adapt the phrases to give other information and you will also sound more fluent.

escuchar *música / un CD / la radio*
jugar *al fútbol / al baloncesto / al billar*
tocar *la guitarra / el piano / la flauta*
ver *la tele / las noticias / una telenovela.*

kerboodle

2.2 Fuera de casa

Objetivos

- Discussing free-time activities outside the home
- Using irregular preterites: *ir*, *ser*
- Using time expressions to recognise whether a statement is in the past tense or the present

1 Ⓥ Look at the photos and answer the question: ¿Qué es para ti un fin de semana genial?

ir a un parque temático

ir a un concierto de rock

ir a un partido de fútbol

salir con los amigos

ir a la playa

practicar deporte

Un fin de semana genial

Me llamo Guillermo. Tengo 15 años y me encanta el deporte y la música. Normalmente, los sábados por la mañana voy a una clase de música, y por la tarde juego al tenis con mi hermano Gerardo. Los domingos hacemos los deberes y jugamos al tenis otra vez. A mí me gusta también la natación y el ciclismo; a mi hermano le gusta el atletismo. Así que de momento no tenemos mucho tiempo libre.

El fin de semana pasado fuimos a un campeonato de tenis en Sitges, una ciudad en la costa. Fueron también nuestros padres. El sábado jugamos varios partidos. Llegamos a la final pero no ganamos la copa. El domingo Gerardo participó en una carrera de mini-maratón. Fui a verle correr.

Por suerte, el lunes no fuimos al instituto porque fue un día festivo. Por la mañana fuimos a la playa y por la tarde fuimos a Port Aventura, un parque temático estupendo. Monté tres veces en la montaña rusa más alta y más rápida del parque. Lo pasé genial.

Me llamo Montse y quiero decirles cómo suelo pasar el finde. Pues generalmente, el sábado por la tarde salgo por ahí con mis amigos. A veces vamos al cine y de vez en cuando vamos a bailar.

Tengo muchos deberes, así que el domingo salgo poco. Sin embargo, la semana pasada lo pasé fenomenal. Había fiesta en mi ciudad y el sábado por la noche salimos toda nuestra pandilla de amigos hasta las dos de la mañana. En la plaza mayor tocaron varios grupos de rock y también vimos un espectáculo de baile increíble.

El domingo un amigo que es jugador juvenil del Villareal me regaló dos entradas para un partido entre Villareal y Valencia. El ambiente en el estadio fue fantástico. En el descanso nos invitó a tomar un refresco en el salón especial para los invitados del equipo. Fue un sueño hecho realidad.

Estrategia

Time expressions: past and present

Use your knowledge of time expressions to help you recognise whether a statement is in the past tense or the present. Words and expressions like *ahora* (now) and *de momento* (at the moment) are for the present. Expressions like *la semana pasada* (last week), *el fin de semana pasado* (last weekend), *el año pasado* (last year) describe past time. How many more past time expressions can you remember?

2a Who usually does these activities, Guillermo, Gerardo and / or Montse?

1 Has a music lesson on Saturday morning.
2 Does homework on Sunday.
3 Likes swimming and cycling.
4 Likes running.
5 Goes out with friends on Saturday.

2b Who did these activities last weekend, Guillermo, Gerardo or Montse?

1 Played in a tennis tournament.
2 Watched / took part in a fun run.
3 Went to a theme park.
4 Saw a rock band.
5 Watched a football match.

Gramática *página 182*

Using irregular preterites: *ir*, *ser*

The verbs *ser* (to be) and *ir* (to go) are the same in the preterite tense:

fui	I was / went
fuiste	you were / went
fue	he, she, it, you (formal) was / were / went
fuimos	we were / went
fuisteis	you were / went
fueron	they, you (formal, plural) were / went

***Fui** al cine anoche pero la película **fue** fatal.* I **went** to the cinema last night but the film **was** terrible.

Also learn some time and place expressions.

See page 70 ➡

3 Copy and complete the dialogue using the correct parts of *ser* / *ir* in the preterite.

Marián: ¿Qué tal tu fin de semana, José Luis? ¿________ a la playa?
José Luis: No, no ________ a la costa. El sábado salí con Jaime y Juan.
Marián: ¿ ________ al cine?
José Luis: Sí, ________ a ver aquella película de ciencia ficción que ponen en el Cine Metro.
Marián: ¿Fue buena o mala?
José Luis: ________ fatal. Después de media hora salí y me fui a casa.
Marián: ¿Y Jaime y Juan?
José Luis: Se quedaron allí hasta el final y luego ________ a tomar unas tapas por ahí.

4a Listen to the conversations. Did each of these people have a good weekend or not?

4b Listen again and answer the questions in English.

1 What event did Laura go to and where did it take place?
2 What event did Pablo take part in and what was the outcome?
3 Why do you think Pablo is still feeling fed up?
4 Why was it a special weekend for Noelia?
5 How would you describe Noelia´s mood now?
6 Where did Raúl go for the weekend and who did he go with?
7 Why do you think the radio presenter asks Raúl if he has won the lottery?
8 What is Raúl's answer?

Consejo

There is no short cut to learning verbs. Read each form of the verb in the grammar box and learn it by heart. Repeat it to yourself. Then try to write it out from memory. Check what you have written.

5 Work in pairs. Take turns to be Marián and José Luis. Adapt the dialogue by changing the underlined words. Refer to the online worksheet for a language structure box to help you.

Marián: ¿Qué tal tu fin de semana, José Luis? ¿Fuiste a <u>un partido de fútbol</u>?
José Luis: No, no fui a <u>un partido</u>.
Marián: ¿Fuiste al cine?
José Luis: Sí, fui a ver una película <u>de ciencia ficción</u>.
Marián: ¿Fue buena o mala?
José Luis: Fue <u>fatal</u>.

2.3 ¿En qué gastas tu dinero?

Objetivos
- Talking about money and shopping
- Using direct object pronouns
- Learning colloquial expressions

El consumismo y los jóvenes

- Los chicos son más consumistas que las chicas, pero ellas gastan la mitad de su dinero en ropa.
- Los chicos se dejan influir más por cuestiones como la moda, las marcas o la publicidad que las chicas.
- Los jóvenes españoles de entre 14 y 24 años gastan alrededor de 120 euros al mes (unos 30 euros a la semana).
- El ocio es lo que importa. Los jóvenes disfrutan más del tiempo libre que los mayores. Gastan el dinero en salir con los amigos y en comer fuera de casa.
- Los jóvenes que trabajan ahorran más y valoran mucho más el dinero que los que siguen recibiendo la paga.
- La paga semanal media de los españoles de 16 y 17 años es algo más de 11.50 euros. Sin embargo, la mayoría dice que siempre hay que ir pidiendo más 'pasta'.
- El 15% de los jóvenes tienen adicción al consumo (son adictos a las compras). Según los psicólogos, compran para mejorar su autoestima y para ser admirados.

1a Read the article and match up these Spanish expressions taken from it with their English equivalents:

el consumismo	fashion and designer labels
la moda y las marcas	to improve their self-esteem
la paga (semanal media)	(average weekly) pocket money
mejorar su autoestima	consumerism

1b Read the article again and answer the following questions in English.

1. According to the survey, who spends more, girls or boys?
2. What do girls spend half their money on?
3. What are boys more influenced by than girls?
4. How much, on average, do young people in Spain spend per week?
5. What is more important to young people than to older people?
6. Who saves more and has a better sense of the value of money?
7. What is the average weekly allowance for Spanish 16- to 17-year-olds?
8. According to the experts, why do people become addicted to shopping?

2 Listen to a Spanish teenager being interviewed for a market research survey. Note his responses to the survey by answering these questions.

1. What does the boy usually spend his money on? (Mention three things.)
2. Where does his money come from? (Mention two sources.)
3. What does the boy say about saving money? (Mention two details.)
4. From what the boy says, do you think his parents are:
   a understanding / generous b strict c unfair?

3 Ⓖ Match up each question with the correct answer.

1 ¿Por qué no llevas tus zapatillas nuevas?
2 ¿Puedo pagar con tarjeta de crédito?
3 ¿Por qué compraste la chaqueta azul?
4 ¿Por qué salisteis con Jaime anoche?

a Porque me va bien este color.
b Porque nos invitó a cenar.
c Porque las dejé en el centro deportivo.
d Sí, puede usarla.

4 Create your own financial profile using expressions from the language structure box. Start like this:

Generalmente gasto dinero en salir con mis amigos y en _______ pero de vez en cuando lo gasto en DVDs, regalos o _______.

Using direct object pronouns

Gramática *página 178*

me	me	*nos*	us
te	you	*os*	you
lo, la	him / her / it / you	*los, las*	them / you

A direct object pronoun replaces the noun (person or thing) which is the object of the verb in a sentence. It usually comes before the verb.

¿En qué gastas tu dinero?	What do you spend your money on?
***Lo** gasto en ropa y en salir con mis amigos.*	I spend it on clothes and on going out with friends.
¿Dónde compraste los zapatos?	Where did you buy the shoes?
***Los** compré en Barcelona.*	I bought them in Barcelona.

Pronouns can be attached to an infinitive:

*¿Podría hacer**te** algunas preguntas?*	Could I ask you some questions?

Also learn about gerunds. *See page 71* ➡

¿De dónde recibes tu dinero?		
Lo recibo de	mis padres mis abuelos mis tíos	cada semana. cada mes. por mi cumpleaños.
Lo gano porque trabajo	los sábados los domingos durante las vacaciones	en una tienda. en un restaurante.
¿En qué lo gastas?		
Lo gasto en	salir con los amigos. comprar ropa. los deportes.	
¿Cuánto dinero gastas y cuánto dinero ahorras?		
Generalmente Normalmente	gasto … libras ahorro … libras	a la semana. al mes.

Learn real language

Estrategia

Make your Spanish more authentic by reading real texts from magazines, newspapers and the internet. Notice the useful expressions and try to include them in your writing and speaking.

Para mí es importante disfrutar de mi tiempo libre y gasto dinero en salir con mis amigos.

Consejo

Using colloquial expressions helps to make your Spanish more authentic, but make sure you know when to use them. For example, you can use *pasta* as a colloquial word for 'money' when talking to someone of your own age, but you should use *dinero* in a more formal situation.

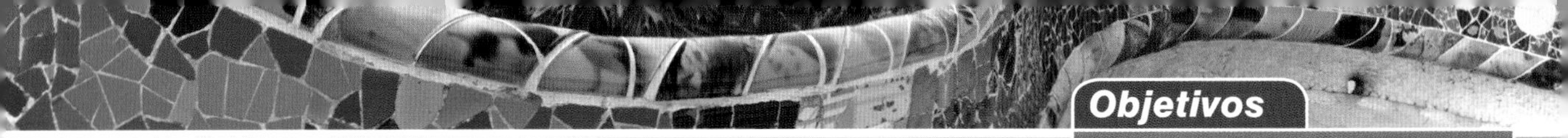

2.4 ¿Te gusta estar de moda?

Objetivos

- Discussing your views on fashion and trends
- Using demonstrative pronouns (*éste*, *ése*, *aquél*)
- Using a variety of words and phrases to express preferences

Mateo

Creo que cada uno debe tener su propia imagen y su propio estilo. Es aburrido si todo el mundo lleva los mismos colores y los mismos estilos simplemente para ir a la moda. Nunca compro ropa de marca porque es muy cara y no vale la pena. Me gusta vestirme de manera original y muy diferente a los demás.

Juan

No compro mucha ropa pero la que tengo es de buena calidad. Prefiero llevar estilos clásicos. Nunca compro ropa en Internet – la compro en los grandes almacenes o en tiendas de ropa porque es importante que esté bien hecha.

Alba

Eso de la moda no me interesa nada. Además, odio ir de compras. Para mí, es más importante la comodidad. Con una camiseta, unos vaqueros y zapatillas de deporte tengo suficiente. Prefiero gastar dinero en disfrutar de mi tiempo libre que en ropa y complementos.

Nicolá

Voy de compras todos los fines de semana y leo muchas revistas porque creo que, para estar de moda, tengo que ver lo que hay en las tiendas de ropa, cuáles son las tendencias del momento y qué colores se usan. Todo eso me encanta. Adoro la ropa y los complementos. También son super importantes para mí el peinado y el maquillaje.

1 Read the accounts of personal style and fashion preference. Match up each person with one of the following descriptions, giving reasons for your choices.

1 The most fashion-conscious person.
2 The least fashion-conscious person.
3 Someone who likes to be different.
4 The person least likely to buy clothes in a sale.
5 The person whose attitude to fashion is similar to yours.

2a Watch the video clip and choose the correct option to complete each of the following sentences.

1 El vídeo tiene lugar en …
a un supermercado.
b una tienda de ropa.
c una zapatería.

2 La chica quiere probarse …
a una chaqueta.
b una falda.
c un vestido.

3 Por fin, la chica decide comprar …
a dos vestidos.
b un vestido y un pañuelo.
c un vestido y un collar.

4 El chico compra …
a una camisa y una corbata.
b unas zapatillas de deporte.
c una camiseta y unos calcetines.

2b Watch again and answer the following questions in English.

1 What does the girl ask the assistant first?
2 Where are the changing rooms?
3 Does the girl pay by cheque, credit card or with cash?
4 How much change does the girl get from 100 euros?

3 G Copy the sentences and fill in the gaps with the correct demonstrative pronoun.

1 Aquella chaqueta es carísima pero _______ es más barata.
éste / ésta / éstas
2 Estos pantalones me quedan bien pero _______ son demasiado grandes.
ése / ésas / ésos
3 Ese vestido te va muy bien pero _______ no te favorece tanto.
éste / ésta / éstos
4 ¿Quiere probarse estos zapatos o _______?
aquél / aquéllas / aquéllos

4 Write your own personal style statement. Use some of the ideas and expressions from the four texts on page 64. Include the following:

- Your attitude to shopping – do you like it or hate it? Why?
- What kind of clothes and accessories you buy.
- Where you usually buy your clothes.
- Your views on designer clothes and 'labels'.
- If you don't like shopping for clothes, what you prefer to spend your money on.

Voy de compras Leo revistas de moda Compro ropa o zapatos	todos los fines de semana / dos veces al mes / nunca o casi nunca.	
Prefiero comprar	ropa de moda (pero no muy cara). ropa deportiva / maquillaje y complementos.	
Creo que es importante	comprar / elegir / llevar	tu propio estilo / estilos clásicos. ropa cómoda y práctica.
Prefiero comprar ropa en	los grandes almacenes / las tiendas de ropa. Internet / las tiendas de segunda mano.	

Consejo

Learn expressions to use in specific situations.
¿Qué talla lleva Ud? What size do you take?
¿Quiere probárselos? Do you want to try them on?
¿Qué tal le van? How are they? / Do they fit you?
Éstos me van bien. These fit me well.

Gramática página 179

Using demonstrative pronouns

A demonstrative pronoun replaces a noun to avoid repeating it.

Estos zapatos son elegantes pero prefiero aquéllos.
These shoes are smart but I prefer those.

There are two words for 'that one' and 'those': *ése, ésa, ésos, ésas* and *aquél, aquélla, aquéllos, aquéllas*. *Ése* refers to something that is nearer to the speaker and *aquél* to something further away.

The neuter forms *eso, esto* and *aquello* represent an idea rather than a thing or person.

Eso de la moda no me interesa nada.

Also learn some indefinite adjectives. *See page 71* ➡

Estrategia

Be expressive about your likes, dislikes and preferences.
***Adoro** la ropa y los complementos.*
***Me gusta** leer revistas de moda.*
***Me encanta** ir de compras.*
***Odio** el color verde.*

Consejo

In Spanish, adjectives usually follow the word they describe:
Me encanta aquella chaqueta roja.
I love that **red** jacket.
But notice the word order when describing the material and shade of colour:
camisa de algodón azul claro
pale blue cotton shirt

2.5 Los jóvenes y la tecnología

Objetivos

- Talking about the advantages and disadvantages of new technology
- Using indirect object pronouns
- Justifying your opinions and adding extra information

Encuesta: la tecnología y tú

Adoro mi móvil. Mis padres me lo regalaron por mi cumpleaños. Tiene cámara de fotos y de vídeo. Más que nada, lo uso para comunicarme con mis amigos. Mando muchos mensajes porque salen más económicos que las llamadas. Sin embargo mis padres me pagan los gastos del móvil. Dicen que se sienten más tranquilos al tener el móvil porque puedo llamarles para decirles con quién y dónde estoy y a qué hora llegaré a casa. ¿Y las desventajas? Veo muy pocas: que son bastante caros los móviles y son fáciles de robar.

Sara, 15 años

¿Cuáles de los siguientes aparatos son más importantes para ti?

- el teléfono móvil
- el ordenador portátil
- el MP3
- la cámara digital
- la videoconsola
- el equipo de música
- la televisión plana o de plasma

¿Cuáles son, en tu opinión, las ventajas de la nueva tecnología?

¿Cuáles son las desventajas?

Tengo un móvil y un ordenador pero lo que más me gusta últimamente es mi videoconsola. Es nueva. No me la regalaron mis padres. La compré con el dinero que gano trabajando los fines de semana. No tengo muchos juegos todavía pero a lo mejor me van a regalar algunos en Navidad o en Reyes. Mis padres a veces se quejan porque paso mucho tiempo jugando en la videoconsola. Pero yo lo paso estupendamente. Es muy entretenido y nunca estoy aburrido. Además, dicen que algunos videojuegos te mejoran la concentración, la coordinación y las reacciones. ¡Vaya excusa para seguir jugando!

Jorge, 16 años

Para mí es imprescindible el portátil. El que tengo no es el último modelo porque antes era de mi hermano. Me lo pasó a mí cuando él compró uno nuevo. Sin embargo es muy útil y tiene muchas ventajas. Por ejemplo, como tenemos banda ancha en casa, puedo conectarme fácilmente a Internet. Navegar en la red es entretenido e incluso educativo. No tengo que ir a la biblioteca o a la librería a buscar datos. También puedo descargar música de la red y esto me sale más económico que comprar discos compactos. El correo electrónico y el mensajero instantáneo los encuentro muy útiles porque puedo chatear y estar en contacto con mis amigos. Además, los deberes se hacen mejor en el ordenador. ¿Y las desventajas? El correo basura que recibes automáticamente con el email. Esto es muy desagradable.

Isabel, 17 años

1 Read the article and for each person write down:

1. The most important item.
2. How he / she acquired it / got it.
3. The advantages.
4. The disadvantages.

2a 🎧 Listen to three people being interviewed about communication technology. Write down which of the following items each interviewee mentions.

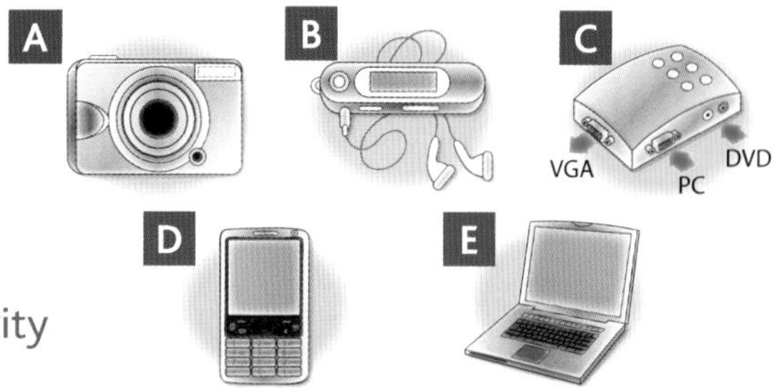

2b 🎧 Listen again. Make a list of the uses mentioned for each item, e.g. keeping in touch with friends, for security reasons, etc.

3 Ⓖ Copy the sentences and fill in the gaps with the appropriate indirect object pronoun.

1 – Tu nueva cámara digital es genial.
 – Sí, me encanta. ______ la regalaron mis padres en Navidad.
2 – ¿Tu padre sabe bajar música de Internet?
 – No, pero voy a enseñar______ a hacerlo.
3 – Recibí tu mensaje anoche. ¿Cuándo me lo mandaste?
 – ______ lo mandé ayer por la mañana.
4 – ¿Vas a mandar un email a tus abuelos?
 – No, voy a escribir______ una carta porque no tienen ordenador.

Using indirect object pronouns

Gramática *página 178*

me	me	*nos*	us
te	you	*os*	you
le	he / she / it / you	*les*	them / those / you

Indirect pronouns are so called because they are not the direct object of the verb in a sentence. They are often translated as 'to' or 'for' e.g. for him, to me.

*Adoro mi móvil. Mis padres **me lo** regalaron.*

In this sentence, ***me*** (= to me) is an indirect object pronoun and ***lo*** (= it) is a direct object pronoun.

'I love my mobile. My parents gave **it** to **me**.'

If an indirect and a direct object pronoun appear together, the indirect one always comes first.

Also learn about comparative and superlative adverbs.

See page 71 ➡

4 Write notes to answer the questions included in the magazine article on page 66. Then work in pairs. Use your notes as prompts for talking to your partner for one minute about the advantages and disadvantages of new technology.

Para mí es imprescindible Lo más importante para mí es	el teléfono móvil el ordenador portátil el MP3	porque ...
Lo uso para	comunicarme con los amigos / hacer los deberes / navegar en la red / escuchar música.	
Me lo	compré	yo.
	regalaron	mis padres / mis abuelos.
Las ventajas son que es	fácil / económico / práctico / útil / entretenido y educativo	comunicarse. buscar información. descargar y guardar música.
Las desventajas son que	son fáciles de robar / son caros. recibes mucho correo basura. es difícil desconectarte.	

Justifying your opinions and adding extra information

Estrategia

The texts on page 66 contain useful expressions that will help you link information and opinions in a sentence. E.g.

más que nada above all / more than anything
sin embargo however

When you read Spanish texts, notice sentences that you can use or adapt to express your own opinions.

Consejo

Use a variety of verbs to avoid repeating verbs like *ser* and *hay*. For example:

Puedo conectarme fácilmente a Internet.

Los deberes se hacen mejor en el ordenador.

Veo muy pocas (desventajas).

Free time and the media

1a Read the cartoon and answer the following questions in English.

1. What are the names of the four characters in this cartoon family?
   a Dad: ***Leo Verdura*** b Mum: ... c Two sons: ... and ...
2. Has Leo tried doing any watersports before? Give reasons for your answer.
3. What does *¡Cuidado!* mean?
4. What was good while it lasted?
5. In the final frame, why is Livingstone worried?

Study tip

Always read the questions first.
Then read the text to get an overall idea of what it is about.
Read the text in detail to find the answers to each question.
You might need to read it a third time to find the answers to questions which ask about less obvious detail such as attitudes and inference.

1b Read the cartoon again. Match up each Spanish expression with its English equivalent.

un rato	we ended up in
la última vez	it was good while it lasted
acabamos en	the last time
la Cruz Roja	this is the life
esto es vida	the Red Cross
fue bonito mientras duró	a little while

1c Choose the sentences which correctly describe the characters in the cartoon. Then choose a sentence from the cartoon to support each of your choices.

1 a Katya is quite impatient and annoyed with Leo.
  b Katya is used to Leo doing crazy things and puts up with his faults.
2 a Leo likes to have fun and enjoy himself.
  b Leo is sensible, careful and sets a good example to his children.
3 a Stanley and Livingstone are both helpful and sympathetic to their dad.
  b One of the brothers makes fun of his dad.

Gramática página 181

The preterite tense

There are four verbs in the preterite tense in the cartoon.

oír – to hear
*La última vez que le **oí** decir eso.*

acabar – to finish
*... **acabamos** en la Cruz Roja*

ser – to be *__Fue__ bonito ...*

durar – to last *... mientras __duró__.*

See page 59

Le

Notice the use of the indirect object pronoun *le* ('him'):

La última vez que __le__ oí decir eso.

See page 67

2 Listen to the five people talking about communication technology. What is the attitude of each person? Choose the correct letter.

A It's essential to my life. B It's useful. C There are disadvantages.

3 Listen to the recorded message and answer the following questions.

1 What must the listener do to hear the message?
  a Press 1 b Press 2 c Press 3
2 Who has left the message?
  a Eva b Carlos c José
3 What has the caller done?
  a booked two seats for a film
  b bought two tickets for a concert
  c got two free tickets to a football match
4 When is the event mentioned, and at what time does it start?
  a today at 8.30
  b on Wednesday at 10.30
  c on Friday at 10.30
5 When did José and Alba go to the event?
  a on Saturday b yesterday
  c on Friday
6 What might they do before the event?
  a have a pizza b have some tapas
  c have a coffee
7 What should the listener do if they are interested in the invitation?
  a go round to his house at 8.30
  b collect the tickets
  c call back or send a text message

G Free time and the media

1a Choose a sentence (1–4 from Activity 1b below) to match each picture.

A

B

C

D

1b Copy and complete the sentences with the correct preterite form of the verb *jugar, llegar, sacar* or *tocar.*

1 En el concierto, toqué la batería y mis amigos Max y David, ______ la guitarra.
2 El sábado jugué en un torneo de tenis pero no ______ a la final.
3 ______ fotos de mi perro para un concurso de fotografía.
4 Mis hermanos ______ en un partido de fútbol.

Regular verbs with spelling changes in the preterite

Gramática página 182

Some regular verbs have spelling changes in the first person form of the preterite. The changes are needed to maintain the sound pattern for the verb when it is pronounced. For example, *jugar* is a regular *-ar* verb so the first person singular ending in the preterite is *-é*.

If just *-é* were added to *jug-*, the sound of the *g* would change. So the *u* must be added to keep the hard *g* sound: *jugué*.

jugar – to play (a sport)	*jugué* – I played
sacar – to take (out)	*saqué* – I took out
tocar – to play (an instrument)	*toqué* – I played
empezar – to start	*empecé* – I started

jugué	*saqué*	*toqué*
jugaste	*sacaste*	*tocaste*
jugó	*sacó*	*tocó*
jugamos	*sacamos*	*tocamos*
jugasteis	*sacasteis*	*tocasteis*
jugaron	*sacaron*	*tocaron*

2 Complete the letter with the following words:

ahora **ahí** **allá** **allí** **aquí**

Hola Eva

¿Cómo estás? (**a**)________ en Aberdeen hace mucho frío y hay bastante nieve en las montañas. El domingo pasado fuimos (**b**)________ a esquiar. Me imagino que hace buen tiempo (**c**)________ en Málaga y con mucho sol.

Todo va bien en el instituto pero (**d**)________ tenemos muchos deberes, por lo menos dos horas al día. De lunes a viernes no salgo. Los sábados por la tarde quedo con mis amigos y vamos por (**e**)________, al cine, o a la pizzería cerca de mi casa.

Escríbeme pronto.

Un beso

Sophie

Time and place expressions

Gramática página 177

Use the following time and place expressions to give detail in your writing and speaking:

***Aquí** tenemos todo muy cerca de casa.*
Here everything is close to home.

*Fue un día festivo así que nos quedamos **allí** un día más.*
It was a holiday so we stayed **there** for one more day.

*Como **ahora** estoy en el cuarto año en el insti, tengo muchos deberes.* **Now** that I'm in the fourth year at secondary school, I have a lot of homework.

Notice the difference between the following words:

aquí	here
ahí	there (but not far away)
allí	there (a bit further away)
allá	there (further away)

3 Copy and complete the Spanish with the words below. Then translate the sentences into English.

disfrutar **hacer** **ir** **tocar**

1 _______ deporte es bueno para mantenerse en forma.
2 _______ la guitarra es mi pasatiempo preferido.
3 _______ al cine es bastante caro.
4 _______ del tiempo libre es importante para una vida sana.

4a Work with a partner. Read the dialogue aloud, completing it with the correct forms of the indefinite adjectives.

Cliente: Hola. Quisiera comprar (**a**) _______ botas. (algunos / algunas)

Dependienta: (**b**) _______ las botas que tenemos están aquí. (Todos / Todas)

Cliente: Me gustan aquellas botas marrones. ¿Tienen el (**c**) _______ estilo en negro? (mismo / misma)

Dependienta: No, pero a lo mejor las tendremos la semana que viene.

Cliente: Muy bien. Suelo venir aquí al centro comercial (**d**) _______ (todos / todas) las semanas así que pasaré (**e**) _______ (otro / otra) día. Adiós.

Dependienta: Adiós. Hasta luego.

4b Work in pairs. Adapt the dialogue in Activity 4a to ask for a different item.

5a Identify the comparative or superlative adverb in each of the following sentences.

1 Los jóvenes entienden mejor los ordenadores que sus padres.
2 Los chicos se dejan influir más por la publicidad y las marcas.
3 Los jóvenes que trabajan gastan su dinero más responsablemente.
4 Para los jóvenes de hoy, todo hay que hacerse más rápidamente, de la comida rápida a la mensajería móvil.

5b Copy the sentences and fill in the missing words to complete the English translations of the sentences from Activity 5a.

1 Young people understand computers _______ than their parents.
2 Boys are _______ influenced by advertising and designer labels.
3 Young people who earn their own money spend it more _______ .
4 For young people today, everything has to be done _______, from fast food to text messaging.

Present participles, the gerund and infinitives

Gramática página 181

In English we use a present participle (a verb form ending in '-ing') or 'gerund' as a noun, for example: **listening** is important in language lessons.

In Spanish, use an infinitive not a present participle in this context:

***Escuchar** es importante en las clases de idiomas.*

Indefinite adjectives

Gramática página 176

Alguno/a, cada, mismo/a, otro/a, todo/a

These agree with the word they describe and usually appear before the word:

todos los precios, todas las tiendas

el mismo estilo, la misma tienda, los mismos colores

otro día, otra camisa, otros colores

algunas camisetas, algunos calcetines

cada always stays the same: *cada semana, cada año*

Comparative and superlative adverbs

Gramática página 177

Adverbs are formed by adding *-mente* to the feminine singular form of an adjective.

rápido – fast, quick

rápidamente – quickly

Put *más* or *menos* before the adverb to make comparatives:

*Gracias al Internet, ahora se puede comunicar **más rápidamente**.*

Thanks to the internet, it's possible to get in touch much more quickly now.

Superlative adverbs are usually the same as the comparative.

Some irregular adverbs do not need *más* before them:

bien (well) *mal* (badly)
mucho (much) *poco* (little)

V Free time and the media

El tiempo libre en casa ➡ *pages 58–59*

la	*batería*	drums
el	*CD, el disco compacto*	CD / compact disc
la	*comedia*	comedy
el	*deporte*	sport
los	*dibujos animados*	cartoons
	escuchar	to listen (to)
	Gran Hermano	Big Brother
la	*guitarra*	guitar
	invitar	to invite
	jugar	to play
	leer	to read
el	*mensaje*	message
la	*música*	music
las	*noticias*	news
el	*ordenador portátil*	laptop computer
el	*portátil*	laptop
el	*partido*	game / match
la	*película*	film
la	*película de acción*	action film / thriller
la	*película romántica*	romantic film
el	*ping-pong*	table tennis
el	*rato, un rato*	(short) time, a little while
	recibir	to receive
la	*serie policíaca*	crime series
la	*telenovela*	soap opera
el	*tiempo libre*	free time
	tocar	to play (a musical instrument)
	ver	to see / watch (a film / television)
el	*videojuego*	video game

Fuera de casa ➡ *pages 60–61*

	aburrido/a	boring
el	*ambiente*	atmosphere
el	*atletismo*	athletics
	bailar	to dance
el	*baile*	dance
el	*campeonato*	championship
la	*carrera*	race
el	*ciclismo*	cycling
la	*ciencia ficción*	science fiction
el	*cine*	cinema
la	*copa*	cup / trophy
	correr	to run
el	*descanso*	break / half-time / interval
el	*día festivo*	holiday / bank holiday
la	*entrada*	ticket / entry
el	*equipo*	team
el	*espectáculo*	performance
el	*estadio*	stadium
la	*fiesta*	party / festival
el	*fin de semana*	weekend
el	*finde*	weekend (colloquial)
	hacer los deberes	to do homework
	ir de compras	to go shopping
el / la	*jugador(a) juvenil*	youth team player
la	*montaña rusa*	roller coaster (theme park ride)
	montar	to ride / go on a ride (at a theme park)
la	*natación*	swimming
el	*parque temático*	theme park
	pasar	to spend (time)
	pasarlo bien / mal	to have a good / bad time
la	*película de horror*	horror film
	regalar	to give (as a present)
	salir	to go out
el	*tenis*	tennis

¿En qué gastas tu dinero? ➡ *pages 62–63*

	ahorrar	to save
la	*chaqueta*	jacket
el	*cumpleaños*	birthday
el	*dinero*	money
	disfrutar	to enjoy
	encontrar	to find / meet

	gastar	to spend
los	*grandes almacenes*	department stores
la	*marca, la ropa de marca*	make, designer clothes
la	*mayoría*	majority
	mejorar	to improve
la	*moda*	fashion
la	*Navidad*	Christmas
el	*ocio*	leisure
la	*paga*	pocket money
	pagar	to pay
la	*publicidad*	advertising
el	*regalo*	present
la	*revista*	magazine
la	*ropa*	clothes
el	*santo*	saint's day
la	*tarjeta de crédito*	credit card
las	*zapatillas de deporte*	trainers

¿Te gusta estar de moda? ➡ *pages 64–65*

las	*botas*	boots
los	*calcetines*	socks
la	*calidad*	quality
de (buena)	*calidad*	(good) quality
la	*camisa*	shirt
la	*camiseta*	t-shirt
el	*cinturón*	belt
el	*collar*	necklace
la	*comodidad*	comfort
la	*corbata*	tie
	costar	to cost
el	*cuero*	leather
	de segunda mano	second hand
el	*descuento*	discount
	estar de moda	to be fashionable
la	*falda*	skirt
la	*gorra*	cap / hat
los	*guantes*	gloves
la	*imagen*	image
	irse bien	to fit / suit (of clothes, etc.)
la	*lana*	wool
	llevar	to wear
las	*medias*	stockings / tights
la	*oferta (especial)*	(special) offer
el	*pañuelo*	scarf
los	*pendientes*	earrings
el	*precio*	price
	probarse	to try on
el	*supermercado*	supermarket
la	*talla*	size (clothes, shoes, etc.)
el	*tamaño*	size
la	*tienda*	shop
la	*tienda (de ropa)*	(clothes) shop
el	*tipo*	type
los	*vaqueros*	jeans
el	*vestido*	dress
la	*zapatería*	shoe shop
los	*zapatos*	shoes

Los jóvenes y la tecnología ➡ *pages 66–67*

la	*banda ancha*	broadband
la	*biblioteca*	library
la	*cámara digital*	digital camera
	chatear	to chat (online)
	conectarse	to connect
el	*correo basura*	junk mail
	descargar	to download
la	*desventaja*	disadvantage
	devolver	to give back
	entretenido/a	entertaining
el	*equipo de música*	music system
	guardar	to keep / save
el	*juego*	game
la	*librería*	bookshop
la	*llamada*	call
	mandar	to send
el	*mensajero instantáneo*	Instant Messenger
el	*móvil (teléfono móvil)*	mobile (mobile phone)
	navegar en la red	to surf the internet
la	*televisión plana*	flatscreen television
la	*ventaja*	advantage
la	*videoconsola*	video console

2.6 Las vacaciones

Objetivos

- Talking about holiday preferences and experiences
- Using irregular preterite verbs
- Showing off the language you know

A

B

C

D

Lucía

Para mí, lo ideal son las vacaciones de sol y playa. Y mi lugar de veraneo preferido es Nerja, que está cerca de Málaga en el sur de España. Estuve en Nerja el mes pasado. Fui sola y además de tomar el sol, bañarme y practicar la vela, visité la famosa Cueva prehistórica. La Cueva de Nerja fue descubierta en 1959. También hay muchos parques temáticos como 'Tivoli World' que tiene más de cuarenta atracciones. Cuando estuve allí monté en la Torre de Caída y la Noria. ¡Qué miedo! Me gusta veranear en Nerja porque me olvido del estrés de los estudios.

Cristobal

A mí me encanta la naturaleza y siempre hago eco turismo. Durante las vacaciones de Semana Santa estuve de vacaciones en los Picos de Europa, las montañas en el norte de España. Fui con mis amigos. Sólo llevamos mochilas, sacos de dormir y un libro de guía. Nos alojamos en albergues juveniles. Conocimos a gente nueva y lo pasamos estupendamente. Practicamos senderismo, alquilamos bicicletas de montaña, montamos a caballo e hicimos piragüismo. Un día fuimos de excursión a un pueblo antiguo con un castillo que fue construido en el siglo X.

Eduardo

Prefiero ir de camping cuando estoy de vacaciones porque estás al aire libre. Este verano fui de camping a Los Pirineos con mi novia. Quisimos unas vacaciones baratas. Fuimos en moto. En el camping hay de todo: desde canchas de baloncesto y mini golf hasta peluquería y tienda de regalos. Alquilé una tienda muy cómoda. Durante el día nadamos en el lago cercano, fuimos de paseo, practicamos la pesca y sacamos fotos. Compramos comida en el supermercado del camping e hicimos barbacoas para cenar. Una noche tuvimos mala suerte porque hubo tormenta.

1a Match up each speech bubble with the correct photo. (There is one extra photo.)

1b Write the name of the person who …

1 went on a walking holiday.
2 went sailing.
3 met new people.
4 stayed in youth hostels.
5 visited a cave.
6 fished.

Consejo

In an active sentence, the subject does the action.

Los habitantes construyeron el castillo. The inhabitants built the castle.

In a passive sentence, the subject has something done to it.

El castillo fue construido. The castle was built.

The passive is formed by using part of the verb *ser* and a past participle.

La Cueva de Nerja fue descubierta en 1959. The Nerja Cave was discovered in 1959.

2a Listen to Gema, Antonio, Paloma and Joaquín talking about their holiday experiences. Are their comments positive (P), negative (N) or both (P + N)?

2b Listen again and write the name of the person who …

1 got sunstroke.
2 lost luggage.
3 had their flight cancelled.
4 had their passport stolen.

3 G Copy the sentences and fill in the gaps with the correct form of the verb in the preterite tense, using the words below.

1 (*I was*) ______ de vacaciones en el extranjero, en Alemania.
2 El policía me (*he gave*) ______ un documento.
3 No (*it was*) ______ buen tiempo.
4 Juan (*he had*) ______ mala suerte.

tuvo **hizo** **estuve** **dio**

Using irregular preterite verbs

Gramática página 182

Learn more irregular verbs in the preterite tense:

Estar	***Hacer***
estuve	*hice*
estuviste	*hiciste*
estuvo	*hizo*
Tener	***Dar***
tuve	*di*
tuviste	*diste*
tuvo	*dio*

Look up *poner, saber, haber, practicar* and *venir.*

Watch out also for radical-changing verbs in the preterite. *-ir* verbs are affected.

Preferir *preferí* *preferiste* *prefirió*

Also learn more about the passive.

See page 84 ➡

4 Do a class survey. Find out what sort of holidays your classmates like. Add reasons to your own answer. If you can, give an example of a recent holiday.

Ejemplo:

A ¿Qué tipo de vacaciones prefieres y por qué?

B Prefiero vacaciones de invierno. Me gusta practicar el esquí.

Estuve de vacaciones en / Fui a	el extranjero / el campo / la playa / la sierra / la montaña.
Me alojé / Me quedé	en un albergue juvenil / hotel / parador / en una pensión.
Visité	parques temáticos / monumentos / pueblos antiguos / espectáculos.
Jugué	a las cartas / al tenis.
Practiqué	deportes acuáticos / el esquí / la vela / la natación.
(No) Me divertí porque (No) Lo pasé bien / mal / regular porque	hizo buen tiempo / mal tiempo / sol / viento / hubo tormentas.
Perdí	el pasaporte / el equipaje / el vuelo.

Showing off the language you know

Estrategia

If you can't remember how to say what you want to say, don't panic. You don't have to tell the truth, but try to produce information in accurate Spanish.

2.7 ¿Adónde vas?

Objetivos
- Talking about holiday plans
- Using the immediate future
- Noting prefixes that are the same in Spanish and English

Este invierno voy a pasar una semana en la nieve. Voy a una estación de esquí en Sierra Nevada que para mí es el lugar número uno para deportes de invierno. Aunque está tan sólo a dos horas de la Costa del Sol, Sierra Nevada es una de las mejores estaciones de esquí en España. Voy a ir con un grupo de amigos y nos vamos a alojar en un chalet con vistas a las pistas. Vamos a poder esquiar y hacer snowboard no sólo por el día sino también por la noche. Para nosotros es importante la vida nocturna y es muy animada en Sierra Nevada. Después de un duro día en la pista vamos a salir de marcha a los bares, pubs y clubes. Vamos a pasarlo estupendamente.

Sergio

Voy a ir a la isla de Cuba a pasar mis vacaciones este año. Mi hermano viene conmigo. Vamos a pasar unos días en La Habana en un hotel de cinco estrellas en el Malecón, el paseo que bordea el mar. La Habana es una ciudad con mucha vida callejera. Vamos a divertirnos en los bares y restaurantes porque hay música en vivo y mucho ambiente. Vamos a pasearnos por las calles estrechas y ver los antiguos coches americanos que conducen los cubanos. Después vamos a pasar cinco noches en Santiago, el corazón de la música cubana, donde voy a asistir a una escuela de salsa. Quiero aprender a bailar salsa y regatón. Luego vamos a ir a la histórica ciudad de Trinidad donde mi hermano va a hacer un curso de buceo. Yo voy a descansar y broncearme en la playa.

Marisa

1a Who is going to do what on holiday this year? Write S (Sergio) or M (Marisa).

¿Quién va a …

1 … tomar el sol?
2 … practicar deporte?
3 … ir a clases de baile?
4 … ir de paseo por la ciudad?
5 … pasarlo bien en las discotecas?
6 … quedarse en una casa?

1b Using the immediate future, write two more things that Sergio and Marisa are each going to do.

Ejemplo: Sergio va a ir con un grupo de amigos.

2a G Copy the sentences and fill in the gaps with the correct form of the verb *ir* and the correct infinitive.

Ejemplo: 1 Consuelo va a jugar al tenis.

1 Consuelo _______ a _______ al tenis.
2 Esta Semana Santa Emilio y yo _______ a _______ a Sevilla.

Using the immediate future

Gramática página 183

To talk about the immediate future use *ir a* + infinitive:

voy a aprender	I'm going to learn
vas a bailar	you are going to dance
va a divertirse	he / she is / you (formal) are going to have a good time
vamos a ir	we are going to go
vais a pasar	you are going to spend
van a salir	they / you (formal, plural) are going to go out

Este invierno voy a pasar una semana en la nieve.
This winter I'm going to spend a week in the snow.

Also learn about disjunctive pronouns.

See page 84

3 ¿Dónde ______ vosotros a ______ las vacaciones?
4 Lorenzo y Luisa ______ a ______ el tren de las 6.00.
5 ¿Y tú? ¿Qué ______ a ______ por las tardes?
6 Yo ______ a ______ en una pensión de dos estrellas.

va	van	vas	vais
voy	vamos	jugar	alojarme
ir	hacer	coger	pasar

2b G Translate the sentences in Activity 2a into English.

Ejemplo: 1 Consuelo is going to play tennis.

3 Listen to Benjamín talking about his holiday plans. Decide whether the following statements are true (T) or false (F). Correct the false statements.

1 Benjamín is going to go to the coast for his holiday.
2 He is going to find it difficult to understand what people are saying.
3 Benjamín is going to be travelling by ferry.
4 Patrick is going to stay for a fortnight with Benjamín.
5 Going to the countryside will be the highlight of Benjamín's stay.
6 Benjamín expects the weather will be good during his visit.

Estrategia

To work out the meaning of an unfamiliar word note prefixes that are the same or similar in Spanish (*re-*, *pre-*, *des-*). Recognising the root verb will also help you to conjugate the verb.

To work out the meaning of *reconocer* in the sentence *¿Cómo te van a reconocer?* remove *re-* from *reconocer. Conocer* means 'to know' so *reconocer* must mean 'to recognise'.

4 Work in pairs. Imagine you have won the lottery. Take turns asking and answering about where you are going to go on holiday and what you are going to do.

Ejemplo:

A ¿Dónde vas a pasar tus vacaciones y qué vas a hacer allí?

B Voy a ir a Grecia y voy a practicar la vela.

Consejo

To say 'for me' and 'with me', use these pronouns after *para*:

mí ti él / ella / usted

nosotros vosotros

ellos / ellas / ustedes

Para mí es el lugar número uno.
For me it's the number one place.

With *con*, there is a special form for the first and second persons:

conmigo with me

contigo with you

Mi hermano va a venir conmigo.
My brother is going to come with me.

5 Prepare an itinerary for an ideal five-day holiday for you or your classmates.

Voy a Vamos a Van a	ir pasar las vacaciones irse de intercambio	al extranjero. a / en la playa. al / en el campo.
	quedarme/nos/se en alojarme/nos/se en	una pensión / una granja.
	practicar / hacer	deportes acuáticos / de invierno.
	salir a los bares y clubes. visitar museos / ir de paseo. asistir a clases de salsa. divertirme/nos/se. hablar español.	

2.8 He ido a la fiesta

Objetivos

- Talking about what to see and do on holiday
- Using the perfect tense to talk about what you have done recently
- Using time phrases in your written work

Este marzo he ido a Valencia a ver las famosas Fallas. Las Fallas es una fiesta espectacular. El ambiente es muy festivo durante las veinticuatro horas diarias, de los casi veinte días que duran las fiestas.

Por las tardes había concursos de grupos pirotécnicos en la Plaza del Ayuntamiento. Y durante cuatro noches seguidas y a partir de la una de la madrugada había 'castillos de fuegos artificiales'. Las explosiones, los fuegos aéreos y volcanes hacían un ruido tremendo.

El momento final de la fiesta ocurre durante la noche del diecinueve, es 'La Cremá' cuando queman todos los ninots de la ciudad al mismo tiempo. Los 'ninots' son figuras enormes de escenas cómicas, de políticos, famosos o deportistas. De esta manera los valencianos queman todo lo aburrido y oscuro del invierno.

Otro evento importante que he visto es una bonita ceremonia en la que miles de Falleras y Falleros llegan a la ciudad de toda la región. Llevan trajes típicos valencianos, bailan por las calles y ofrecen flores a la estatua enorme de la Virgen María.

Hay muchas otras actividades durante las Fallas. He ido a las corridas de toros, he visto los desfiles y he probado muchos platos de paella en los concursos de paella. La paella es la especialidad de la región. Es una de las fiestas más originales de España. ¡No te la pierdas!

Marcos

1a Read Marcos's account of his visit to the Fallas festival. Find the Spanish for these words and phrases in the text.

1 The atmosphere is completely festive.
2 From one in the morning
3 They burn all the Falla figures.
4 They wear local costumes.
5 I've been to the bullfights.
6 I've seen the parades.
7 The regional speciality
8 Don't miss it!

1b Answer the following questions in Spanish.

1 ¿Adónde ha ido Marcos?
2 ¿Cuánto tiempo ha durado la fiesta?
3 ¿Qué ha visto Marcos en la Plaza del Ayuntamiento?
4 ¿Qué han quemado los valencianos la noche del diecinueve?
5 ¿Qué ha comido Marcos durante la fiesta?

2 Listen to the conversation and answer the following questions in English.

1 Why hasn't Sara seen Marcos?
2 How many days running has he visited the City of Arts and Sciences?
3 Which museum is in the shape of a dinosaur?
4 What has impressed him about the aquarium?
5 What two things impressed him about the flamenco show?
6 Why did he like the Planetarium best?

Gramática — página 182

Using the perfect tense to talk about what you have done recently

To form the perfect tense, use the appropriate form of *haber* and the past participle.

To form the past participle add *-ado* to the stem of *-ar* verbs and *-ido* to the stem of *-er* and *-ir* verbs.

He estado de vacaciones.
I've been on holiday.

Also learn about interrogative pronouns. *See page 84* ➡

3 Ⓖ Copy the sentences and fill in the gaps with the correct form of the verb *haber* and the correct past participle.

1 Javier y Pili ___ ___ un plato de paella valenciana.
2 ¿Vosotros ___ ___ el espectáculo de flamenco?
3 Yo ___ ___ el museo de ciencias.
4 ¿Tú ___ ___ en Valencia?
5 A Marcos le ___ ___ mucho el acuario.
6 Nosotros ___ ___ a las corridas de toros.

he **has** **ha** **hemos** **habéis**
han **visitado** **comido** **estado**
visto **ido** **gustado**

4 Work in pairs. Look at the pictures and ask each other about recent holidays to the places in the pictures.

1 ¿Adónde has ido de vacaciones?
2 ¿Qué has hecho / visto?
3 ¿Te ha gustado?

Consejo

To ask questions, use interrogative pronouns such as *¿cuándo?* (when?), *¿dónde?* (where?) *and ¿qué?* (what?) at the beginning of the sentence.

¿Cómo has viajado? How have you travelled?

Remember that these words have accents when they are used as interrogatives.

5 Write a postcard about a recent holiday.

He estado	una semana / quince días	en Semana Santa / Navidades. en primavera / verano / otoño / invierno.
He visto / He ido a He visitado	las fiestas / las corridas de toros. los jardines / el museo. el castillo / el concierto.	
Me ha gustado Me ha encantado Me ha impresionado	porque	el ambiente es festivo. es espectacular. es emocionante. es interesante. lo he pasado bien he aprendido mucho. he probado la paella.

Estrategia

Using time phrases in your written work

To express frequency:
a diario daily

To express sequence:
a partir de from
antes (de) before

Queman todas las figuras al mismo tiempo. They burn all the figures at the same time.

He ido tres días seguidos. I've been three days running.

Objetivos

- Talking about getting around on holiday
- Using imperative verb forms
- Using high numbers and 24-hour time

2.9 ¡Vamos de viaje!

1 Read the dialogues and find the correct word for each gap from the lists below. Then listen and check.

En la oficina de alquiler de coches

Cliente: Quisiera alquilar un coche. ¿Me puede decir cuánto cuesta?

Empleado: ¿Qué modelo de coche quiere alquilar?

Cliente: Un Seat Ibiza.

Empleado: ¿Por cuántos días quiere alquilarlo?

Cliente: Por cuatro días.

Empleado: La tarifa por un SEAT Ibiza es 73.25 euros por día pero por cuatro días son 219.76. Incluye seguros de robo y colisión y el IVA.

Cliente: ¿Tiene aire (1) ...?

Empleado: Sí, y equipo de música.

Cliente: Está bien.

Empleado: Rellene esta (2) ..., por favor. Y déme su carnet de (3) ...

Cliente: Tome usted.

Empleado: Enséñeme su (4) ... de identidad o su pasaporte.

Cliente: Tenga.

Empleado: ¿Va a pagar con tarjeta de crédito o en efectivo?

Cliente: Con tarjeta de crédito.

Empleado: Perfecto. Firme aquí.

Cliente: Queremos ir a Ávila.

Empleado: Mire el mapa de la región. Tome la (5) ... con dirección a Burgos.

documento | ficha | acondicionado | autopista | conducir

En la taquilla de RENFE

Viajero: Quiero ir a Barcelona pasado mañana.

Taquillero: Hay varias opciones. El tren más rápido es el AVE.

Viajero: ¿A qué hora sale el primer tren?

Taquillero: A las 6h. Hay trenes cada media hora hasta las 22h.

Viajero: ¿Cuánto tarda el (6) ... ?

Taquillero: Dos horas 43 minutos. La llegada a Barcelona es a las 8h43.

Viajero: ¿Hay que cambiar?

Taquillero: No, es (7) ...

Viajero: ¿Hay (8) ... para jóvenes?

Taquillero: Sí, un 20%. ¿Tiene carné joven?

Viajero: Sí, tome. Déme un (9) ... de ida y vuelta en el AVE para el jueves a las 13h30.

Taquillero: ¿Cuándo va a regresar?

Viajero: El domingo.

Taquillero: Son 125 euros.

Viajero: Tome usted.

Taquillero: Hay máquinas de auto check-in en la estación. Puede utilizar su billete también en los trenes de cercanías.

Viajero: Hay servicio de cafetería en el (10) ..., ¿no?

Taquillero: Sí, y hay música y vídeo por canal individual.

Viajero: ¡Qué bien!

tren | billete | viaje | descuento | directo

2 Listen to the conversations and answer the questions in English.

1 What platform does the Malaga train leave from?
2 What do you have to do at the crossroads?
3 What is cheaper than driving?
4 What is after the traffic lights?
5 What is the person looking for?
6 How does the person suggest travelling?

Estrategia

Using high numbers and 24-hour time

Numbers and times nearly always come up in the exam.

Practise high numbers and 24-hour times with a partner.

3 G Copy the sentences and fill in the gaps with the correct form of the verb in the imperative.

1 ______ su carnet de conducir. (traer – tú)
2 ______ tu carnet de identidad o tu pasaporte. (tomar – vosotros)
3 ______ tu equipaje en la consigna. (dejar – vosotros)
4 ______ por el paso subterráneo. (bajar – vosotros)
5 ______ el mapa de la región. (mirar – tú)

Gramática *página 184*

Using imperative verb forms

To form *vosotros* imperatives, remove the *-r* from the infinitive and replace it with *-d*. To form *tú* imperatives just remove the *-s* from the present tense *tú* form.

Familiar

	tú	***vosotros***
-ar	*toma*	*tomad*
-er	*bebe*	*bebed*
-ir	*vive*	*vivid*

Baja la calle. Go down the street.
Mirad el mapa. Look at the map.

See page 85 ➡

4 Work in pairs. Take turns to make up an instruction to go with each picture.

5 Write an email to a friend giving instructions for a journey to meet you. Tell your friend what to do if you aren't there on time.

Consejo

To say 'let's' use *vamos a* + infinitive.

Vamos a viajar en primera clase.

Vamos a coger un autobús.

Para ir a (Barcelona)		compra	un billete de ida (y vuelta).	
En la estación En la parada	coge toma	el tren el autobús el autocar	de las (15.30).	Cambia en (Atocha).
Enseña Muestra		tu el	carné de conducir. carnet / documento de identidad (DNI).	
Si no estoy,		mira (el mapa / las direcciones) / espera.		

Holidays

Queridos primos:

a Estoy de vacaciones aquí en Cancún en México con mis padres. Es la primera vez que he visitado el extranjero. Para mí es una aventura porque siempre he querido visitar un país latinoamericano. Hemos venido en avión. El vuelo era directo y tardó ocho horas. Nuestro hotel es de cinco estrellas. Tiene dos piscinas y tres restaurantes. También tiene varias tiendas de recuerdos donde puedes comprar regalos y postales.

b Las playas son largas con arena blanca y el azul del mar Caribe. Hay muchas sombrillas. El clima es subtropical y ha hecho sol y calor todos los días. Pasamos los días tomando el sol o haciendo deportes acuáticos.

c No tenemos pensión completa. Tenemos media pensión y todas las noches hemos cenado en diferentes restaurantes de la ciudad. Hemos probado platos típicos como el guacamole, los tacos y las enchiladas aunque tengo que admitir que para mí la comida de aquí no es muy buena y tampoco es barata.

d En noviembre en México se celebra el Día de los Muertos. Es una mezcla de costumbres cristianas y aztecas. Es una fiesta muy alegre. La gente visita los cementerios con comida y flores para los muertos y tocan grupos de mariachis. La gente se viste de esqueletos y hay muchos bailes muy divertidos. Por lo general la vida nocturna es muy animada en Cancún. Hay muchas discotecas y clubes que están abiertos toda la noche.

e Hay un mercado con mucho ambiente donde venden artículos de artesanía. Lo malo es que todo es caro. Sin embargo hemos comprado joyas de plata como collares y pendientes.

f Hoy hemos ido en ferry a la Isla de Mujeres a pasar el día donde hemos practicado el buceo entre los corales. Me ha divertido mucho aprender un deporte nuevo pero para mí lo mejor ha sido ver los peces tropicales. Mañana vamos a ir de excursión con guía en autocar a ver las ruinas mayas. He leído sobre la civilización Maya en la guía. Quiero conocer más sobre la cultura y las costumbres de los Mayas. Va a ser impresionante. Voy a sacar muchas fotos.

Un beso

Guadalupe

1a Read Guadalupe's letter about her holiday in Cancún. What opinion does she have about the following aspects of her trip? Write P (positive), N (negative) or P + N (positive and negative).

1 her first trip abroad
2 the food
3 the market
4 tomorrow's excursion

1b Answer the following questions in English.

1 Why is Guadalupe excited to be in Mexico. (Give two reasons.)
2 What have Guadalupe's family booked at the hotel?
  a B&B b half board c full board
3 What does Guadalupe think of the Day of the Dead celebrations? They are … a fun b sad c boring.
4 Why exactly is the nightlife so lively in Cancún?
5 What did Guadalupe like the most about today's trip?
  a learning a new sport b seeing the fish
  c seeing the ancient ruins
6 What does Guadalupe hope to gain from her visit to see the ancient ruins?

2a Listen to the conversations in a Mexican restaurant. Match up each conversation with the correct picture.

2b Listen to the conversations again and answer the following questions in English.

1 Where will the customers be seated tonight?
  a on the terrace b in a corner c by the window.
2 Why does the waitress recommend the tourist menu?
  a it is good value b it has local dishes c there is more to choose from.
3 What two advantages does the customer see in ordering a *plato combinado*?
4 Do you think the customer is satisfied? Give reasons for your answer.
5 Why does the customer want an extra spoon?
6 Do you think the customers enjoyed their visit to the restaurant? Give a reason for your answer.

Gramática página 182

The perfect tense

Use the perfect tense for things that have happened recently in the past:

Hemos probado *platos típicos.*

See page 85

The immediate future

Use the immediate future for things that are going to happen in the near future:

Mañana ***vamos a ir*** *de excursión.*

See page 85

Vocabulario

la arena	sand
la cuchara	spoon
el guía	guide
la guía	guidebook
media pensión	half board
pensión completa	full board
la propina	tip
la queja	complaint
la sombrilla	sunshade

Study tip

Learning vocabulary

Write new words in a notebook or on cards. Group words in opposites, word families or make up spidergrams of related words.

Note the gender of nouns.

List high-frequency words: *pero, muy, más, así*. Always learn meaning, gender, spelling, accents and pronunciation.

Look, cover, write and check!

G Holidays

1 Identify which of the following sentences are in the passive voice. Translate the sentences into English.

1. La catedral es admirada por todo el mundo.
2. Los cheques de viajero fueron cambiados en el banco.
3. Los jóvenes fueron a la Oficina de Turismo para informarse.
4. El museo fue cerrado durante dos meses.
5. A mi amiga le regalé un abanico.
6. El portero trae las maletas a la habitación.

2 Copy the sentences and fill in the gaps with the correct prepositional pronoun.

1. La paella es _______ (*for us*).
2. Esta postal es _______ (*for you, singular informal*).
3. ¿Las limonadas son _______ (*for you, plural informal*)?
4. Va a ir a la montaña _______ (*with them*).
5. ¿Quieres venir _______ (*with me*)?
6. Yo hablé _______ (*with him*).

3 Choose the correct interrogative pronoun to complete these questions. Then work in pairs and make up more questions.

1. ¿_______ te gusta más? (*which*)
2. ¿_______ te dio el regalo? (*who*)
3. ¿_______ vienes? (*from where*)
4. ¿_______ quieres ir a los Estados Unidos? (*why*)
5. ¿_______ vamos a ir al aeropuerto? (*how*)
6. ¿_______ es la fiesta de San Fermín? (*when*)
7. ¿_______ necesitamos otra maleta? (*for what*)
8. ¿_______ quieres hacer hoy? (*what*)

Recognising the passive voice

In a passive sentence the subject has something done to it, him or her:

Los billetes fueron comprados por el viajero. The tickets were bought by the traveller.

Remember that the passive is formed with *ser* and a past participle.

Gramática página 186

How to say 'for me'

After *para* use these disjunctive pronouns:

mí	*nosotros/as*
ti	*vosotros/as*
él / ella / usted	*ellos / ellas / ustedes*

E.g. ***Para mí**, las vacaciones de invierno son las más divertidas.* For me, winter holidays are the most fun.

How to say 'with me'

With *con*, there is a special form for the first and second persons:

conmigo with me *contigo* with you

E.g. *Ester quiere cenar* ***conmigo***. Ester wants to have dinner with me.

Iremos a Italia ***con ella***. We'll go to Italy with her.

Gramática página 179

Interrogatives

Use interrogative pronouns to form a question:

¿cómo?
¿cuál? ¿cuáles?
¿cuándo?
¿cuánto / cuánta / cuántos / cuántas?
¿dónde?
¿adónde?
¿de dónde?
¿por dónde?
¿qué?
¿para qué?
¿por qué?
¿quién(es)?
¿de quién?
¿Dónde fuiste de vacaciones?
¿Con quién fuiste?

Remember that these words have accents when they are used as interrogatives.

Gramática página 180

4 Copy the sentences and fill in the gaps with the past participles of the verbs in brackets. Then translate the sentences into English.

1 Mi amigo me ha _______ (invitar) a pasar una semana en Bilbao.
2 Julia, ¿has _______ (ver) la nueva película de Penélope Cruz?
3 Ellos no han _______ (comer) el cordero asado en este restaurante.
4 ¿Vosotros habéis _______ (hacer) un viaje a la Costa Azul?
5 No he _______ (ir) de vacaciones este año.
6 Nosotros nos hemos _______ (quedar) en casa.

5a Choose the appropriate form of the imperative by deciding whether the requests are formal or familiar.

1 No beba / bebas tanta cerveza, Manolo.
2 ¡Ve / Vaya al hospital enseguida, señora!
3 Cruce / Cruza la plaza, Mónica.
4 Rellena / Rellene el formulario, señor.
5 Señores, visitad / visiten nuestro pueblo.
6 Patricio, pon / ponga los platos en el lavaplatos.

5b Look at the pictures and write a caption for each one using *vamos a …* Then write five more sentences using *vamos (a)* …

A

B

The perfect tense

Gramática — página 182

To say what you have done recently, use the perfect tense.

Use the appropriate form of *haber* + the past participle.

To form the past participle add *-ado* to the stem of *-ar* verbs and *-ido* to the stem of *-er* and *-ir* verbs.

***Hemos visitado** Polonia.* We have visited Poland.

Watch out for irregular past participles. E.g. *ver – visto, hacer – hecho, decir – dicho.*

Imperatives

Gramática — página 184

Imperatives give commands and instructions.

On page 81 you learnt how to form *tú* and *vosotros* imperatives. *Usted(es)* imperatives work differently: they use the subjunctive form.

	Familiar		**Formal**		
	tú	***vosotros***	***usted***	***ustedes***	
-ar	*cierra*	*cerra**d***	*cierre*	*cierre**n***	close
-er	*come*	*come**d***	*coma*	*coma**n***	eat
-ir	*abre*	*abri**d***	*abra*	*abra**n***	open

***Compra** este recuerdo.* Buy this souvenir.

Look out for irregular verbs.

C

How to say 'let's'

Gramática

To say 'let's', use *vamos* or *vamos a* + infinitive.

***Vamos** al extranjero.*	Let's go abroad.
***Vamos** a salir.*	Let's go out.

V Holidays

Las vacaciones ➡ *pages 74–75*

el	*aire libre*	open air
el	*albergue juvenil*	youth hostel
	Alemania	Germany
	alojarse	to stay
	alquilar	to hire
	antiguo/a	old
el	*avión*	aeroplane
	bañarse	to swim
montar a	*caballo*	to go horse riding
la	*cancha (de baloncesto)*	(basketball) court
jugar a las	*cartas*	to play cards
el	*castillo*	castle
ir de	*camping*	to go camping
	cómodo/a	comfortable
	conocer	to meet / get to know
	construir	to build
	descansar	to rest
el	*equipaje*	luggage
el	*espectáculo*	show
los	*Estados Unidos*	the United States
el	*estrés*	stress
ir de	*excursión*	to go on a trip
el	*extranjero*	abroad
la	*ficha*	form
la	*hamburguesería*	hamburger joint
la	*heladería*	ice-cream parlour
la	*insolación*	sunstroke
	Irlanda	Ireland
el	*lago*	lake
	libre	free
el	*libro de guía*	guidebook
la	*mochila*	rucksack
	mojarse	to get wet
la	*montaña*	mountain
	nadar	to swim
la	*naturaleza*	nature
	olvidarse	to forget
el	*parador*	state-run hotel
el	*pasaporte*	passport
	pasarlo bien / mal	to have a good / bad time
la	*peluquería*	hairdresser's
	practicar la pesca	to go fishing
	rellenar	to fill in
el	*retraso*	delay
el	*saco de dormir*	sleeping bag
la	*Semana Santa*	Easter Holidays / Holy Week
la	*tienda*	tent
	tomar el sol	to sunbathe
	veranear	to spend your summer holidays
el	*vuelo*	flight

¿Adónde vas? ➡ *pages 76–77*

el	*ambiente*	atmosphere
	broncearse	to sunbathe
la	*costumbre*	custom / tradition
el	*deporte de invierno*	winter sport
	descansar	to rest
el	*equipaje*	luggage
la	*estación de esquí*	ski resort
	Grecia	Greece
el	*inglés*	English
el	*intercambio*	exchange
	irlandés	Irish
la	*isla*	island
la	*nieve*	snow
el	*paraguas*	umbrella
	pasar	to spend (time)
	pasearse	to walk / stroll
la	*pista*	ski slope

	quedarse	to stay
la	*sierra*	mountain range
la	*vista*	view
	en vivo	live (music)

He ido a la fiesta ➡ *pages 78–79*

	aprender	to learn
el	*concierto*	concert
la	*corrida de toros*	bullfight
el	*edificio*	building
el	*espacio*	space
la	*especialidad*	speciality
el	*espectáculo de flamenco*	flamenco show
la	*fiesta*	festival / party
los	*fuegos artificiales*	fireworks
el	*museo*	museum
el	*plato*	dish
	quemar	to burn
el	*traje*	costume / outfit / suit

¡Vamos de viaje! ➡ *pages 80–81*

el	*aeropuerto*	airport
el	*aire acondicionado*	air conditioning
	alquilar	to hire / rent
el	*alquiler*	hire
el	*andén*	platform
el	*asiento*	seat
el	*autocar*	coach
el	*barco*	boat
el	*billete*	ticket
	cambiar	to change
el	*carné joven*	student card
el	*carnet de conducir*	driving licence
el	*carnet / documento de identidad (DNI)*	ID
la	*carretera*	road
el	*cheque de viaje*	travellers' cheque
el	*coche*	car
	coger	to pick / take
	conducir	to drive
la	*consigna*	left luggage
el	*cruce*	junction / crossroads
en	*efectivo*	in cash
	enseñar	to teach
la	*estación*	station
estar	*ocupado/a*	to be occupied
la	*gasolina*	petrol
el	*IVA*	VAT
la	*llegada*	arrival
la	*maleta*	suitcase
el	*mapa*	map
la	*máquina*	machine
el	*metro*	underground train system
	mostrar	to show
la	*moto(cicleta)*	motorbike
	pagar	to pay
la	*parada*	stop
el	*permiso de conducir*	driving licence
	preguntar	to ask
	primera clase	first class
el	*puerto*	port
	regresar	to return
	RENFE	Spanish state railway
la	*sala de espera*	waiting room
la	*salida*	exit
el	*seguro (del coche)*	car insurance
los	*semáforos*	traffic lights
el	*suplemento*	supplement
la	*taquilla*	ticket office
	tardar	to take (time)
la	*tarjeta de crédito*	credit card
	tomar	to take
el	*tren*	train
el	*tren de cercanías*	local train
	utilizar	to use
la	*vía*	track
	viajar	to travel

2 Las vacaciones

You are talking to a Spanish friend about holidays. He / She wants to know:

1 What type of holiday you prefer
2 What you did last summer
3 What destination you would recommend and why
4 How to get to your suggested destination
5 Where you will be going on your next holiday
6 What is important for you when choosing a type of holiday
7 **!**

! Remember you will have to respond to something that you have not yet prepared.

Study tips

Start your plan. For example, you could write a maximum of six words for each of the seven sections that make up the task, remembering that the total maximum is 40, so two sections will need to have only five. Here are some suggested words for the first section:

esquí, gustar, divertido, chalet, semanas, padres

Remember to include one verb in each list of words. The verbs must be either infinitives or past participles.

1 What type of holiday you prefer.

- Mention the type of holiday you like and why
- Say where you have been recently
- Mention the type of accommodation you usually stay in
- Say how long you go for and who with

Study tips

You could start off with *Para mí, lo ideal son las vacaciones …*

You could use *me gusta(n)*, *prefiero* or *me encanta(n)* to say you like a type of holiday. See page 186.

Use the perfect tense to describe what you have done recently, e.g. *He ido a Grecia, he visitado las Islas Canarias*. See page 182.

To say that you usually do something use *normalmente* or *generalmente*.

Use either *me alojo* or *me quedo* to say where you usually stay.

Use *para* to say how long you go on holiday for. See page 187.

2 What you did last summer.

- Say where you went last summer
- Say what you did there
- Say whether you had a good time or not
- Mention any good or bad experiences you had

Study tips

Remember to use the preterite tense of the verb *ir* to say where you went. Watch out for other irregular verbs in the preterite, e.g. *hacer, tener.* See page 182.

You could add verbs to your list to help you remember to give details of what you did: *ir*, *comer*, *jugar*, *practicar*, *visitar*, *comprar*.

To say you had a good or bad time use *pasarlo bien / mal, divertirse, disfrutar.*

3 What destination you would recommend and why.

- Suggest a holiday destination and say where it is
- Mention what the weather is like there normally
- Say what there is to do and see and what it is like
- Describe the type of food you can eat there

Study tips

Recommend a country, city, area or resort and say where it is. You can begin your answer with *Recomiendo …* e.g. *Recomiendo Barbados, Menorca, una isla en el Mediterráneo.*

To describe the weather you can use the verbs *hacer* and *haber*, e.g. *hace frío / buen tiempo / sol / viento* and *hay tormentas / nieve / niebla*.

Use *hay* to say what there is, e.g. *Hay fiestas en agosto.* Use *es* to say what something is like, e.g. *Es impresionante*.

Mention any local dishes and specialities and say if the food is good (*bueno*), hot (*picante*), tasty (*rico*), fresh (*fresco*).

4 How to get to your suggested destination.

- Mention the best way to get to the location
- Compare other types of transport
- Mention ticket prices
- Say how to get to the airport / port / station to the hotel or other accommodation

Study tips

You could begin with *Para ir a (Barcelona)* …

To compare types of transport use *más* and *menos*, e.g. *El avión es más barato que el tren.*

Make sure you know your high numbers and how to say 24-hour times so that you can give prices and departure and arrival information.

Use *hay que* and *debes* to give instructions, e.g. *Debes alquilar un coche. Hay que tomar la autopista hasta Gerona.*

5 Where you will be going on your next holiday.

- Say where you will be going
- Say why you will be going there
- Mention when you will be going
- Say what you plan to do there

Study tips

Use the immediate future tense to talk about future plans: *Voy a ir a (Italia).* See page 183.

Make sure you know the words for the seasons and months of the year.

Try to avoid repeating information more than once and give alternative activities to those already mentioned.

6 What is important for you when choosing a type of holiday.

- Mention local festivals and customs
- Mention learning new things
- Talk about ways to relax
- Mention ways to be active on holiday

Study tips

To say what is important / good / fun / interesting use *Para mí, lo importante / bueno / divertido / interesante es …*

When talking about festivals mention dates and special attractions such as fireworks or parades.

Customs can include things like meal times, markets, music and clothing.

You can talk about different sports that you can do on holiday such as cycling, horse riding and walking.

Don't just copy the models in textbooks or online. You will find it easier to remember information that is personal and that you have prepared yourself.

7 !

At this point, you will be asked another question which you don't know in advance. However, you can try to guess what it might be and prepare various options:

- Describe your friend's last holiday
- Talk about your ideal holiday
- Talk about the benefits of taking holidays
- Talk about your local area as a holiday destination

Study tips

Listen carefully to what the examiner is asking you. Make sure you know a variety of interrogative pronouns such as *¿Cómo?, ¿Cuándo?¿Cuánto? ¿Dónde?* and shape your answer to the question.

Make sure you prepare answers for all the above possibilities by making three different points for each possibility, e.g. bullet point 3: meeting new people, enjoying the nightlife, resting. Write three or four words for the each of the two most likely options.

Check the **total** number of words. It should not be more than 40.

You should now have completed your plan and prepared your answers. Give your plan to your teacher for feedback. Compare your answers to the online sample version – you might find some useful hints to make yours even better.

2 El tiempo libre

You are writing a section of an article for a Spanish online magazine on teenagers in the EU. The title of the article is '*Los jóvenes y el tiempo libre*'. In your section you could include:

1. What you do at home on a typical weekend
2. What you do outside the home in your free time
3. Money, how you get it and what you spend it on
4. Your views on fashion
5. Your own tastes and style
6. How you use communication technology
7. An overview of how young people spend their leisure time

Study tips

Start your plan by writing a list of key words for each of the seven sections in the task. The maximum is 40 words in total. Any words are allowed as long as they are not conjugated verbs. Here are some suggestions for the first section: *guitarra, dibujos animados, música, videoconsola*.

Remember to include some verbs in your lists. Write them in the infinitive but make sure you know how to use them in the correct form.

1 What you do at home on a typical weekend.
- Say what time you usually get up
- Describe your usual free-time activities
- Say what you and your family did last weekend
- Say what your plans are for next weekend

Study tips

You could start off with *Normalmente, los fines de semana me levanto a las …*

Use *a veces* to say what you sometimes do: *A veces saco al perro a pasear.*

Use time expressions to describe when you do or did things at the weekend: *el sábado por la mañana, por la tarde, después …*

Use the preterite tense to describe what you or your family did: *toqué el piano, arreglé mi dormitorio, mi padre lavó el coche …*

Use *ir a* + infinitive to talk about plans for the near future: *Este fin de semana voy a descansar mucho. Voy a levantarme tarde. Voy a escuchar música, tocar la guitarra, jugar en mi videoconsola y ver la tele.*

2 What you do outside the home in your free time.
- Describe the sports you do and when you do them
- Say when and where you go with your friends
- Describe a weekend when you did something special
- Say whether you enjoyed the weekend or not

Study tips

You can use *el sábado* or *los sábados*, *el fin de semana* or *los fines de semana* to say 'on Saturday' or 'on Saturdays', 'at the weekend' or 'at the weekends'.

Remember to use the preterite tense of the verb *ir* to say where you went.

Use words like *fenomenal* or *genial* to describe events you enjoyed.

3 Money – how you get it and what you spend it on.
- Say if you work to earn money or if your parents give you money
- Say how much money you have each week or each month
- Say what you spend your money on
- Say if you save money regularly, how much and what for

Study tips

Remember some key words for talking about money: *ganar* – to earn, *gastar* – to spend, *ahorrar* – to save, *la paga* – pocket money.

Use *a la semana* or *al mes* to say how much money you earn, receive or spend 'a week' or 'a month': *Trabajo en una cafetería y gano 50 libras a la semana.*

4 Your views on fashion.
- Say whether you are interested in fashion or not
- Say what kind of clothes, colours and accessories are fashionable at the moment
- Give your views on designer labels
- Say whether you think males and females are equally interested in fashion

Study tips

Find the words for the clothes and accessories you want to mention in your writing on pages 72–73 and make a list. Start with a sentence that sums up your attitude to fashion: *La moda (no) me interesa mucho / bastante / nada*. Include key vocabulary: *estar de moda* (to be fashionable).

5 Your own tastes and style.
- Describe your own fashion style
- Describe your shopping habits: how often you go shopping, where you usually buy your clothes, whether you like shopping for clothes, etc.
- Describe the kind of clothes and accessories you like to buy and wear
- Say what else you spend money on

Study tips

Look at the four texts on page 64 which give opinions on fashion and personal style. Notice the expressions they use and adapt them to give your own views. Use a variety of verbs and phrases to describe your likes and dislikes: *adoro, me encanta, me gusta, no me gusta, odio, detesto*.

6 How you use communication technology.
- Say which items you use most: mobile, lap top, MP3, etc.
- Say why they are useful to you
- Describe the advantages and disadvantages of communication technology
- Say why you think communication technology is important for young people

Study tips

Find the expressions in the texts on page 66 that match your own views on communication technology. For example: *Para mí es imprescindible (el portátil). Adoro (mi móvil). Lo uso para …*
Don't attempt to give a complex explanation if you are unsure of the language needed. For example, look for a simple way of describing the advantages (*ventajas*) and disadvantages (*desventajas*) of communication technology. Adapt the sentences in the text on page 66 to express your own ideas.

7 An overview of how young people spend their leisure time.
- Describe how other people you know spend their free time and give examples
- Say which leisure facilities in your local area are good
- Say what could be improved to offer young people facilities in your area
- Say why you think having free time is important

Study tips

Make sure you use the correct part of the verb to describe what other people do:
A mi hermana le gusta la música. Toca la guitarra en un grupo. Mi amigo Alex practica muchos deportes. Los fines de semana juega al rugby y al fútbol.
En mi barrio tenemos una piscina pero sería fantástico tener una pista de atletismo también.
Being able to express opinions raises the level of your writing. For example: *Creo que el tiempo libre es importante porque …*
para evitar el estrés, es necesario descansar / de lunes a viernes trabajamos mucho y tenemos muchos deberes / es importante estar con la familia y con los amigos.

Have you completed your plan and prepared your answers? Make sure your teacher checks it and gives you feedback.
Compare your answers to the online sample version – you might find some useful hints to make yours even better.

kerboodle

Resumen

1 Copy and complete the following sentence with the correct verbs in the present tense. Use *escuchar, jugar, tocar, ver.*

En mi tiempo libre _______ la guitarra, _______ música, _______ en mi videoconsola y _______ la tele.

2 In the following sentence, replace *genial* with another word to give the opposite meaning.

Lo pasé genial.

3 Copy and complete this sentence with the correct forms of *jugar* and *ganar* in the preterite tense.

El domingo por la tarde mi hermano y mi padre _______ en un partido de fútbol de padres contra hijos. ¡Y claro, _______ los hijos!

4 Translate these sentences. Make sure you know the difference between *fui* and *fue.*

El sábado fui a un concierto con Nieves. También fue nuestro amigo, Juan.

5 Complete the conversation with the correct demonstrative pronoun.

– Me gustan aquellas botas marrones en el escaparate. Pero son muy caras.

– Pruébate _______. Son muy parecidas pero a mitad del precio.

6 Write a definition in Spanish for the following expression:

la paga semanal

7 Give an appropriate response in Spanish to the following question.

¿Cuáles son las desventajas de los móviles y de Internet?

8 Copy and complete this sentence with the correct verbs in the preterite tense.

En agosto fui a Cornualles pero _______ mala suerte porque _______ camping y hacía mal tiempo.

9 Give an appropriate response to this question, using *ir a* + infinitive:

¿Qué vas a hacer en Semana Santa?

10 Translate this question into English.

¿Has estado alguna vez en Sevilla?

¿Lo sabes?

- Los españoles se pasan casi las mismas horas semanalmente navegando por Internet que viendo la televisión (10 y 11 horas respectivamente).
- Un 55% de los españoles invierten un 48% de sus ingresos en ocio, ropa y moda, uno de los porcentajes más altos de Europa y del mundo.

3 Home and environment

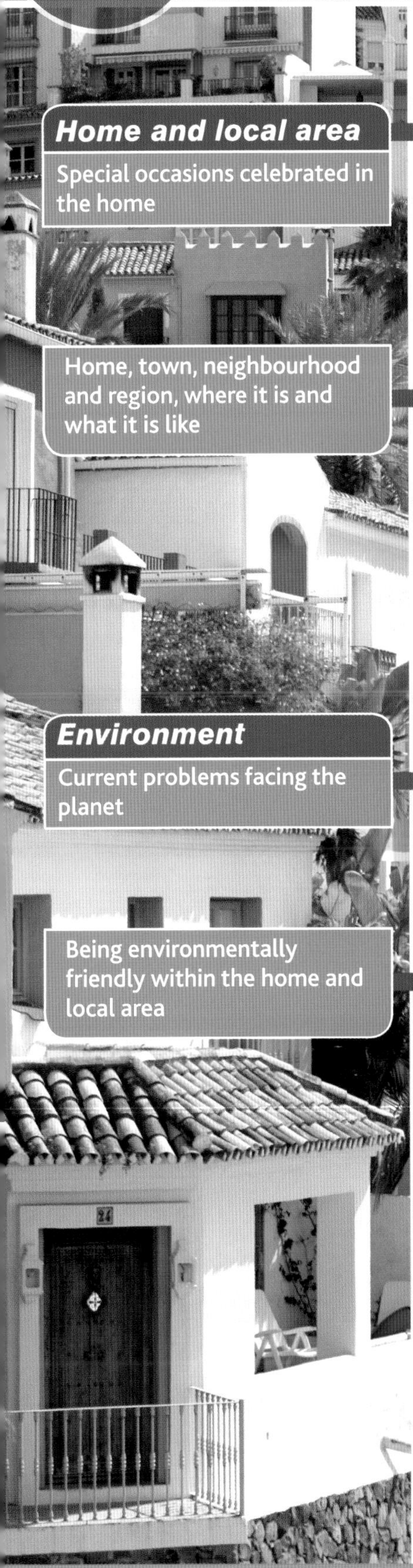

Rooms in the house, things in the house

1a Read the following descriptions of houses and match up each one with the correct plan.

1

Mi casa es bastante grande, es de dos plantas. En la planta baja hay un salón, un comedor, una cocina y un aseo. Arriba, en la primera planta están el cuarto de baño, el dormitorio de mis padres y el dormitorio de mi hermana y mío. No tenemos garaje pero tenemos un jardín grande detrás de la casa y otro más pequeño delante.

2

Tenemos una casa nueva y vivimos aquí desde hace dos meses. Me encanta porque es moderna y todo está nuevo. En la planta baja hay una cocina grande, un salón y un aseo. Arriba están los tres dormitorios, el dormitorio de mis padres con baño adjunto, el mío y el cuarto de huéspedes. También hay otro cuarto de baño y la escalera al ático donde está el despacho de mi madre.

A

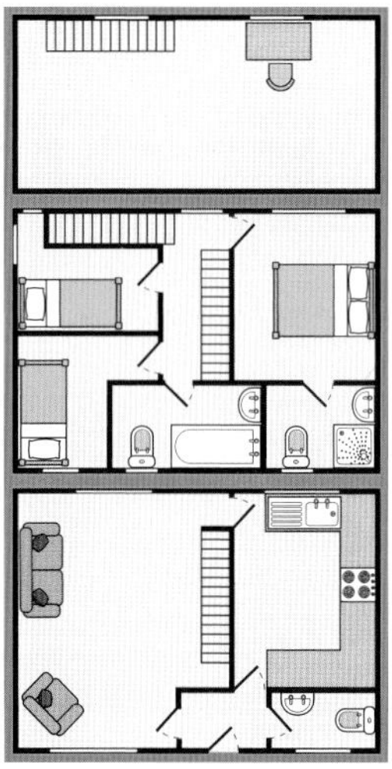

B

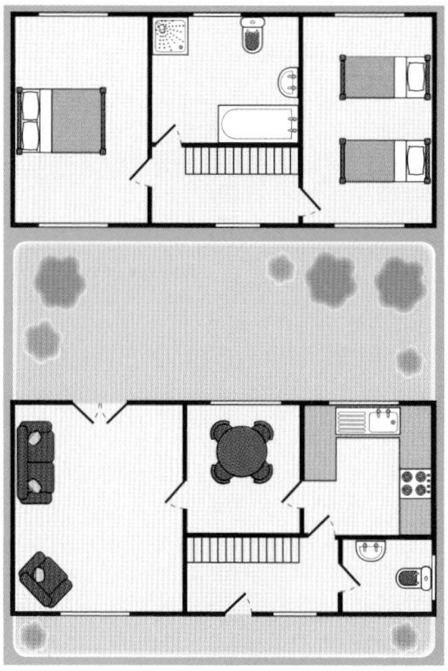

Vocabulario

el aseo	toilet
la cocina	kitchen
el comedor	dining room
el cuarto de baño	bathroom
el despacho	study
el dormitorio	bedroom
el salón	lounge
la terraza	terrace

Prepositions

Use these prepositions with *estar* to say where things are:

arriba	upstairs
debajo de	under
delante de	in front of
detrás de	behind
encima de	on top of
enfrente de	opposite
a la derecha de	to the right of
a la izquierda de	to the left of

Gramática página 187

Vocabulario

la alfombra	rug
la butaca	armchair
las cortinas	curtains
el escritorio	desk
la pared	wall

1b Look at the picture of the room and say if the following sentences are true or false. Correct the sentences that are false.

1. La cama está debajo de la ventana.
2. La mesa está detrás del sofá.
3. La butaca está delante del televisor.
4. La alfombra es azul y las cortinas son verdes.

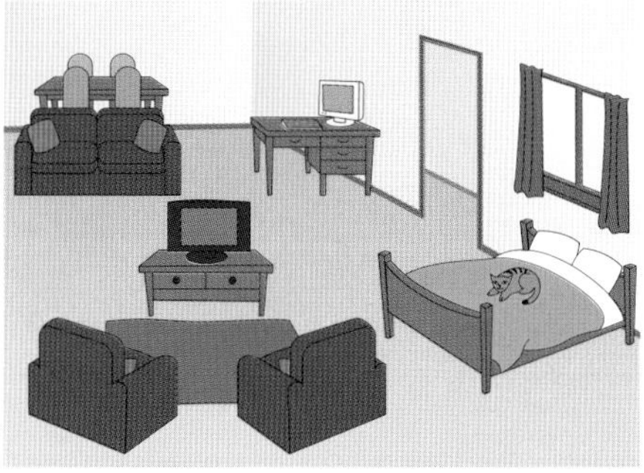

1c Work in pairs. Partner A asks questions about the room and Partner B answers. Then swap roles.

2 Write a description of your own house in Spanish.

House types and locations

Matilde

Mi dirección es Calle Francisco de Goya, número 10, 3°. Vivo en un piso moderno. Mi bloque es de cinco plantas y vivimos en la tercera planta. Es parte de una construcción nueva. Antes vivía en una casa adosada en otro barrio. Me gusta vivir aquí más que en la otra casa porque el piso es más grande.

Ignacio

¿Cómo es mi casa? Pues, es una casa adosada antigua de dos plantas en un pueblo cerca de Cáceres. Todas las casas en la calle son iguales. Preferiría vivir en una casa más grande. Necesitamos más espacio. Esta casa es muy pequeña.

Elvira

El año que viene mi familia y yo vamos a mudarnos a una casa nueva en las afueras de Segovia. Ahora vivimos en un piso duplex con dormitorios arriba y los demás cuartos abajo. Vamos a comprar un chalet de tres plantas, con sótano y desván.

1 Read the descriptions and name the person who says each of the sentences below.

1 I live in a street of two-storey houses.
2 We are moving to a three-storey house next year.
3 I live in a village not far from the city.
4 I used to live in a terraced house but now I live in a flat.
5 I live on the outskirts of the city.
6 I'd like to live somewhere with more space.
7 Our flat is on two floors.
8 I live on the third floor.

2 Write some questions in Spanish to ask other students about their houses. You could include:

- what type of house they live in
- how long they have lived there
- what they think of their home

¿Cómo es tu casa?

Vivo en una casa adosada.

¿Qué opinas de tu casa?

Me gusta mi casa porque es más grande que mi piso antiguo.

Vocabulario

una casa	house
una casa adosada	semi-detached / terraced house
un chalé / chalet	detached house
una construcción nueva	new development
un piso	flat
una torre / un bloque	tower block

Gramática *página 187*

Ser and *estar*

Ser and *estar* both mean 'to be'.

Ser is used to describe what things and people are and what is unlikely to change.

E.g. *Mi bloque **es** de cinco plantas.*

Estar is used to describe where things are, and something which is likely to change.

E.g. ***Estoy** muy mal.*

See page 108

Vocabulario

Mi (casa) está …	Mi (house) is …
cerca (de)	close (to)
lejos (de)	far (from)
en el campo	in the countryside
en la costa	on the coast
en el centro	in the centre
en una zona céntrica	in a central area
en las afueras	in the suburbs
a (cinco) minutos andando	(five) minutes walk away
a (media hora) en autobús	(half an hour) by bus
a (veinte) kilómetros	(twenty) kilometres away

Normal routine

Me despierto muy temprano, a las 6h15 de la mañana. Después de ducharme y vestirme, me tomo un café y una tostada para desayunar. Me lavo los dientes y a las 7h15 salgo para el instituto.

No vuelvo hasta las 3h45.

Prefiero comer en el instituto porque vivo lejos. Las clases empiezan a las ocho y terminan a las tres. Creo que es un día escolar muy largo.

Todos los miércoles tengo que ir a mi clase de inglés.

Normalmente cenamos a las 9h. Veo la tele un rato después de cenar. Me acuesto a eso de las 10h30. Me gusta leer en la cama pero me duermo enseguida. Siempre estoy cansado.

Los sábados por la tarde salgo por ahí con mis amigos. A veces vamos al centro comercial, al cine o a una fiesta. Los domingos por la mañana juego al fútbol en el equipo de mi insti. Al mediodía comemos en casa de mis abuelos y después vamos de paseo al parque.

Miguel

1a Read Miguel's account of his daily routine. Match up the two halves of the sentences below.

1 Miguel se despierta a las …
2 Va al instituto a las siete y cuarto …
3 En su opinión las clases empiezan demasiado …
4 Los miércoles tiene …
5 Cena a las 9h y ve …
6 Se acuesta a las diez y media, lee …
7 De vez en cuando va al cine con sus amigos …
8 Da una vuelta por el parque …

a los sábados por la tarde.
b y vuelve a las cuatro menos cuarto.
c una clase particular de inglés.
d después de comer con los abuelos.
e temprano y terminan muy tarde.
f un poco y se duerme enseguida.
g 6h15 y se levanta a las 6h30.
h un poco de televisión antes de acostarse.

1b Make up an interview with Miguel about his daily routine. Work in pairs. Partner A plays the part of the interviewer and Partner B plays the part of Miguel. Then swap roles.

1c Write a letter to Miguel telling him about your own routine.

Radical-changing verbs

Gramática

página 181

Some verbs follow a pattern in which the middle letters change:

jugar	*preferir*
juego	*prefiero*
juegas	*prefieres*
juega	*prefiere*
jugamos	*preferimos*
jugáis	*preferís*
juegan	*prefieren*

Miguel se despierta temprano.
Prefiero navegar por Internet.

Vocabulario

me acuesto	I go to bed
me arreglo	I get (myself) ready
me despierto	I wake up
me ducho	I shower
me duermo	I go to sleep
me lavo los dientes	I brush my teeth
me levanto	I get up
salgo	I leave / go out
me visto	I get dressed
vuelvo	I return

Helping at home

Buscar

Inicio | Índice | Sitemap | Ayuda | Versión texto

FAQs
Noticias
Acceso directo
Arriba

En mi familia todos ayudamos en casa porque somos muchos. Mi padre y mi hermana cocinan muy bien y normalmente preparan la cena entre los dos.
Mi hermano pequeño tiene que poner la mesa antes de comer. Mis dos hermanos quitan la mesa y también friegan los platos. A mí me gusta planchar. Plancho las camisas. También limpio el cuarto de baño todas las semanas. Mi hermana mayor no hace mucho porque tiene que estudiar y tiene un trabajo parcial. Ella hace las camas y cambia las sábanas todas las semanas.
Mi padre saca la basura y mi madre pasa la aspiradora y hace la compra en el supermercado. Mi hermanita pequeña no hace nada porque es un bebé.

Enrique

Vocabulario

arreglar el dormitorio	to tidy the bedroom
cocinar / preparar la cena	to cook / prepare the dinner
fregar los platos / el suelo	to wash the dishes / floor
hacer la cama	to make the bed
hacer la compra	to do the shopping
limpiar el cuarto de baño	to clean the bathroom
pasar la aspiradora	to hoover
planchar	to do the ironing
poner la mesa	to set the table
quitar la mesa	to clear the table
sacar la basura	to take out the rubbish
no hacer nada	to do nothing

1a Read Enrique's account and write the letters of the pictures in the order in which the household tasks are mentioned.

A
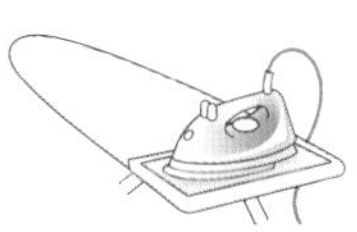

B

C
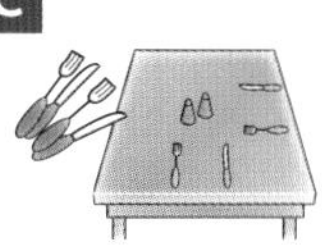

D
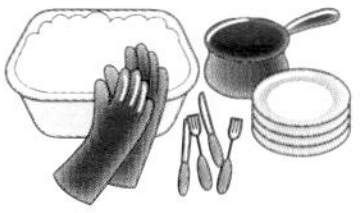

E

F
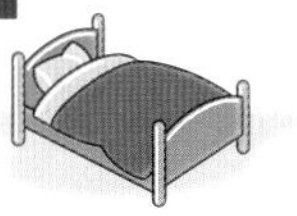

G

H
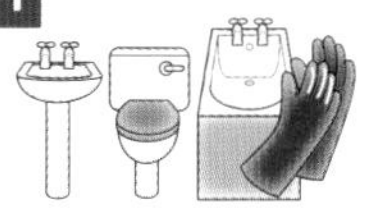

I

1b Read Enrique's account again and indicate who does each of the household tasks in the pictures: Enrique (E), father (F), mother (M), older sister (OS), younger brother (YB), other brothers (OB).

2 Who does what in your house? Work in pairs. Partner A asks the questions and Partner B answers. Then swap roles.

¿Quién lava los platos?

Yo lavo los platos.

3 Adapt Enrique's description to write, in Spanish, about how you help at home.

Present & preterite tenses in the same sentence

Gramática página 181

Use the present tense to talk about activities you do regularly and the preterite to talk about activities you have done. The following time expressions can also be used:

Present

ahora	*de lunes a viernes*
hoy	*los domingos*
normalmente	

Preterite

ayer	*la semana pasada*
anteayer	*hace dos días*

Los sábados hago *la compra en el supermercado pero* ***el sábado pasado hice*** *la compra en el mercado.*

kerboodle

3.1 De fiesta

Objetivos

- Talking about special occasions
- Using the imperfect tense
- Making use of social and cultural contexts

Las fiestas de Navidad – los recuerdos de Nicolás

Buscar

Inicio | Índice | Sitemap | Ayuda | Versión texto

FAQs
Noticias
Acceso directo
Arriba

A Cuando era pequeño las fiestas de Navidad eran las mejores del año. Era cuando la familia se reunía y mis padres preparaban comida especial y comíamos dulces como el mazapán y el turrón que contiene almendras y miel. A veces mis primos y yo íbamos por la calle cantando villancicos – canciones típicas de Navidad – y la gente nos daba algo de dinero. En el salón siempre poníamos un belén que es una escena en miniatura del nacimiento del Niño Jesús.

B El 24 de diciembre es la víspera de la Navidad y se celebra la Nochebuena. Todos los años cenábamos con los abuelos, los tíos y los primos. El plato principal solía ser pescado. Después de la cena íbamos a la iglesia a celebrar la Misa de Gallo a medianoche.

C La Nochevieja se celebra el 31 de diciembre. A las 12 de la noche, tomábamos 12 uvas para tener suerte los próximos 12 meses. Después, los adultos brindaban con cava, sidra o champán. Muchas veces poníamos música y bailábamos toda la noche. Lo pasábamos muy bien.

D Los Reyes Magos es el 6 de enero. Es un día mágico para los niños, pues los tres Reyes nos traen los juguetes que hemos pedido en una carta. Cada año en nuestra ciudad el 5 de enero, víspera de Reyes, a las seis de la tarde, los Reyes se paseaban por las calles a caballo o en camello, cargados de paquetes de juguetes. Repartían caramelos entre la gente, que los esperaban por las calles para verlos pasar. Luego, de madrugada, cuando estábamos en la cama, pasaban casa por casa repartiendo regalos. Ponían los regalos en los zapatos que se dejaban en el balcón.

1

2

3

4

1a Match up each photo with the correct paragraph.

1b Answer the following questions in English.

1. Where did Nicolás sing Christmas carols?
2. Where did the family set up the Nativity scene?
3. At what time did the family go to church?
4. Why are 12 grapes eaten for each stroke of 12 midnight on *Nochevieja*?
5. When do Spanish children get their Christmas presents?
6. When do the Three Kings parade around the town?

Estrategia

Making use of social and cultural contexts

Use what you know about Spanish-speaking countries to help you work out the meaning of unfamiliar words. For example, if you know that *Día de Reyes* is the 6th January, you can deduce from *día 5 de enero, víspera de Reyes* that *víspera* means 'the eve of' or 'the day before'.

2a Ⓖ Copy the sentences and fill in the gaps with the correct verb from the list.

1. Mi familia ______ pescado en la cena de Nochebuena.
2. Mis hermanos ______ un belén.
3. ¿______ vosotros a la Misa de Gallo?
4. Mi madre ______ los regalos en los zapatos.
5. ¿Tú ______ 12 uvas para tener suerte?
6. Ustedes ______ para ver la cabalgata.

tomabas **esperaban** **ibais**

ponía **hacían** **comía**

2b Ⓖ Make a list of the verbs in the imperfect tense in Nicolás' memories of Christmas celebrations in Activity 1.

3a 🎧 Listen to Guadalupe's account of her 15th birthday celebrations.
Which of the following does she mention?

A

B

C

D

E

3b 🎧 Decide whether the following statements are true (T), false (F) or not mentioned (?). Correct the ones that are false.

1. Guadalupe had a *quinceañera* party in July.
2. She was woken up by a band of musicians.
3. She was given a camera as a present.
4. She wore a pink designer dress.
5. She sat at the top table with her friends.
6. The party finished at four in the morning.

4 Work in pairs. Take turns to ask and answer questions about how you celebrate a special occasion now, and how you used to when you were younger. Then write about the occasion you chose to talk about. Refer to the online worksheet for a language structure box to help you.

Cuando eras pequeño/a …	Ahora …
¿Cómo te preparabas para la fiesta?	¿Cómo te preparas para la fiesta?
¿Qué ropa llevabas?	¿Qué ropa llevas?
¿Qué comías?	¿Qué comes?
¿Qué hacías?	¿Qué haces?

Gramática

página 182

Using the imperfect tense

Use the imperfect tense for things that used to happen regularly in the past and to describe incomplete actions in the past.

The imperfect is formed by replacing the infinitive endings with the following:

-ar verbs: *-aba, -abas, -aba, -ábamos, -abais, -aban*

-er and *-ir* verbs: *-ía, -ías, -ía, -íamos, -íais, -ían*

Cenaba pescado. I used to eat fish.

Comíamos dulces. We used to eat sweets.

The only irregular imperfects are *ir, ver* and *ser*.

ir – iba *ver – veía* *ser – era*

Also learn about when to use the imperfect and preterite tenses. *See page 108* ➡

Consejo

Use the imperfect to express habitual actions in the past, and the preterite to express an action completed at a definite time. These time expressions indicate habit and should be used with the imperfect tense:

siempre / con frecuencia

frecuentemente / a menudo

a veces / de vez en cuando

muchas veces

cada año / día / mes

todos los días (jueves)

3.2 ¿Cómo es tu casa?

Objetivos

- Describing what your home is like
- Using possessive pronouns
- Remembering to use quantifiers and intensifiers

1 Read the following blog and find the Spanish words in each paragraph which match the English expressions below. Work in pairs: test each other on these words and phrases from the text.

1. It's like a palace.
2. There are lots of stairs to climb.
3. Ours is rented.
4. There is only a shower.
5. It's very cosy.

La casa de Julia Pérez

Buscar

Inicio | Índice | Sitemap | Ayuda | Versión texto

FAQs

Noticias

Acceso directo

Arriba

El blog de Trini

A

Julia Pérez es mi cantante preferida y ésta es su casa. Es igual que un palacio, ¿verdad? ¿Cuántas habitaciones y cuartos de baño tiene? Demasiados. ¿Tendrá gimnasio, cine o biblioteca? No tengo idea, es enorme. Sin embargo mi piso aquí en Madrid es muy pequeño con dos dormitorios, el de mis padres y el mío que comparto con mi hermana mayor. Hay un cuarto de baño y tiene un salón comedor.

B

Mira la piscina y las fuentes en el césped de la casa de Julia. Mi casa no tiene patio, sólo tiene una terraza. Su casa es de dos plantas con ático. Nuestra casa está en el séptimo piso y da a la calle mientras que la mansión de Julia tiene jardines con árboles y flores. El ascensor en mi bloque está roto y hay muchas escaleras que subir. No tenemos aparcamiento mientras que su casa tiene garajes para todos sus coches.

C

Su casa vale millones de dólares, la nuestra es alquilada. La suya está lejos de sus vecinos. Tiene paredes altas y cámaras de seguridad. Nuestro bloque tiene la mínima seguridad y puede entrar cualquiera.

D

¿Cómo está decorada la casa de Julia? Sin duda tiene alfombras caras, muebles de lujo, lámparas de cristal, cortinas de seda y espejos gigantescos por toda la casa … Mi piso está pintado todo de blanco con una moqueta azul y persianas en las ventanas. Nuestra cocina es tan pequeña que no cabe la nevera, la tenemos en el pasillo. No tenemos ni lavaplatos ni tampoco microondas. Y no hay bañera en el cuarto de baño, sólo hay una ducha.

E

¿Me gusta más la casa de Julia que la mía? Es claramente más grande, más lujosa y cómoda que la mía. Aunque mi casa es pobre y pequeña es muy acogedora. No me gusta tanto la mansión de Julia como mi hogar querido.

2 Read the sentences and identify which home, if any, is being referred to in each case. Write J for Julia's house, T for Trini's flat or N for neither of them.

Ejemplo: 1 J

1. Es parecida a un palacio.
2. Es adosada.
3. El ascensor no funciona.
4. Está menos aislada.
5. El edificio es antiguo.
6. Hay mejores muebles.
7. Hay pocos electrodomésticos.
8. Es la más grande.

3 Listen to the interview with María Ángeles about her house. In which section of the interview (a–e) are the following mentioned?

1 The house is warm in winter and cool in summer.
2 The house didn't have lighting and heating before.
3 María Ángeles lives in a village.
4 Her home is modernised.
5 Her room is on the top floor.

Estrategia

Remembering to use quantifiers and intensifiers

Sometimes you need to listen for clues to the speaker's emotional attitude to her house. Words like *muy, bastante, demasiado, poco* and *mucho* can help you to answer the question.

4 **G** Choose the appropriate possessive pronoun and copy out the sentences correctly.

1 No me gusta su casa pero me gusta mucho la vuestra / las vuestras.
2 Nuestro piso es pequeño, pero la suya / el suyo es muy pequeño.
3 Mi cocina es grande. ¿Y la tuya / el tuyo?
4 ¿Es éste vuestro dormitorio? Sí, es el nuestro / las nuestras.
5 El chalet es muy moderno. No es como el mío / la mía.

Gramática página 179

Possessive pronouns: mío, tuyo, suyo, nuestro, vuestro, suyo

Use these with *el / la / los / las* and remember to make them agree with the nouns they replace.

La casa de Julia es más grande que la mía.

Also learn about interrogative adjectives.

See page 109 ➡

5 Work in pairs. Look at the pictures and each choose a house. Partner A asks Partner B questions to work out which is their chosen house. Also ask which your partner prefers and why. Then swap roles.

Consejo

Use these expressions to make comparisons:

La casa de Julia es más lujosa que la mía.

La casa de Julia no es tan acogedora como la mía.

Vivo en La mía / La tuya (es)	un piso una casa (adosada)	en	las afueras / el campo. la ciudad / un pueblo.
Es		bastante / demasiado / muy	antiguo/a / grande / pequeño/a.
En mi / tu casa En la mía / la tuya	hay / no hay	aparcamiento / planta(s) / dormitorios / cuartos de baño / un patio / una terraza.	
La mía / La tuya Mi / Tu casa	es más no es tan	acogedora / cómoda / lujosa / moderna	que la mía / la tuya. como la mía / la tuya.
Me gusta (más) / Prefiero	mi / tu casa la mía / la tuya	porque	tiene vistas bonitas. está en el centro.

3.3 ¿Cómo es tu barrio?

Objetivos

- Talking about your neighbourhood
- Using relative pronouns
- Using common patterns within Spanish

Mi barrio

A

Mi barrio está en las afueras de la ciudad. Es residencial. Antes había mucha industria y fábricas pero ahora hay mucho paro. El barrio es feo y no está muy limpio. Hay mucho tráfico y ruido porque la autopista pasa por el medio del barrio por lo tanto hay bastante contaminación. Es un poco peligroso y hay cámaras de seguridad en algunas calles. No hay mucha diversión y por lo tanto no hay mucho que hacer para los jóvenes. Lo bueno es que van a construir un polideportivo el año que viene. Lo que me gusta de mi barrio es que hay un centro comercial donde hay un multi-cine. Pero lo que necesitamos también es una zona peatonal y lo más importante, lugares verdes.

B

Vivo en un pueblo muy bonito en la costa. Hay mucho turismo aquí en verano porque hay playas muy cerca y un puerto pesquero pintoresco. También hay un parque de atracciones. En el centro histórico las calles son estrechas con tiendas turísticas y una plaza donde hay un mercado de artesanía los jueves. Hay muchos restaurantes y bares animados pero lo malo de mi barrio es que no hay mucho para los jóvenes. En invierno es aburrido y no hay nada que hacer porque todo está cerrado. Hay diversión en la ciudad pero está lejos y no hay autobuses. Antes había una discoteca pero ahora está cerrada. Hacen falta instalaciones para los jóvenes como un club de jóvenes o una piscina. También necesitamos una red de transporte eficiente.

1 Make notes for each local area described in the texts: location, what it is like, what it has, what there is for young people and what it needs.

2 Work in pairs. Each choose one text and take turns to ask each other the following questions about the neighbourhoods described.

¿Cómo es el barrio?
¿Qué tiene?
¿Qué hay para los jóvenes?
¿Qué necesita?

Estrategia: Using common patterns within Spanish

Look for common patterns in families of words.

Change the following nouns to adjectives by adding *-oso, -osa*, e.g. *ruido – ruidoso*

peligro, espacio

Change the following verbs to nouns by adding *-ión* or *-ción*, e.g. *animar – animación*

habitar, participar

Add *-ería* endings to these nouns to change them into the names of shops, e.g. *zapato – zapatería*

pescado, pastel, libro

3a 🎧 Listen to Isidro and Cristina talking about their neighbourhoods and answer the questions.

1 Where does Isidro live? 2 Where does Cristina live?

3b Listen again and put the information each speaker gives into the order in which you hear it.

Isidro

a It's not clean, there's rubbish in the streets.
b Even the police won't enter the neighbourhood.
c People don't have jobs.

Cristina

a You have to drive into the centre if you want some fun.
b The housing estate was built recently.
c There are good sporting facilities.

4 G Translate the following sentences into English.

1 La piscina que van a construir es olímpica.
2 Lo que necesitamos son canchas de tenis.
3 El policía con quien hablé, me dio la dirección.
4 El monumento que me gusta más, es el castillo.
5 La basura en las calles es lo que no me gusta.
6 La chica a quien invité es argentina.

5 ✏ Write a report about your neighbourhood. Include the following:

- Where it is.
- What it's like.
- What facilities it has for young people.
- What it used to be like.
- What it needs to improve it.

Gramática *página 179*

Using relative pronouns

Que (who / what / that / which) can refer to people or things.

Use *que, quien* (who) to give more information about someone or something.

La chica, que trabaja en el polideportivo, es muy simpática.
The girl who works in the sports centre is very friendly.

After a preposition, use *quien* to refer to a person.

No me gusta la chica con quien sale. I don't like the girl he is going out with.

Use *lo que* (what) to refer to an idea.

Lo que me gusta de mi barrio es que es tranquilo.
What I like about my area is that it's quiet.

Also learn to use *hay* and *había*. *See page 108* ➡

Consejo

Lo + adjective translates as 'the ... thing':

Lo bueno es que van a construir un polideportivo.
The good thing is that they are going to build a sports centre.

To say what is needed use:

necesita, necesitamos, se necesita, hace falta.

Hace falta un parque infantil.
It needs a children's playground.

Es / Está	ruidoso / tranquilo / seguro / peligroso / sucio / limpio.		
(No) Hay (No) Tiene	mucho/a(s)	contaminación lugares de diversión	un centro comercial. una autopista.
Para la gente joven	(no) hay	mucho que hacer. instalaciones deportivas.	
Antes había	mucho tráfico	pero ahora hay	zonas verdes.
Necesita Se necesita Hace falta	un multi-cine. un parque infantil. una red de transportes eficiente.		

kerboodle

3.4 Mi región

Objetivos

- Talking about your region
- Describing past weather conditions
- Recognising percentages, common fractions and temperatures

En el norte

Vivo en una zona rural a 120 kilómetros al norte de Barcelona. Es un lugar tranquilo aunque hay una ciudad a poca distancia, con todos los servicios, y es fácil llegar a las playas de la Costa Brava. Además hay buen acceso a la autopista.

El pueblo está situado en un valle muy bonito con muchas granjas y casas de piedra. Alrededor hay bosques, ríos y montañas. A lo lejos se ven los picos de los Pirineos. Normalmente, desde diciembre a abril, están cubiertos de nieve y se puede ir a esquiar. Pero este año no hacía mucho frío en invierno y casi no nevaba.

El valle está a 500 metros sobre el nivel del mar y tiene un clima bastante variable. Este verano hacía mucho calor, con temperaturas de más de 30 grados. Pero en invierno la temperatura baja mucho por la noche, hasta quince grados bajo cero.

Lo mejor de mi zona son las noches de luna llena, con cielos despejados y miles de estrellas.

En el sur

Vivo en las afueras de Sevilla, en el sur de España. La zona alrededor de la ciudad es muy llana pero a unos kilómetros hacia el oeste se encuentra la Sierra de Aracena y al este están las montañas de Sierra Nevada.

Al sur de Sevilla hay pueblos pequeños, con casas antiguas, todas pintadas de blanco y muy típicas de la región. Además hay ciudades antiguas con monumentos históricos, como La Mezquita de Córdoba y la Alhambra de Granada, un impresionante palacio árabe.

Lo bueno de mi región es que tiene un clima estupendo con más de un noventa por ciento de días de sol al año. En verano a veces hace más de 40 grados. Los inviernos son suaves – no hace frío y raras veces se baja de los 0º Celsius. Pero hay excepciones, por ejemplo, fuimos de excursión a la sierra en septiembre y hacía mal tiempo casi toda la semana: había tormentas y hasta inundaciones.

1a Match up each caption a–f with one of the two parts of the article.

a La autopista está cerca y es fácil llegar a Barcelona o Francia.

b En mi región hay ciudades interesantes con monumentos históricos.

c La región tiene un clima muy agradable: hace buen tiempo todo el año.

d La zona alrededor de la ciudad es muy llana.

e Mi pueblo está en el campo, en medio de granjas, bosques, ríos y montañas.

f Hace mucho frío en invierno.

Estrategia

Look at the context in which numbers relating to weather conditions and geographical locations appear. Also look for words that are similar in English.

sobre el nivel del mar	above sea level
bajo cero	below zero
noventa por ciento	90%
40 grados	forty degrees

1b Answer the following questions in English.

En el norte

1 How high is the valley?

2 How hot is it in summer?

3 How cold is it in winter?

En el sur

1 Is it sunny most of the year in Seville? How do you know?

2 How hot is it in summer?

3 What is the weather like in winter?

Would you prefer to live in the north or the south of Spain? Why?

Consejo

Notice that you use verbs for describing the weather only in the third person singular.

2 🎧 Listen to four people (Carlos, Sandra, José María and Noemí) talking about places they have visited. For each person, note down in English the place visited, activities they could do, some positive aspects and what the weather was like.

3 Ⓖ Copy and complete the sentences using the appropriate verbs in the past: *hacía* (use three times), *estaba* (use once), *nevaba* (use once).

Este año no (1) hacía mucho frío en invierno y no

(2) ______  en las montañas hasta finales de marzo.

Sin embargo, durante el verano (3) ______ 

mucho calor.

Pero según Sandra, (4) ______ 

frío por la noche en los

Pirineos y durante el día (5) ______ sol y el cielo

(6) ______  despejado.

> ### Describing past weather conditions
> **Gramática** *página 182*
>
> To talk about weather in the past, with *buen / mal tiempo, calor, frío, sol, viento*, use *hacía*:
>
> *Hacía mal tiempo casi toda la semana.*
>
> With *despejado, nublado (nuboso)*, use *estaba*:
>
> *Estaba casi siempre nublado.*
>
> Here are two more verbs for describing weather:
>
> *llover* – to rain *llueve* – it rains *llovía* – it rained
>
> *nevar* – to snow *nieva* – it snows *nevaba* – it snowed
>
> Learn more about the imperfect tense.
>
> *See page 182* ➡

4 📖 Decide whether these descriptions are true or false for where you live.

- Es fácil llegar al centro de la ciudad.
- Es un lugar tranquilo.
- Está en el campo.
- El paisaje es impresionante.
- Se puede esquiar en invierno.
- Hay muchas playas y puedes hacer surfing en verano.
- No hace mucho frío en invierno.
- Llueve poco y casi nunca está nublado.
- En la región hay pueblos típicos y ciudades antiguas con monumentos históricos.
- Hay museos interesantes, galerías de arte, cines y teatros.
- Hay tiendas estupendas.

5 ✏ Write a description of your region for a Spanish-speaking visitor. Use the following questions as a guide:

- ¿Dónde vives exactamente?
- ¿Cómo es tu región?
- ¿Qué actividades puedes hacer allí?
- ¿Qué tiempo hace en verano y en invierno?
- ¿Qué tiempo hacía este verano / en el invierno / el año pasado?
- ¿Qué es lo mejor de tu región?

Vivo en	las afueras de (Londres). un pueblo (pequeño / grande). el campo / la costa.	
Es Está	una zona una región	hermosa / industrial / llana / montañosa / residencial / ruidosa / rural / tranquila / verde. en el norte / sur / este / oeste de (Inglaterra / Gales / Escocia / Irlanda).
Tiene un clima	agradable / estable / variable.	

kerboodle

Home and local area

ALQUILER VACACIONAL

Zona: Costa Tropical – Almuñécar
Tipo de alojamiento: Piso, 3 dormitorios
Nº de personas: 8

Descripción:

Apartamento situado en la playa, a tan sólo 500 m del Parque Acuático. La terraza da vistas al mar. Tiene aire acondicionado. La cocina está totalmente equipada con lavadora, tostador, frigorífico con máquina de hielo y microondas. Hay un patio con una barbacoa.

Los dormitorios tienen armarios empotrados. En el salón hay sofá-cama, TV y chimenea.

El edificio tiene piscina y una farmacia en la planta baja. En los alrededores hay todo tipo de comercios, tiendas de comestibles, un pequeño supermercado, tiendas de recuerdos además de bares, restaurantes y chiringuitos de playa.

La parada de autobús está cerca.

Precio:

	Día	Semana	Mes
	€	€	€
Temporada baja	50	331	513
Temporada media	60	431	613
Temporada alta	70	531	713

1 Read the advert for the holiday apartment and choose the correct pictures to answer the following questions.

1 Which rooms are mentioned?

a

b

c

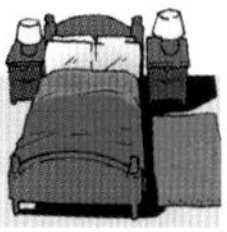
d

2 Which household items are mentioned?

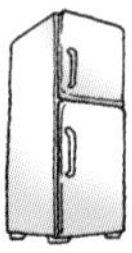
a

b

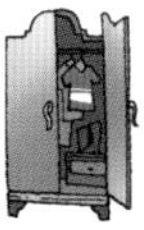
c

d

2 Read the advert again and decide which of the following statements are true.

1 It has a view of the water park.
2 There is a barbecue on the terrace.
3 There are bars and restaurants in the next village.
4 There is a fireplace in the living room.
5 There is a swimming pool on the ground floor.
6 The nearest public transport is the bus service.
7 It costs 431€ to rent the apartment for a month in low season.
8 It costs 513€ to rent the apartment for a week in high season.

3 Listen to the interview with Miguel and answer the following questions.

1 How does Miguel describe his town?
 a pretty and touristy b touristy and historic
 c pretty and modern.
2 What was the weather like last summer?
 a hot and windy b stormy and windy c stormy and hot.
3 What is the train service like?
 a There are delays because of the weather.
 b There are two trains a day to the capital.
 c It is cheaper than the bus service.
4 What does Miguel like about his town?
 a There are plans to open a bowling alley.
 b There is a new cinema.
 c There is a lot to do for young people.

Vocabulario

el aire acondicionado	air conditioning
la chimenea	fireplace
el edificio	building
empotrado	fitted

4 Listen to the interview with Penélope about a festival in her neighbourhood and answer the following questions.

1 When does the most enjoyable fiesta in her neighbourhood take place?
 a 1st August b 3rd May c 15th September.
2 What does Penélope think of the plans to change the location of the craft market?
 a it is a good thing b it is a bad idea c it is not important.
3 Why does Penélope come home so late during the festival?
 a playing in a band b DJing every night
 c dancing in the town square.
4 What do Penélope's parents think about her coming home late from the festival?
 a not bothered b worried c angry.
5 What two benefits does the festival bring to the town?

Study tip

When tackling a listening task, read the questions before you start. The questions will help you to listen out for specific information.

If you are listening to a dialogue, keep track of who is speaking.

Keep track of what question you are on.

Listen out for categories of words such as time phrases and opinions.

G Home and local area

1a Copy and complete the following sentences with the appropriate form of *ser* or *estar*.

1 Madrid _______ la capital de España.
2 Gerona _______ en Cataluña.
3 Mi padres _______ contentos.
4 Yo _______ de Bilbao.
5 Las sillas _______ de plástico.
6 Nosotros _______ en la plaza.

1b Work in pairs. Use *ser* and *estar* to make up a conversation about your home and local area. Take turns to ask and answer the questions.

- ¿Cómo es tu casa?
- ¿Cómo es tu pueblo / barrio?
- ¿Qué es lo mejor / peor de tu barrio / pueblo?

2a Choose the correct verb forms to complete the following text.

Nosotros siempre **(1)** comíamos / comimos pavo el día de Navidad pero el año pasado **(2)** íbamos / fuimos a casa de mis amigos vegetarianos y **(3)** probábamos / probamos garbanzos por primera vez. Generalmente mis padres no **(4)** gastaban / gastaron mucho dinero en regalos pero hace dos años mis padres me **(5)** regalaban / regalaron una bicicleta de montaña. Con frecuencia **(6)** salíamos / salimos al centro a ver las luces en las calles principales. Generalmente **(7)** celebrábamos / celebramos la Nochevieja en casa pero un año **(8)** viajábamos / viajamos a Australia y lo **(9)** pasábamos / pasamos en la playa.

2b Write three sentences in the imperfect tense and three in the preterite tense, using the time expressions in the grammar box.

3 Translate the following sentences into English.

1 En invierno hay mucha nieve.
2 Siempre había mucho ruido en la calle.
3 Ahora hay una zona peatonal en el centro.
4 Hace diez años había una bolera en mi pueblo.
5 Este verano había tormentas.

Ser and *estar*

There are two verbs in Spanish that mean 'to be'.

Ser is used to describe what things and people are and what is unlikely to change:

Mi casa ***es*** *antigua.*

Estar is used to describe where things are and things which are likely to change:

Mi barrio ***está*** *en las afueras de la ciudad.*

Gramática página 187

When to use the imperfect and preterite tenses

Time expressions like these indicate habit and should be used with the imperfect tense:

siempre / a veces / todos los días

E.g. *Cuando* ***era*** *pequeño, siempre* ***iba*** *a la escuela a pie.*

Time expressions like these indicate one-off actions and should be used with the preterite tense:

ayer / el otro día / hace tres años

E.g. *Ayer hizo sol.*

Gramática página 183

Hay and *había*

To say 'there is' and 'there are' use *hay*:

E.g. *En mi barrio hay una comisaría y dos bancos.*

To say 'there was' and 'there were' use *había*:

E.g. *Antes* ***había*** *un teatro.*

Gramática página 184

4a Copy and complete the following sentences wth the correct form of the possessive pronoun.

1 Este libro es ___ (*mine*).
2 Yo tengo mis billetes pero Carlos no tiene los ___ (*his*).
3 El piso de Fátima tiene más dormitorios que el ___ (*ours*).
4 Aquellas bolsas son ___ (*hers*).
5 Hoy es mi cumpleaños. ¿Cuándo es el ___ (*yours, informal singular*)?
6 La cocina de mi casa es más pequeña que la ___ (*yours, informal plural*).

4b Make up some sentences of your own using possessive pronouns, writing the Spanish and the English. Work in pairs. Partner A gives Partner B the English version to translate into Spanish, then checks with their own Spanish translation. Then swap roles.

5a Copy the sentences and fill in the gaps with *cuánto*, *cuánta*, *cuántos* or *cuántas*.

1 ¿___ alumnos hay en tu clase?
2 ¿___ idiomas hablas?
3 ¿___ personas hay en tu familia?
4 ¿___ gramos de jamón quiere usted?
5 ¿___ tiempo hace que vives en tu casa?

5b Using *cuánto*, *cuánta* or *cuántos*, *cuántas* write a question for each of the following answers.

Ejemplo: Hay tres dormitorios. ¿Cuántos dormitorios hay?

1 Hay un jardín detrás de la casa y otro delante.
2 La casa tiene tres plantas.
3 Hay un cuarto de baño en el piso.
4 Mi madre tiene 40 años.
5 Tengo tres hermanos.

6 Translate the following sentences into English.

1 La casa que está a la izquierda es bonita.
2 El vestido que compró Marina es barato.
3 La chica con quien habla Marcos es francesa.
4 La persona para quien compro el regalo es mi abuela.
5 Los amigos a quienes llamo viven en otro barrio.
6 La información que necesito está en mi agenda.

Using possessive pronouns

Gramática página 179

mío, mía, míos, mías

tuyo, tuya, tuyos, tuyas

suyo, suya, suyos, suyas

nuestro, nuestra, nuestros, nuestras

vuestro, vuestra, vuestros, vuestras

suyo, suya, suyos, suyas

Use them with *el / la / los / las* and remember to make them agree with the nouns they replace.

El pueblo de Miguel es más grande que ***el mío***.

Cuánto, cuánta, cuántos, cuántas

Gramática página 177

Use *cuánto, cuánta, cuántos* and *cuántas* to ask 'how much?' or 'how many?'. It must agree with the noun that follows it:

¿Cuántos dormitorios hay?

Relative pronouns

Gramática página 179

Que can refer to people or things.

El hombre ***que*** *habla.*

No hay mucho ***que*** *hacer.*

Use *que, quien, quienes* to give more information about someone or something.

El hombre ***que*** *habla es mi profesor.*

Home and local area

De fiesta ➡ *pages 98–99*

	acabar	to finish
el	*baile*	dance
el	*balcón*	balcony
	cada	every / each
la	*canción*	song
el	*caramelo*	sweet
	cargar	to load
	celebrar	to celebrate
el	*dulce*	sweet
	empezar	to begin
	especial	special
	esperar	to wait
la	*fiesta*	party / festival
la	*flor*	flower
la	*gente*	people
el	*invitado*	guest
el	*juguete*	toy
la	*medianoche*	midnight
el / la	*mejor*	the best
la	*Navidad*	Christmas
la	*Nochebuena*	Christmas Eve
la	*Nochevieja*	New Year's Eve
	Papá Noel	Father Christmas
el	*paquete*	parcel / packet
	pedir	to ask for
el	*pescado*	fish
el	*regalo*	gift
	repartir	to share / give out
el / la	*santo/a*	name / saint's day
la	*uva*	grape

¿Cómo es tu casa? ➡ *pages 100–101*

	adosado/a	semi-detached
	antes	before
el	*aparcamiento*	parking
el	*árbol*	tree
el	*ascensor*	lift
	aunque	although
la	*bañera*	bathtub
el	*bosque*	forest
la	*calefacción*	heating
	caliente	warm
el	*campo*	field / countryside
	caro/a	expensive
el	*césped*	lawn
la	*chimenea*	fireplace / chimney
por	*cierto*	certainly / by the way
el	*comedor*	dining room
	compartir	to share
el	*cristal*	glass
	dar a	to have a view of
	demasiado/a	too much / many
por	*dentro*	inside
la	*ducha*	shower
sin	*duda*	without a doubt
el	*electrodoméstico*	household appliance
	entrar	to come in / enter
el	*espacio*	space
la	*flor*	flower
	fresco/a	cool
	funcionar	to work
la	*granja*	farm
	grueso/a	thick
la	*habitación*	room
el	*hogar*	home
	igual	same
la	*lámpara*	lamp
la	*luz*	light
	mientras que	while
la	*moqueta*	fitted carpet
el	*mueble*	furniture
el	*nuestro (la nuestra)*	ours
	parecido/a	similar
la	*persiana*	blind
estar	*pintado/a*	to be painted
la	*planta*	floor / storey
	pobre	poor
	pocos/as	few
	seguro/a	safe / secure

	subir	to go up
(ni)	*tampoco*	neither
	tan	so
	tanto/a	so much
	tranquilo/a	quiet / calm
	valer	to be worth
el / la	*vecino/a*	neighbour
la	*ventana*	window
	viejo/a	old

¿Cómo es tu barrio? ➡ *pages 102–103*

	ahora	now
	algunos/as	some
	animado/a	lively
	antes	before
la	*autopista*	motorway
el	*barrio*	neighbourhood
	bastante	quite
la	*basura*	rubbish
	bonito/a	pretty
lo	*bueno*	the good thing
estar	*cerrado*	to be closed
	construir	to build
la	*contaminación*	pollution
la	*diversión*	entertainment
	estrecho/a	narrow
hacer	*falta*	to be needed
	feo/a	ugly
la	*industria*	industry
la	*instalación*	facility
	limpio/a	clean
el	*lugar*	place
lo	*malo*	the bad thing
por el	*medio*	through the middle
	necesitar	to need
el	*paro*	unemployment
el	*parque infantil*	playground
	peligroso/a	dangerous
un	*poco*	a little
	por lo tanto	therefore
el	*puerto*	port
el	*ruido*	noise
	también	also

Mi región ➡ *pages 104–105*

el	*acceso*	access
	además	also / besides
	agradable	pleasant
	alrededor	around
	bajar	to go down
	caluroso/a	hot
	casi	almost
el	*cielo*	sky
el	*clima*	climate
	desde … a …	from … to …
	despejado/a	clear
la	*distancia*	distance
	durante	during
	encontrar	to find
la	*gente*	people
el	*grado*	degree
	hasta	up to
	hay que	you have to
la	*inundación*	flood
	llegar	to arrive / get to
	lleno/a	full
	más de	more than
en	*medio de*	in the middle of
lo	*mejor*	the best
la	*mezquita*	mosque
	nunca	never
	precioso/a	beautiful
	saber	to know
	según	according to
	siempre	always
	sin embargo	however
el	*teatro*	theatre
	tener razón	to be right
	tranquilo/a	calm / quiet

3.5 La contaminación

Objetivos

- Understanding and giving opinions about pollution
- Using *por* and *para*
- Learning complete phrases to promote fluency

1 Work in pairs. Read the opinions on the banners and put them in order of priority according to your own views. Compare your ideas with your partner.

Me molesta el ruido del tráfico
La contaminación mata. Quiero respirar aire puro.
Me fastidia ver basura en la calle.
Apaga las luces. Queremos ver las estrellas

1 La suciedad molesta más

Según la encuesta, lo que más molesta a los habitantes de Barcelona es la suciedad. El 20,9% se queja de los papeles, las bolsas y los envases de plástico que se encuentran en las calles. Unos comentan que no duermen bien, dicen que la luz excesiva durante la noche les impide dormir. Otros dicen que los edificios muy altos y mal diseñados y el exceso de anuncios, dañan el aspecto visual de la ciudad.

2 La contaminación acústica – noches de pesadilla

Los habitantes de los barrios alrededor del aeropuerto han presentado una denuncia por exceso de ruido. La apertura de la tercera pista del aeropuerto se ha convertido en una pesadilla para los vecinos de las urbanizaciones cercanas: los aviones pasan a poca altura de sus casas y el ruido no les deja dormir.

3 Más de la mitad de los españoles respiran aire contaminado

Un informe sobre la calidad del aire concluye que el 53% de los españoles respira aire contaminado. Por consiguiente, en Barcelona, el gobierno ha aprobado un paquete de 73 medidas para reducir la contaminación del aire, provocada especialmente por el tráfico. Una de las medidas más controvertidas es limitar la velocidad a 80 km/h.

4 Residuos químicos peligrosos

Este martes, a las 6.30 de la mañana, se ha producido una fuga en una fábrica al Río Ebro. Esta fuga estaba compuesta por una solución de 30 metros cúbicos, que contenía 12 gramos de mercurio por litro. La división de medio ambiente de la policía está investigando el vertido. En estos casos se suelen poner multas muy fuertes a los empresarios responsables.

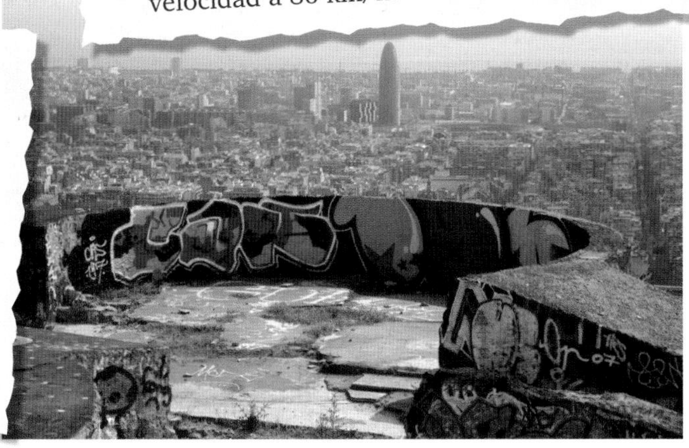

2 Read the newspaper cuttings and answer the following questions in English.

1 What did 20.9% of people surveyed complain about?
2 Which two other kinds of pollution were mentioned in the Barcelona survey?
3 What kind of pollution affects people living near the airport?
4 What affects 53% of Spaniards?
5 How has the River Ebro been affected by pollution recently?

3 Watch the video clip, then answer the following questions.

1 Which two kinds of pollution are caused by traffic in Esther's and Jaime's town?
2 What point do they make about rubbish and recycling?
   a There are lots of recycling bins so the streets are clean.
   b There are recycling bins but people still leave rubbish in the street.
   c The recycling bins aren't in the right places.
3 What spoils the look of the old streets and squares?
   a Traffic noise and fumes.
   b Ugly posters and signs.
   c Modern buildings that don't fit in.
4 Which two of the following measures are needed to protect the environment?
   a Reduce traffic in city centres and make more cycle ways.
   b Raise awareness about recycling and stop people dumping rubbish.
   c Restrict building in cities and in green belts.

4 G Copy and complete the sentences with *por* or *para*.

1 Ponemos todas las botellas de vidrio y de plástico en un cajón y una vez ______ semana lo llevamos al reciclaje.
2 En las grandes ciudades el aire está contaminado ______ los gases de escape del tráfico y de las fábricas.
3 Tenemos que reducir el tráfico ______ controlar la contaminación.
4 Cuando paseo ______ las calles de mi barrio, no veo mucha basura.
5 Esto es porque hemos tenido una campaña ______ mejorar el medio ambiente.

Gramática página 187

Using *por* and *para*

Use *por* to mean:

- 'per': *12 gramos de uranio por litro.*
- 'because of': *Por exceso de ruido.*
- 'for' (substituting one thing for another): *cambiar el coche por la bicicleta.*
- 'through', 'along': *Cuando paseo por el parque.*

Use *para* to mean:

- 'in order to', 'for the purpose of': *El gobierno ha aprobado un paquete de 73 medidas para reducir la contaminación del aire.*

Also learn about the perfect tense. See page 120

Consejo

por todas partes – everywhere
por ahí – around there
por eso – for this reason, so
por lo tanto – so, as a result
por lo general – generally
por fin – finally

5 Prepare a presentation to answer the following questions. Refer to the online worksheet for a language structure box to help you.

¿Qué aspectos de la contaminación y del medio ambiente te afectan más?
¿Qué hay que hacer para solucionar estos problemas?

Estrategia

Learning complete phrases about key issues rather than separate words will help you to think in Spanish and be more fluent.

3.6 El futuro del planeta

Objetivos

- Understanding the main threats to the environment
- Using the future tense
- Expressing ideas: use phrases you know

Creo que el problema más grave para el futuro del planeta es que suben las temperaturas y cambia el tiempo en todas partes del mundo. Si no reducimos las emisiones de CO_2, la situación será irreversible. Como resultado del efecto invernadero, los veranos serán más calurosos y el hielo en los polos norte y sur desaparecerá. Dicen que subirá el nivel del mar y habrá inundaciones. Ya es muy caluroso el verano aquí en México.

Natalia, *Ciudad de México*

Están desapareciendo rápidamente las selvas tropicales. Es un aspecto muy preocupante del medio ambiente en Sudamérica y en todo el mundo. Los árboles ayudan a mantener el equilibrio de nuestros ecosistemas. Si destruimos los bosques y las selvas nos faltará oxígeno. Además se destruirá el hábitat de muchos animales. Las especies en peligro de extinción desaparecerán por completo y para siempre.

Jorge, *Caracas, Venezuela*

Las tormentas, los huracanes y las inundaciones son un problema preocupante en todos los países caribeños. No hay manera de protegerse contra la fuerza de estos desastres. Lo único que se puede hacer es estar alerta a los peligros. Se cree que habrá más tormentas y que hará más calor en el futuro.

Alex, *Trinidad, Cuba*

En el futuro faltarán recursos importantes como el petróleo y los alimentos. La población mundial sigue creciendo y no habrá suficientes recursos para todos. Hay que buscar soluciones, como energías renovables por ejemplo, pero a fin de cuentas creo que el mayor problema es que hay demasiada gente y éste es el problema más grave para el futuro de nuestro planeta.

Cecilia, *Buenos Aires, Argentina*

1a Read the letter extracts and say which of the following environmental problems each person addresses. There may be more than one answer for some speakers.

1 Las catástrofes naturales.
2 El calentamiento global y el cambio climático.
3 La deforestación.
4 La escasez de recursos y la sobrepoblación.

Consejo

Don't be put off by the complexity of vocabulary on environmental issues. Many of the terms are easy to recognise. For example:

Reducir el acelerado ritmo del cambio climático.
To slow down the rapid pace of climate change.

Limitar el uso de combustibles fósiles.
To limit the use of fossil fuels.

1b Identify the person who expresses each of the following opinions.

1 We must protect woods and forests because we need trees to give us oxygen.
2 The polar ice caps will melt and sea levels will rise.
3 Overpopulation is the biggest problem for the future of the world.
4 Summers will be hotter.
5 Global warming and climate change are the biggest threats.
6 There will be shortages of key resources such as oil and food.
7 Many species will become extinct if their habitat is destroyed.

2 Listen to the interviews and choose the correct option.

1 The interviews are for a programme about: a noise b natural disasters c climate change.
2 Ignacio talks about: a higher temperatures in summer b drought conditions c forest fires.
3 Gloria mentions: a cold winter weather b changeable weather and floods c hurricanes.
4 Gloria thinks that: a climate change is already happening b unusual weather patterns are normal c climate change will happen in the future.

3a Find 10 verbs in the future tense in the letters on page 114.

3b Copy the sentences, putting the verb in brackets into the future tense.

1 Si reducimos el tráfico en las ciudades, el aire (estar) menos contaminado.
2 Si se organizan campañas para erradicar las bolsas de plástico, (haber) menos basura en las calles.
3 El calentamiento global y el cambio climático (ser) irreversibles si no se reducen las emisiones de CO_2.
4 La deforestación (matar) a muchos animales.
5 Dicen que (hacer) más calor en verano y menos frío en invierno.
6 (Faltar) alimentos, agua y combustibles si la población mundial sigue aumentando.

4 Summarise the main environmental threats to the planet.

Using the future tense

Gramática *página 183*

Add the following endings to the infinitive of the verb to make the future:

ser – to be *ser**é**, ser**ás**, ser**á**, ser**emos**, ser**éis**, ser**án***

Some verbs have an irregular stem in the future, but the future endings are the same:

hacer – to make, to do *haré, harás, hará, haremos, haréis, harán*

tener – to have *tendré, tendrás, tendrá, tendremos, tendréis, tendrán*

haber – hay – there is, there are *habrá* – there will be

Learn also about ways to avoid using the passive.

See page 121 ➡

Expressing ideas: use phrases you know

Estrategia

Use phrases you know that give your opinions. Avoid ideas if you are not certain how to put them into Spanish.

Tenemos que reducir las emisiones de CO_2.

Todos debemos cambiar el coche por la bicicleta.

Debemos usar más materiales renovables y menos combustibles fósiles.

Creo que Pienso que	el problema más	grave serio	para	el planeta mi región	es	el efecto invernadero y el calentamiento global. la sobrepoblación.
Porque	desaparecerá(n) habrá (más) faltará(n) subirá	el hielo en los polos / los hábitats de muchos animales. catástrofes naturales / tormentas. alimentos / recursos de energía. el nivel del mar.				

3.7 Cómo cuidar el medio ambiente

Objetivos

- Giving suggestions for being environmentally friendly
- Using verbs of obligation: *deber, haber de, hay que, tener que*
- Using variety to make your Spanish more interesting

¿Te apuntas a cambiar de hábitos? Lee nuestros consejos para reducir CO_2 en tu casa.

En el salón

Apaga las luces al salir del salón. Debes apagar también el televisor y el ordenador, asegurándote de que la luz de standby está apagada.

Si tienes frío, ponte un jersey. Puedes reducir tu consumo de calefacción y aire acondicionado si llevas manga larga en invierno y ropa ligera en verano.

Las cortinas y persianas ayudan a mantener fresca tu casa en verano y caliente en invierno.

En la cocina

No tires todo a la basura. Reutiliza y recicla los residuos. Sepáralos y ponlos en los contenedores de reciclaje.

Recicla los envases de vidrio, de plástico y los metálicos. Recicla también el cartón y el papel.

No pongas alimentos calientes en la nevera. Déjalos que enfríen. Abre la puerta de la nevera lo menos posible.

No abras innecesariamente el horno cuando lo tengas encendido.

Ahorrarás agua y energía si sólo pones el lavaplatos cuando esté lleno.

En el dormitorio

¿Eres friolero? Usa un buen edredón nórdico en invierno.

Cuando compras algo nuevo para la casa, busca aparatos de eficiencia energética. Por ejemplo, elige lámparas electrónicas (LED) porque duran más y consumen un 90% menos que otras lámparas.

En el baño

Ahorra agua. No dejes los grifos abiertos cuando te lavas los dientes.

Dúchate en vez de bañarte. Ahorrarás agua y energía.

Entre 30°C y 35°C es una temperatura adecuada para el agua. Ahorras grados y ahorras energía.

En el garaje

Los viajes a pie, en bicicleta o en el transporte público ayudan a reducir emisiones y ahorran combustibles.

Si tienes que usar tu coche, conduce de manera eficiente y reducirás el consumo de petróleo y las emisiones contaminantes.

A la hora de comprar un coche, hemos de elegir un modelo de bajo consumo y con bajas emisiones de CO_2.

1 Read the leaflet and match up each section with the appropriate English sentences (1–10).

1 When buying new appliances, choose the most energy-efficient models.
2 Don't open the oven when it's on and don't leave the fridge door open.
3 Save on heating by wearing warm clothes in winter.
4 Only put the dishwasher on when it is full.
5 Cut down on fuel and emissions by driving efficiently.
6 Save on air conditioning by keeping the blinds and curtains drawn in summer.
7 Save water and heating by having a shower instead of a bath.
8 Recycle glass, plastic and metal containers as well as cardboard and paper.
9 Make sure that the TV, computer and lights are switched off when not in use.
10 If you feel the cold, use a warm duvet on your bed in winter.

2 Work in pairs. Partner A reads out one of the statements below and Partner B decides whether the speaker is eco-friendly or not. Then swap roles.

a Me ducho rápido e intento usar poca agua.

b En invierno me pongo dos camisetas y una sudadera con capucha.

c Me da pereza apagar las luces al salir del salón.

d Nunca tiro las latas y botellas a la basura.

e No voy al instituto a pie o en bicicleta. Prefiero que mis padres me lleven en coche.

3 Listen to Daniel and Nati. What are their answers to the following questions? Select the correct option for each person.

1 ¿Qué haces tú para cuidar el medio ambiente?
   - a Intento conservar energía.
   - b Voy al instituto a pie.
   - c Reciclo todo lo posible.

2 ¿Conoces a alguien que sea un buen protector del medio ambiente? ¿Cómo es? ¿Qué hace?
   - a Mi madre, porque lleva todos los envases al reciclaje.
   - b Tengo un amigo super ecológico que va a todas partes en bicicleta.
   - c Mi padre: sólo pone la calefacción cuando hace mucho frío.

3 ¿Qué medidas o instalaciones hay en tu instituto para cuidar el medio ambiente?
   - a No hay ninguna.
   - b Placas solares.
   - c Persianas en las ventanas de las aulas.

4 ¿Qué crees que se debe hacer para reducir emisiones en tu ciudad o región?
   - a Se deben crear más carriles para bicicletas.
   - b Hemos de elegir coches de bajo consumo y de bajas emisiones.
   - c Hay que reducir el tráfico en el centro de la ciudad.

Using verbs of obligation

Gramática *página 186*

Use the verbs according to the degree of necessity you want to express.

Weakest

haber de …

Hemos de elegir coches de bajo consumo y de bajas emisiones.

We should choose economical cars with low emissions.

tener que …

Si tienes que usar tu coche, conduce de manera eficiente.

If you have to use your car, drive efficiently.

deber

Debes apagar la tele y el ordenador.

You must turn off the TV and computer.

Strongest

Also learn about indefinite pronouns. *See page 121* ➡

4 **G** Copy the sentences and fill in the gaps with correct verb from the list.

1 Mis padres me dicen: 'No ______ llevar ropa ligera en invierno. Ponte un jersey.'

2 El último alumno que salga del salón ______ apagar las luces.

3 Siempre ______ de apagar el televisor y el ordenador cuando no estamos usándolos.

4 En verano en el instituto ______ que cerrar las persianas si queremos mantener fresca el aula.

hemos **debes** **tenemos** **debe**

5 Write a leaflet giving 10 tips on ways to reduce CO_2 emissions and save energy at home and at school. Refer to the online worksheet for a language structure box to help you.

Estrategia

Start some sentences with statements or questions rather than instructions, to add variety.

Information:

Las cortinas y persianas ayudan a mantener fresca tu casa en verano.

Questions:

¿Eres friolero? Usa un buen edredón nórdico.

Environment

Fuente Vaqueros, Andalucía

1

Estados Unidos ha cancelado una deuda de 25 millones de dólares a Perú a cambio de la conservación de 54 millones de hectáreas de bosques amazónicos.

Dos tercios de Perú es selva amazónica prácticamente deshabitada. Sin embargo, una gran parte de este terreno está en peligro debido a la deforestación y a la explotación de petróleo y minerales. Estados Unidos ha cancelado la deuda a cambio de que el dinero se destine a proteger la selva.

2

Fuente Vaqueros, un pueblo pequeño en Andalucía, instalará energía solar en los edificios públicos. El gobierno local ha decidido utilizar las energías renovables por sus ventajas medioambientales y económicas. Las placas solares se instalarán en el ayuntamiento, el polideportivo, el teatro, y en otros edificios de uso público.

Este ayuntamiento también ha comprado 5.000 m^2 de terreno, con el objetivo de que cada niño pueda plantar un árbol.

3

La electricidad de origen solar podría contribuir a cubrir las necesidades de dos tercios de la población mundial – incluyendo las poblaciones remotas – hacia 2030. Ésta es la principal conclusión del informe Generación Solar.

Según este estudio, la energía solar tiene el potencial de proporcionar energía a 4.000 millones de personas en 2030.

1 Read the news stories and match up each one with the most appropriate title below.

a El futuro del mundo será solar

b Sudamérica: dinero para la protección de los árboles

c El sol ayudará a una comunidad rural a ahorrar dinero y a proteger el medio ambiente

2 Read the news stories again and answer the questions.

1 Why did the USA cancel a 25 million dollar debt owed by Peru?
 a to help victims of natural disasters
 b to protect the forests
 c to promote use of alternative energy sources
2 What is the Amazon area threatened by?
 a forest clearance and prospecting for oil and other resources
 b natural disasters such as floods and earthquakes
 c tourism
3 What kind of renewable energy is a small Spanish town planning to use for public buildings?
4 Which three public buildings in Fuente Vaqueros are mentioned?
5 How can the children from Fuente Vaqueros help to protect the environment?
6 According to a report by Generación Solar, what can solar energy provide by 2030?
 a heating for four thousand million people
 b enough electricity for two-thirds of the world's population
 c free electricity for three-quarters of the world's population

Vocabulario

a cambio de	in exchange for
cubrir	to cover
debido a	because of / owing to
la deuda	debt
las placas solares	solar panels
proporcionar	to provide
el terreno	land

Gramática página 182

The perfect tense (for reporting recent events)

*El gobierno local **ha decidido** utilizar las energías renovables por sus ventajas medioambientales y económicas.*

See page 120

Study tip

You will hear each listening activity twice.

Firstly, listen to find out what the conversation is about. If you can get a general idea of the context and the issues you will then find it easier to understand more detail when you listen for the second time.

3a Listen to the interviews. What are they about?

 a better public transport
 b more people cycling
 c congestion charging

3b Listen again and note each person's point of view. Write F (for), A (against) or N (neither for nor against) for each interviewee: the young man, the girl and the older woman.

4a Listen to the market research interview and choose the correct letters of the issues mentioned.

A Cutting down on plastic bags
B Recycling
C Global warming
D Climate change
E Chemical waste
F Reducing CO_2 emissions
G Protecting forests

4b Listen again and choose the correct letters of the opinions expressed by the interviewee.

A It's important to cut down on plastic bags at supermarkets.
B Global warming is one of the most important issues.
C We have to stop climate change before it becomes irreversible.
D Recycling and energy conservation are key factors.
E To reduce global warming we must reduce CO_2 emissions and protect forests.

G Environment

1a Choose the correct verb form to complete each sentence.

1. El ayuntamiento <u>ha introducido / han introducido</u> un sistema de recogida de materiales reciclables.
2. Las medidas para controlar la velocidad del tráfico en la ciudad <u>ha reducido / han reducido</u> el número de accidentes.
3. Este año yo <u>he intentado / has intentado</u> comprar menos y reciclar más.
4. <u>¿Has notado / Habéis notado</u> el cambio climático en tu región?
5. En nuestro pueblo <u>hemos notado / han notado</u> un aumento de ruido como resultado de los vuelos baratos.

1b Use the perfect tense and the prompts below to write six sentences about how you have helped to protect the environment in the last week.

Ejemplo: He apagado las luces al salir del aula.

A apagar las luces / cerrar la puerta y las ventanas al salir del aula
B poner un jersey o una sudadera cuando hacía frío
C (no) tirar todo a la basura
D reutilizar / reciclar los residuos
E reciclar los envases de vidrio, de plástico y los metálicos
F (no) poner alimentos calientes en la nevera

The perfect tense

Irregular past participles of irregular verbs:

caer – caído	*leer – leído*
dar – dado	*poner – puesto*
decir – dicho	*traer – traído*
hacer – hecho	*ver – visto*

Irregular past participles of regular verbs:

abrir – abierto	*morir – muerto*
cubrir – cubierto	*romper – roto*
escribir – escrito	*volver – vuelto*

Always put pronouns before *haber*, not before the past participle:

He ahorrado agua y energía porque ***me he duchado*** *en vez de bañarme.*

Gramática página 182

2a Write the present participles for the following verbs.

1. cambiar (to change)
2. crear (to create)
3. desaparecer (to disappear)
4. reducir (to reduce)
5. vender (to sell)

The present continuous tense

You have already learnt how to form the present continuous tense.

-ar verbs	*-er* verbs	*-ir* verbs
-ando	*-iendo*	*-iendo*
hablando	*comiendo*	*viviendo*

Remember to use the present continuous rather than the ordinary present tense when you want to emphasise the continuity of the action:

Las selvas tropicales están desapareciendo rápidamente.

Gramática página 181

2b Copy the sentences and fill in the gaps with the present continuous of the verb in brackets.

1. En Ciudad de México, el gobierno ___ carriles o 'ciclovías' para bicicletas. (crear)
2. Las medidas para limitar vehículos en el centro de la ciudad ___ la congestión y la contaminación del aire. (reducir)
3. Como resultado de la destrucción de los bosques y selvas, ___ muchas especies de plantas y animales. (desaparecer)
4. Los fabricantes de coches ___ cada vez más coches híbridos y otros vehículos de bajas emisiones. (vender)

3 Choose the correct English translation for each of the following signs.

1 For sale.
2 Spanish spoken.
3 Breakfast is served from seven thirty.
4 No entry to under-18s.
5 Apartments to let.
6 Credit cards are accepted.

4 Copy the sentences and fill in the gaps with *algo* or *alguien*.

1 – ¿Quiere ___ más?
– No, nada más, gracias.
2 Muy bien, ___ ha cerrado las persianas.
3 Llámame cuando llegues a casa. Tengo ___ bueno que contarte.
4 Tenemos ___ en común. Nos interesa el medio ambiente.
5 Si no sabes la respuesta, puedes llamar a ___ .

5 Replace the imperatives in the following instructions with a verb of obligation plus an infinitive.

Ejemplo: 1 Hay que regar el jardín por la mañana temprano o al atardecer.

Hay que ...
Debes / No debes ...
Tienes que ...

1 **Riega** el jardín por la mañana temprano o al atardecer.
2 **Adapta** la calefacción a tus necesidades.
3 **Apaga** la luz cuando salgas de la habitación.
4 **No dejes** en stand-by el televisor y el ordenador.
5 **Repara** los escapes de agua.
6 **Cierra** el grifo cuando te lavas los dientes.

Gramática página 186

Avoiding the passive by using the reflexive pronoun *se*

This construction is widely used in written and spoken Spanish. It is often seen in signs and announcements too.

E.g. *Se abre de las 7.30 a la 1.30.* Open from 7.30 to 1.30.

Gramática página 180

Indefinite pronouns: *algo*, *alguien*

Indefinite pronouns always have the same form because they do not refer to a specific thing or person.

algo something
alguien someone, somebody, anyone, anybody

Gramática página 184

Avoiding imperatives

You can use imperatives in Spanish to give instructions without sounding impolite.

Deme un kilo de naranjas. Give me a kilo of oranges.

Traiga la cuenta, por favor. Bring the bill, please.

Haga este trabajo para mañana. Do this work by tomorrow.

But if you want to give instructions in a more indirect way, you can use verbs of obligation:

Hay que hacer este trabajo para mañana. You must do this work by tomorrow.

V Environment

La contaminación ➡ *pages 112–113*

el	*aeropuerto*	airport
el	*accidente*	accident
el	*aire*	air
el	*anuncio*	advert
	apagar	to turn off
	a pie	on foot
	aprobar	to pass (exam, law)
la	*basura*	rubbish
la	*bolsa de plástico*	plastic bag
la	*calidad*	quality
	cambiar	to change
	cercano/a	near
la	*contaminación*	pollution
	dañar	to damage / spoil
la	*denuncia*	complaint
el	*edificio*	building
las	*emisiones*	emissions
la	*encuesta*	survey
el	*envase*	container
la	*fábrica*	factory
	fastidiar	to annoy
me	*fastidia*	it annoys me
	impedir	to impede / prevent
la	*luz*	light
	matar	to kill
la	*medida*	measure
el	*medio ambiente*	environment
la	*mitad*	half
	molestar	to annoy / bother
me	*molesta*	it bothers me
la	*multa*	fine
la	*naturaleza*	nature
el	*peligro*	danger
	peligroso/a	dangerous
la	*pesadilla*	nightmare
la	*pista*	runway
	preocuparse	to worry
	puro/a	pure, clean
	quejarse de	to complain about
	reducir	to reduce
los	*residuos químicos*	chemical waste
	respirar	to breathe
el	*ruido*	noise
	según	according to
	solucionar	to solve
el	*tráfico*	traffic
	tóxico/a	poisonous / toxic
el / la	*vecino/a*	neighbour
la	*velocidad*	speed
el	*vertido*	spillage

El futuro del planeta ➡ *pages 114–115*

el	*alimento*	food
	aumentar	to increase
el	*calentamiento global*	global warming
	caluroso/a	hot
el	*cambio climático*	climate change
la	*catástrofe*	disaster
la	*catástrofe natural*	natural disaster
	crecer	to grow
la	*deforestación*	deforestation
	demasiado/a	too much
	desaparecer	to disappear
	destruir	to destroy
el	*efecto invernadero*	greenhouse effect
el	*equilibrio*	balance
la	*escasez*	shortage
la	*extinción*	extinction

	faltar	to lack
	grave	serious
el	*hielo*	ice
el	*huracán*	hurricane
el	*incendio*	fire
la	*inundación*	flood
	irreversible	irreversible
el	*mundo*	world
el	*nivel del mar*	sea level
el	*oxígeno*	oxygen
el	*petróleo*	oil
el	*planeta*	planet
la	*población*	population
el	*polo norte*	north pole
el	*problema*	problem
	proteger	to protect
	reciclable	recyclable
el	*recurso*	resource
	renovable	renewable
las	*selvas tropicales*	tropical forests
la	*sequía*	drought
la	*sobrepoblación*	overpopulation
	subir	to go up / rise

Cómo cuidar el medio ambiente ➡ *pages 116–117*

	apagar	to switch off
	apuntarse	to sign up
	caliente	hot / warm
el	*cartón*	cardboard
el	*combustible*	fuel
el	*consejo*	advice
	consumir	to consume
el	*consumo*	consumption
el	*contenedor*	container
la	*cortina*	curtain
	cuidar	to look after
	ducharse	to have a shower
	durar	to last
el	*edredón nórdico*	quilt
la	*energía*	energy
el / la	*friolero/a*	person who feels the cold
el	*horno*	oven
el	*lavaplatos*	dishwasher
	ligero/a	light
	lleno/a	full
la	*nevera*	fridge
la	*persiana*	blind
a	*pie*	on foot
	reciclar	to recycle
el	*residuo*	waste
	reutilizar	to reuse
	separar	to separate
	tirar	to throw / throw away
el	*transporte público*	public transport
	usar	to use
el	*vidrio*	glass

3 El medio ambiente

A Spanish TV company is making a programme about young Europeans' views on the environment and they want to interview you. Prepare for the interview by preparing the following points to mention:

1 A description of your region
2 Climate and weather
3 Pollution in your local area
4 Your views on the greatest environmental threats to the planet
5 Being eco-friendly at home and at school
6 How to reduce CO_2 emissions and combat climate change
7 ! Remember you will have to respond to something that you have not yet prepared.

Study tips

Start by making a plan. First, provide an introduction to the topic, such as:
Creo que el medio ambiente es un tema muy importante.
Creo que es muy importante proteger el medio ambiente.

1 A description of your region.
- Say where you live and describe your area
- Say where your home town is in relation to the nearest well-known city or where your neighbourhood is in relation to the centre or the airport
- Describe the main features of your region, e.g. industrial, suburban, rural
- Say which part of the country your region is in, e.g. north, south, east, west

Study tips

Use *ser* for descriptions of your region and *estar* for geographical location.
Es una región muy industrial.
Está en el norte del país.
Remember that you will be speaking to a Spanish audience so you should use information they will understand. For example, for distance refer to kilometres, not miles.
Mi pueblo está a unos ciento cincuenta kilómetros al norte de Londres.

2 Climate and weather.
- Describe the natural features near your town, e.g. mountains, rivers, woods, coast
- Describe the climate in your region and give details of summer and winter temperatures
- Say what the weather was like last summer or last winter
- Mention any unusual or extreme weather conditions in your region in the last year

Study tips

Note down useful terms linked to the climate and weather in your area and make sure you know how to say the relevant numbers in Spanish.
(500 / quinientos) metros sobre el nivel del mar
(15 / quince) grados bajo cero
(40 / cuarenta) grados
Remember to use the imperfect for describing past weather conditions. See page 182.
Hacía mucho calor / frío / viento.
(No) Llovía (mucho).
(No) Nevaba.
Había tormentas / inundaciones.

3 Pollution in your local area.
- Say what worries you most about pollution in your area, e.g. air pollution, chemical waste
- Say what other negative aspects of your local environment bother you, e.g. noise, litter, traffic
- Explain what kind of problems the negative factors cause, e.g. difficult to sleep, dangerous to cycle, dangers to wildlife
- Say what we need to do to reduce the problems

Study tips

Look at pages 112–113 and make a list of all the kinds of pollution mentioned.
Use the appropriate verbs to give your opinions.
(lo que más) me molesta = what bothers me most
(lo que más) me preocupa = what worries me most
me pone de los nervios = it gets on my nerves

4 Your views on the greatest environmental threats to the planet.

- Say which global environmental issues worry you
- Say which of these issues most threaten the future of the planet
- Explain the possible outcomes of these threats
- Say what we should do to prevent these things happening

Study tips

Look at pages 114–115 and the language structure box on the online worksheet and draw a spidergram showing key global environmental issues, their causes and likely outcomes.

Use a variety of verbs to introduce your opinions.

Creo que …

Pienso que …

En mi opinión ….

Me parece que …

5 Being eco-friendly at home and at school.

- Say what you recycle, e.g. types of packaging, food, clothes, plastic bags, paper
- Give your suggestions for saving energy, e.g. saving on heating, lighting, air conditioning, electricity
- Give your suggestions for saving water
- Say what you have done recently to be eco-friendly at home and at school

Study tips

Use verbs of obligation to say what we should do. *Debemos / Tenemos que.* See page 186.

Use *hay que* or the third person impersonal forms with *se* to say what should be done.

Se debe

Se podría

6 How to reduce CO_2 emissions and combat climate change.

- Talk about ways of reducing the number of cars in your area or city
- Mention vehicles that are less polluting and more energy efficient
- Say how ways of driving can help the environment
- Say what you think individuals can do and what the government should do

Study tips

Make a list of useful phrases for talking about ways to protect the environment. Make separate sections, e.g. things individuals can do and what the government should do.

Todos debemos …

cambiar el coche por la bicicleta.

elegir coches de bajo consumo y de bajas emisiones (coches híbridos).

El gobierno debe …

mejorar el transporte público.

instalar placas solares en edificios públicos.

poner multas a las empresas que contaminan el agua o el aire con residuos químicos.

7 **!** At this point, you will be asked another question which you don't know in advance. However, you can try to guess what it might be and prepare various options:

- Which policies to protect the environment have been successful in your town or local area?
- What are your views on climate change?
- How do you think climate change will affect your country or region?
- What must people do now and in the future to protect the environment?

Study tips

Show that you know different ways of referring to the past.

Use the perfect tense to talk about the recent past. *En mi región hemos reducido la cantidad de basura y hemos reciclado más.*

Use the preterite to talk about events that happened in the past. *El año pasado los supermercados decidieron no dar bolsas de plástico a los clientes.*

Use the future to give predictions. *Los veranos serán más calurosos. Habrá más tormentas. Subirá el nivel del mar y tendremos inundaciones.*

You should now have completed your plan and prepared your answers. Give your plan to your teacher for feedback. Compare your answers to the online sample version – you might find some useful hints to make yours even better.

3 Donde vivo

Your Spanish friend Javier is coming to stay with you and your family for a holiday. He has asked you to write him an email in Spanish describing your house and local area to give him an idea of what to expect. Call the email 'Where I live'. You could include:

1. Your house
2. Your bedroom
3. Your neighbourhood now and in the past
4. Things for young people to do
5. Your region
6. A special occasion in your home
7. Where you would like to live in the future

Study tips

Try starting your email with a greeting, such as *Querido Javier:* or *Hola amigo:*

Your first sentence could be a reference to his earlier email, e.g. *Me preguntas sobre mi casa.* Or you could introduce what you are going to write about with a phrase like:

Voy a describir mi casa.

Finish your email with a suitable phrase, such as *Saludos*, *Un abrazo*, *Recuerdos a tu familia* or *Hasta pronto.*

1 Your house

- Say whether you live in a house or flat and what type of building it is
- Mention the number and types of rooms and if it has a garden, garage, balcony, etc.
- Say whether you like your house or not and why
- Say how long you have lived there and if you liked your previous house

Study tips

Now start your notes. Write down six words, such as:

casa, dormitorios, cocina, arriba, jardín, balcón

Think of a verb for each word, such as:

vivir, ser, tener, haber, estar

Think of some adjectives that go with each noun, for example:

pequeño, moderno, limpio, acogedor, tranquilo

Make sure that the adjectives agree with what they are describing. Remember that *casa* is feminine and *piso* is masculine.

E.g. *La casa es modern**a**. El piso es antigu**o**.*

To say how long you have lived somewhere use *desde hace*:

Vivo aquí desde hace diez años.

To give an opinion of your old house remember to use the imperfect tense:

No me gustaba mi antigua casa porque era pequeña.

2 Your bedroom

- Say where it is in the house
- Mention how it is decorated
- Compare your bedroom to Javier's
- Say what you do in your room

Study tips

Use *estar* to say where things are, e.g. *está arriba / en el ático.*

Unlike most colours the words for orange and pink don't agree with the noun they are describing: *Las cortinas son de color naranja / rosa.*

To compare your house or bedroom with Javier's, use *el mío / la mía* to say 'mine' and *el tuyo / la tuya* to say 'yours', e.g. *Mi dormitorio es más grande que el tuyo.*

To say what you do in your room use phrases from pages 58–59. *Me gusta navegar por Internet. Leo y dibujo.*

3 Your neighbourhood now and in the past

- Say what your neighbourhood is like now and what it used to be like
- Mention what it has and what it used to have
- Say what you like about it and why
- Say what you dislike about it and give a reason

Study tips

Add six more words to your notes to help you describe things in your local area

To say what there is in your neighbourhood use *hay*. To say what there used to be use *había*.

To say what your neighbourhood is like use *es*. To say what it used to be like use *era*.

Use *lo que* to say 'the ... thing': ***Lo malo** es que no hay mucho para los jóvenes.*

***Lo que** me gusta de mi barrio es que es limpio.*

Remember that *¿por qué?* means 'why?' and *porque* means 'because'.

4 Things for young people to do
- Mention what there is for young people to do.
- Say what you do there at weekends
- Mention what you did last weekend
- Say what you think would improve your local area

Study tips

To say what you do in your local area try using phrases from pages 102–103. *De vez en cuando voy al cine.*

Make sure that you use different tenses correctly. Use the preterite tense to say what you did last weekend: *El fin de semana pasado fui al polideportivo.* See page 181.

To say what is needed in your area use: *Necesita, necesitamos, se necesita, hace falta.*

5 Your region
- Say where your region is
- Write about what it has and what it is like
- Talk about the weather and the seasons
- Mention what the weather was like this time last year

Study tips

Add six geographical words to describe your region: *bosque, río, montaña …*

To say how far away something is use *está a*: *Está a unos 40 minutos de Londres. Está a 120 kilómetros al norte de Edimburgo.*

Use *estar* and *hacer* for weather expressions: *Hace sol, está lloviendo.*

Use the preterite tense to talk about weather in the past: *El año pasado hizo mucho frío en invierno.* See page 181.

6 A special occasion in your home
- Say what the special occasion is and what you are celebrating
- Say when the special occasion is
- Mention how you celebrate the occasion
- Compare how you used to celebrate the occasion when you were younger

Study tips

Add another six words to your list to help you describe a special occasion, for example: *vestido, pastel, regalar, tarjeta, divertirse, pasarlo bien.*

Remember how to write dates: *el primero / uno de mayo, el quince de noviembre.*

Use time expressions to show that you do or did something habitually: *siempre, con frecuencia, a veces, todos los años.*

Use the imperfect tense to talk about how you used to celebrate special occasions: *Cuando era pequeño/a comía muchos dulces.* See page 182.

7 Where you would like to live in the future
- Say what your ideal house would be like
- Say what town, country or area you would like to live in and give reasons for your choice
- Talk about what makes an area a good place to live
- Mention what improvements you would make if you were mayor of a town

Study tips

Use the conditional tense for saying what you would do: *sería, tendría, habría, viviría, compraría*. See page 184.

Use *me gustaría* + verb in the infinitive to say what you would like to do: *Me gustaría vivir en el extranjero.*

You could begin to describe what makes an area a good or bad place to live by using the following sentence as a model: *Un pueblo en el campo es un lugar ideal para las familias porque es tranquilo y no hay crimen.*

To describe improvements you would make to a town, you could begin your sentences as follows: *Si fuera alcalde …* 'If I were mayor …', *Mejoraría …* 'I would improve …', *Construiría …* 'I would build …', *Daría …* 'I would give …'.

Check that you have a complete set of 40 cue words in seven groups to complete this assessment. Hand in a first draft to your teacher.

Have you completed your plan and prepared your answers? Make sure your teacher checks it and gives you feedback. Compare your answers to the online sample version – you might find some useful hints to make yours even better.

Context summary

Resumen

1 Copy these sentences and fill in the gaps with the correct possessive pronouns.

¿Es ésta vuestra casa? Sí, es la ______ y éste es el piso de Juan, es el ______ .

2 Answer the following question in Spanish.

¿Qué muebles hay en tu salón?

3 Translate the following sentence into English.

De vez en cuando en Nochebuena comíamos pescado.

4 Answer the following question in Spanish.

¿Qué es lo que necesita tu barrio?

5 Complete this sentence with an appropriate ending.

Las afueras de la ciudad no son tan peligrosas …

6 Translate the following sentence into Spanish.

In winter it was cold and it snowed; the temperature was usually below zero.

7 Copy this sentence and fill in the gaps with either *por* or *para*.

Tenemos que cambiar el coche ______ la bicicleta ______ reducir el tráfico en las ciudades.

8 What is the Spanish expression for the following definition:

Changing world weather patterns caused by factors including excessive CO_2 emissions and the destruction of tropical forests.

9 Complete the following sentence with the correct verbs in the future tense.

En el futuro ___ el nivel del mar, no ___ agua limpia y el campo se ___ desierto.

10 Put these words into the correct order to make a sentence.

convertir podemos importante nuevos en es porque materiales reciclar basura la

¿Lo sabes?

Una encuesta internacional sitúa a Barcelona, junto con Nueva York, Londres y París, entre las cuatro mejores ciudades del mundo para vivir. Su elección, delante de Sydney, Roma, Buenos Aires y Los Ángeles, se basa en aspectos como 'la gente, el ambiente, el clima, el mar, la creatividad, el ocio y la acogida'.

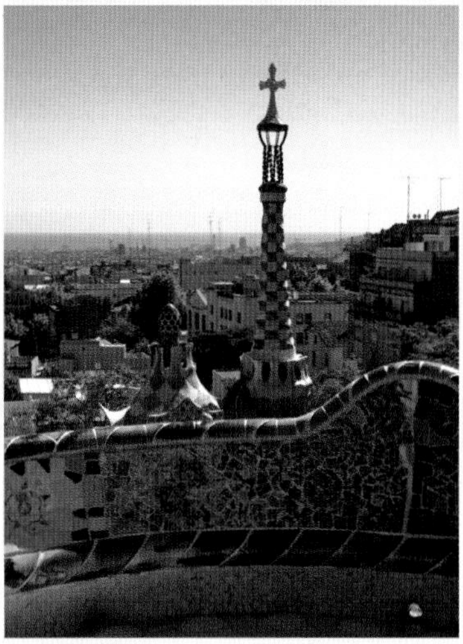

4 Work and education

Key Stage 3 Revision

School / college and future plans

What school / college is like

4.1 Bienvenidos al colegio
- Using impersonal verbs
- Developing answers to questions

4.2 Colegios británicos y españoles
- Using different tenses
- Spotting tense usage

Pressures and problems

4.3 ¡Cuánto estrés!
- Using *desde hacía* and the imperfect tense
- Making sure you give all the information that you are asked to give

4.4 ¿Qué piensas de tu colegio?
- Using the conditional tense
- Looking for clues to help understanding

Current and future jobs

Looking for and getting a job

4.5 El trabajo a tiempo parcial
- Recognising the pluperfect tense
- Including different tenses in speaking and writing

4.6 Buscando trabajo
- Asking questions using the preterite tense
- Using context to work out meaning

4.7 Poniéndose en contacto
- Using *quisiera*
- Using knowledge of grammatical categories

Advantages and disadvantages of different jobs

4.8 Después de los exámenes
- Using imperatives (commands)
- Finding different ways to say similar things

4.9 Comparando empleos diferentes
- Using irregular adverbs
- Checking grammar in written work

School subjects, school buildings

Me llamo Ricardo. Me gusta mi instituto porque es un edificio bastante antiguo que tiene aulas e instalaciones nuevas. Es un instituto mixto con más de mil alumnos en total y no tenemos que llevar uniforme.

Hay aulas para cada asignatura y hay laboratorios de ciencias y de idiomas. Me encanta usar el laboratorio de idiomas, porque es moderno y tenemos la oportunidad de hablar en inglés la mayoría del tiempo.

Lo malo es el comedor, que está en la parte vieja del instituto. Es demasiado pequeño y a veces tenemos que pasar veinte minutos esperando la comida.

1 Read Ricardo's text and decide if the following statements are true (T), false (F) or not mentioned (?).

1 Ricardo likes his school.
2 All of his school is modern.
3 His school is for boys only.
4 There are fewer than 1000 pupils in his school.
5 He hates being in the language lab because he has to speak English.
6 The dining room is too small.
7 The food is good.

2a Work in pairs. Partner A starts by naming in Spanish either a school subject or a part of your school. Partner B repeats that word and adds another, then Partner A repeats both words and adds another, and so on. When one of you hesitates or cannot give another word, the other person scores a point. The first to three points is the winner.

2b Write some questions to ask each other about your school. Partner A asks the questions and Partner B answers. Then swap roles.

Forming the negative

Gramática

Remember that making a sentence negative in Spanish is easy – simply place *no* before the verb.

Tenemos que llevar uniforme. We have to wear a uniform.

***No** tenemos que llevar uniforme.* We don't have to wear a uniform.

Me gusta el inglés. I like English.

***No** me gusta el inglés.* I don't like English.

página 186

Vocabulario

el aula (f)	classroom
el comedor	dining room
el edificio	building
el laboratorio	laboratory
el alemán	German
las ciencias	science
el dibujo	art
el español	Spanish
el francés	French
la geografía	geography
la historia	history
la informática	ICT
el inglés	English
las matemáticas	maths
la música	music
la tecnología	technology
me encanta(n)	I love
me gusta(n)	I like

Jobs and careers

Vocabulario

el / la azafata	flight attendant
el / la camarero/a	waiter / waitress
el / la carnicero/a	butcher
el / la dependiente/a	shop assistant
el / la granjero/a	farmer
el / la jardinero/a	gardener
el / la mecánico/a	mechanic
el / la médico/a	doctor
el / la panadero/a	baker
el / la policía	policeman/ policewoman
el / la profesor(a)	teacher

1a Match up each job with its correct description. There are two descriptions you don't need. Do you know the Spanish for all these jobs?

Jobs

1 Police officer
2 Waiter
3 Doctor
4 Teacher
5 Farmer
6 Vet

Descriptions

A Está bien ayudar a personas enfermas a sentirse mejor.
B Los alumnos en mi clase son muy simpáticos.
C A veces es triste cuando la gente viene al consultorio con su mascota.
D Es fantástico trabajar en el campo y estar al aire libre.
E Reparando coches todo el día puede ser un poco aburrido.
F Llevo el correo a más de trescientas casas cada día.
G Es muy duro pero puede ser emocionante cuando trato de coger a un ladrón.
H Paso toda la noche sirviendo la comida a los clientes y limpiando las mesas.

1b Make up similar sentences in Spanish for these jobs.

1 dependiente/a
2 secretario/a
3 dentista
4 carnicero/a
5 jardinero/a
6 carpintero/a

1c Work in pairs. Partner A reads out a sentence and Partner B says which job it is describing. Then swap roles.

Gramática

Job titles

For jobs, remember that most of them have a masculine and a feminine version. For example: *profesor* (male teacher), and *profesora* (female teacher); *camarero* (waiter), and *camarera* (waitress).

página 174

4.1 Bienvenidos al colegio

- Describing what school / college is like
- Using impersonal verbs
- Developing answers to questions

1 Ⓥ In three minutes, see how many of the following words and phrases you can find in Spanish in the text below.

1 pupils
2 atmosphere
3 sports hall
4 library
5 take place
6 support lessons

Bienvenidos al Instituto Cervantes

En el Instituto Cervantes, ofrecemos cursos de Educación Secundaria Obligatoria, de Bachillerato y de Formación Profesional. Nuestros alumnos consiguen un nivel muy alto en sus estudios en un ambiente feliz y amistoso.

Tenemos laboratorios de idiomas, informática y ciencias así como aulas específicas para las diferentes asignaturas. En sus clases de deporte los estudiantes disponen de piscina (exterior y climatizada), polideportivo, pistas de tenis, patinaje, atletismo, campos de fútbol y gimnasios.

Hay alrededor de novecientos cincuenta alumnos en el instituto, que actualmente tiene sesenta y cinco profesores. Estos profesores son expertos en la asignatura que enseñan.

La biblioteca del colegio ahora cuenta con más de 4.500 libros y los alumnos suelen utilizar su servicio de préstamo y consulta todos los días. Hay también más de treinta ordenadores allí.

Durante el año tienen lugar numerosos viajes de estudios y visitas extraescolares. Por ejemplo el febrero pasado un grupo de estudiantes de arte fue al museo de cerámica y otro grupo fue a ver un espectáculo de baile tradicional. Esas actividades y otras se repiten cada año.

En la hora de la comida muchos departamentos dan clases de apoyo no solamente para los que tienen problemas con el trabajo, sino también para los que quieren mejorar sus conocimientos.

2 Read the following sentences and decide whether they are true (T), false (F) or not mentioned in the text (?).

1 The atmosphere in the school is friendly.
2 The outdoor pool is bigger than the indoor one.
3 There are 75 teachers in the school.
4 The computers in the library are available after school.
5 There was a visit to a traditional dance show last year.
6 Support lessons take place at lunchtime.

3 Listen to four students speaking about their schools. Copy and complete the table by writing 'yes' or 'no' in each box.

School	Is it mixed?	Is there a uniform?	Is there a pool?	Is there a hall?
1				
2				
3				
4				

4 Ⓖ Copy the sentences and fill in the gaps with the missing pronoun or verb from the boxes below. Then translate each sentence into English.

Ejemplo: *Me gusta la geografía.*
I like geography.

1 ______ gusta el inglés.
2 Nos ______ las aulas.
3 ______ interesan las matemáticas.
4 Les ______ sus profesores.
5 ______ encanta el colegio.
6 Me ______ la tecnología.

Pronoun	me	te	le	nos	os	les

Verb	gusta	interesa	molesta	encanta
	gustan	interesan	molestan	encantan

Impersonal verbs

These are used in the third person singular and plural of the verb. They are preceded by an indirect object pronoun.

Me gusta el dibujo means 'I like art'. The literal translation is 'Art pleases me'.

Interesar, encantar and *molestar* work in the same way.

Also learn more about the words for 'this' and 'that'.

See page 142

Gramática *página 186*

5 Prepare a presentation about your school, to last between one and two minutes. Use the language structure box to help you.

Mi colegio / Este colegio	está (situado) en	Manchester.
Mi instituto / Este instituto	tiene	profesores simpáticos. un polideportivo.
Tenemos	un comedor un salón de actos	moderno. estupendo.
	una biblioteca una piscina	bastante grande. maravillosa.
Es un colegio / instituto	mixto / masculino / femenino.	
En España suelen	comer	a las dos. a las doce y media.
En Inglaterra solemos	tener	muchos deberes.

Estrategia

Developing answers to questions

When you are asked a question in Spanish, either orally or in written form, try to expand on your answer as much as possible. Aim to give at least two sentences in your reply.

¿Qué opinas de tu colegio?

Es bastante divertido. Tiene muchas instalaciones deportivas, lo que me gusta mucho.

Consejo

Try to find alternatives to words that you find you use all the time, for example *hay, tiene, es.*

En mi colegio hay muchos laboratorios / tenemos muchos laboratorios.

4.2 Colegios británicos y españoles

Objetivos

- Talking about school routine and comparison with Spanish schools
- Using different tenses
- Spotting tense usage

1 Work in pairs. Your task is to form a sentence about your school by saying one word each in turn. You must use at least one of the following words in each sentence:

termina; empieza; comida; recreo; comedor; uniforme; informática; chicle

Ejemplo: El – colegio – empieza – a – las – nueve – menos – cuarto.

Buscar

Inicio | Índice | Sitemap | Ayuda | Versión texto

Hola Juan

Estoy un poco estresado con todo el trabajo que tengo que hacer de momento. Los días parecen muy largos, ya que tengo que levantarme antes de las siete, desayunar y ponerme el uniforme, que incluso tenemos que llevar en colegios públicos como el mío. Pasan lista a las ocho y media, aunque la primera clase no empieza hasta las nueve menos diez. Las clases terminan a las tres, así que es duro.

La semana pasada perdí mi libro de historia y tuve que comprar otro, lo que me parece muy injusto.

La comida en el instituto es fatal y no podemos salir durante la hora que tenemos para comer. Por eso si no llevamos bocadillos de casa, tenemos que comer la basura que sirven en el comedor.

Espero con impaciencia el fin de los exámenes en junio y las nueve semanas de vacaciones que voy a tener – normalmente tengo seis.

Danny

Buscar

Inicio | Índice | Sitemap | Ayuda | Versión texto

Hola Danny

Como ya sabes, voy a un colegio privado y tenemos que llevar uniforme, a diferencia de los colegios públicos en mi ciudad.

Tienes suerte que solamente tienes que comprar los libros que pierdes, porque mis padres tienen que comprármelos todos. Y esto ocurre también en los colegios públicos.

Empiezo a las nueve y termino a las cinco o a las seis, dependiendo del día. Hay dos horas para la comida, cuando voy a la cafetería en el pueblo. Hoy fui allí y tomé una tortilla española.

En mi colegio pasan lista en todas las clases, y como consecuencia no hay una clase especial como en el tuyo. Sin embargo, cada estudiante tiene un tutor personal que fija objetivos académicos y que te ayuda con problemas personales. Hablamos con el tutor cada tres semanas y hay reuniones con los padres una vez cada trimestre.

Todavía no sé lo que voy a hacer durante los tres meses de vacaciones de verano, pero seguro que voy a visitarte otra vez.

Juan

Estrategia

Using different verb tenses will allow you to access the higher marks for speaking and writing Controlled Assessment.

Read through the texts. Pick out the verbs. Which tense and which person of the verb is being used?

2a Read the emails and decide to which school each of the following statements applies. Write D (for Danny's school), J (for Juan's school) or D + J (for both schools).

1 Lunchtime lasts one hour.
2 The register is taken in every lesson.
3 Uniform is compulsory.
4 The students can go out of school at lunchtime.
5 The school is a state school.

2b Copy the sentences and fill in the gaps with a suitable word from the emails.

1 Normalmente ______ al patio durante el recreo.
2 Las ciencias son fáciles, pero el inglés es muy ______.
3 Tengo clase de matemáticas ______ los días.
4 La última ______ que hice un examen de matemáticas, lo aprobé.
5 Ayer ______ que ver a la directora.
6 ______ no sé lo que voy a hacer el año que viene.

3 Listen to four Spanish students speaking about the English schools they have visited during an exchange visit. Note whether each person's opinion is positive (P), negative (N) or positive and negative (P + N). Then write a summary in English of what each person says, showing why you have chosen P, N or P + N.

4 Choose the correct tense of the verbs.

1 Durante las próximas vacaciones fui / iré / he ido de excursión con el colegio.
2 Actualmente comemos / comimos / comeremos en el comedor del instituto.
3 Anoche haré / hago / hice mis deberes antes de cenar.
4 La semana pasada tuve / tengo / tendré una reunión con mi tutora.
5 El año que viene creo que mi amigo estudiaba / estudiará / estudió en la universidad.
6 Cuando vuelvo a casa, siempre leeré / leí / leo el periódico digital.

Gramática *página 180*

Using different tenses

As you have already seen, verb endings in Spanish tell us the person and the tense of the verb. You will need to use language that requires different tenses of the verb and will therefore have to be familiar with endings for those tenses. *See page 180* ➡

Also revise comparative adjectives.

See page 143 ➡

5 Write in Spanish what you have found to be some of the differences in Spanish schools compared to your own. Write an imaginative account, focusing on a Spanish student's school day, either in the present tense saying what normally happens or in the past, describing what was done yesterday. Refer to the online worksheet for a language structure box to help you.

Consejo

When you have written something in Spanish, check each verb and make sure you have used the correct tense. Ask yourself these questions:

- Who or what is the subject of the verb?
- Does the action take place in the present, past or future?

kerboodle

4.3 ¡Cuánto estrés!

- Discussing pressures and problems in school
- Using *desde hacía* and the imperfect tense
- Making sure that you give all the information that you are asked to give

1 Ⓥ Find the odd word out in the following groups. Then make up one of your own using school vocabulary. Test it out on the rest of the class.

1	director	profesor	comedor	tutor
2	deberes	trabajo	tarea	estuche
3	castigar	apoyar	ayudar	enseñar
4	me gusta	me encanta	me enfada	me interesa

Las preocupaciones de los estudiantes

Aquí están los resultados de un sondeo realizado con un grupo de estudiantes españoles entre 14 y 16 años:

Problema	**Porcentaje afectado**
Exámenes / evaluaciones	76%
Deberes	59%
Comportamiento de compañeros	42%
Acoso escolar	38%
Padres	31%
Profesores	29%
Ropa	23%
Castigos	11%
Falta de libertad	8%

Es evidente al observar este sondeo que a los estudiantes entrevistados les preocupan sobre todo los asuntos relacionados con el trabajo escolar. La necesidad de sacar buenas notas es cada vez más importante hoy en día tanto para los que buscan trabajo como para los que quieren seguir con los estudios. Había gran número de alumnos que estaban a favor de un sistema de evaluación continua como alternativa a los exámenes, porque éstos provocan demasiado estrés.

Con respecto al comportamiento había dos problemas para los encuestados. Primero, les enfadaba a muchos estudiantes que algunos de sus compañeros de clase se comportaran mal y eso hace el trabajo del profesor o de la profesora muy difícil. La consecuencia de esto es que a menudo los que quieren aprender no pueden. Segundo, había muchos que sufrían violencia física y verbal por parte de otros estudiantes. Algunos estudiantes sufrían desde hacía muchos años.

La presión por parte de los adultos (padres y profesores) afecta a ciertos estudiantes, aunque generalmente reconocen que esta presión puede ser beneficiosa cuando no es demasiado y cuando los castigos en casa y en el colegio no son graves.

La ropa es algo que causa problemas en colegios donde no hay uniforme, porque puede ser muy caro comprar cosas de última moda.

2a Find the Spanish equivalent in the text for these words and phrases.

1	bullying	4	behaviour
2	punishments	5	pressure
3	good marks	6	although

Consejo

When reading material that is not immediately understandable, focus on what a paragraph is dealing with before tackling exercises on it. For a true or false activity, narrow down the area of a text to where you are likely to find the answer and concentrate on that section.

2b Answer the following questions in English.

1 Who took part in the survey?
2 What has become more important for those students who want to find a job?
3 Why were a lot of students in favour of continuous assessment?
4 What are the **two** consequences of bad behaviour by students?
5 What has been affecting some students for many years?
6 How can not having a uniform be a problem?

3 Listen to the three teenagers. For each person, decide which of the following statements are true.

María

1 a I have never been bullied.
  b I am bullied sometimes.
  c I have to admit that I am a bully sometimes.
2 a I find homework quite easy.
  b My teachers don't explain things well enough.
  c I spend a lot of time doing homework.

Carlos

3 a Some of my friends have been bullied.
  b My friends have a bad effect on my studies.
  c I am an unlucky person.
4 a I don't like sport of any description.
  b I don't have any problems at school.
  c Basketball is never played at my school.

Lucía

5 a My parents aren't interested in what I do at school.
  b My parents put a lot of pressure on me.
  c My parents always help me with my homework.
6 a My teachers sympathise with the problems I have at home.
  b I go out too often.
  c My parents don't mind me going out.

4 Change the infinitive of the verb in brackets to the imperfect tense. Translate each sentence into English.

1 (Estudiar, ellos) en ese colegio desde hacía cuatro años.
2 (Sufrir, nosotros) acoso escolar desde hacía mucho tiempo.
3 (Esperar, ella) a su amigo en el patio desde hacía quince minutos.
4 (Vivir, él) en la casa al lado de su víctima desde hacía un mes.

5 With a partner, or in groups of three or four, answer the following questions. You could play the role of someone who is more or less affected by these problems than you are. Refer to the online worksheet for a language structure box to help you.

- Dame ejemplos de comportamiento bueno y malo en la clase.
- ¿Qué te preocupa más de los problemas mencionados en el sondeo? ¿Por qué?
- ¿Es mejor tener exámenes o evaluación continua? ¿Por qué?
- ¿Cuáles son los aspectos positivos y negativos de llevar uniforme?
- ¿Cómo son las relaciones entre tu familia y tú con respecto al trabajo escolar?

Gramática página 187

Using *desde hacía* and the imperfect tense

To say that something **had** been happening for a certain amount of time, use *desde hacía* with a verb in the **imperfect** tense. For example:

Iba al colegio en autobús desde hacía diez años.

See also the notes on using the subjunctive in exclamatory phrases. *See page 142*

Estrategia

For speaking and writing activities, where you have a series of bullet points, try to say or write something about all of them. Focus on the question word, as this will enable you to begin an answer. If the question word is *¿dónde?*, you will be giving a place as part of your answer.

kerboodle

4.4 ¿Qué piensas de tu colegio?

- Discussing opinions of school
- Using the conditional tense
- Looking for clues to help understanding

1 Work in pairs. Partner A gives their opinion, in Spanish, of the following aspects of your school. Then swap roles.

los servicios; el uniforme; el comedor; el horario; los castigos; el inglés; las ciencias

It is election time for the candidates who want to be chairman of the School Council (*Consejo Escolar*) in the *Instituto Cervantes*. Two students have written their manifesto.

¡Vota por Natalia Sánchez!

No te olvides de votar por mí. Soy la persona que va a cambiar todas las cosas malas que pueda. He hablado con muchos estudiantes para conocer sus ideas y ahora voy a seguir sus sugerencias.

- Primero, los servicios, que muchas veces están sucios. Necesitamos ser más responsables en mantenerlos limpios. No somos niños y no es justo que nos quejemos de un problema que depende de nosotros mismos.
- ¿Qué piensas del horario? Hay muchos que están en contra de empezar clase a las ocho. Es demasiado temprano en mi opinión. Habrá que hablar con el director y con los otros profesores, pero estoy segura de que podríamos comenzar una hora más tarde.
- La comida en nuestra cantina a veces es fatal. La próxima vez que estés allí, mira la cantidad de comida basura que hay: pizza, hamburguesas, patatas fritas. Tenemos que hacer algo.

Natalia

¡Elige a Iker Gutiérrez!

Considera bien los cambios que propongo. Es posible que pienses que en parte son raros, pero estamos aquí para estudiar y prepararnos para el futuro.

- No tenemos uniforme desde hace treinta años. Mi padre asistía a este instituto cuando había uniforme y me dice que había mucho más respeto no solamente para los profesores sino también para los alumnos por parte del público en general. Además, me fastidia que todas las mañanas tenga que decidir lo que me voy a poner. Sería mucho mejor llevar uniforme.
- Piensa un minuto en los castigos que existen. Un minuto es suficiente, porque hay pocos. Creo que no será popular con muchos estudiantes si tenemos castigos más graves, pero opino que la mayoría estará a favor ya que saben que a largo plazo va a ayudarles a sacar buenas notas, y finalmente conseguir un trabajo bien pagado.

Iker

2 Answer the following questions in English.

1. Why has Natalia spoken to lots of students?
2. What is her suggestion for improving the toilets?
3. What does she want to happen with the school day?
4. Why does something need to be done about the school meals?
5. According to Iker, why should students think hard about his suggestions?
6. What does his father say about uniform?
7. Is Iker in favour or against having a school uniform? Why?
8. How does he want the punishments to change?

3 Listen to Manolo talking about school subjects. Match up each subject with the correct comment.

Subject	Comment
1 History	A I would like to change to another subject.
2 English	B My teacher for this subject is really boring.
3 Geography	C It's a shame I'm not good at the subject because I like it.
4 Art	D We never have to take notes in the lessons.
	E I'm enjoying the subject much more than in the past.
	F I've not had any problems with this subject.

Looking for clues to help understanding

Estrategia

If you do not understand a particular word, listen carefully to what comes before and after to try to find clues. Listen especially for words connected to a particular topic.

4 G Copy and complete the sentences, choosing the correct part of the conditional tense.

1 En mi opinión, el colegio sería / serían / seríamos mejor con una piscina.
2 Me gusta / gustaría / gustarían tener más laboratorios de ciencias.
3 Mis amigos y yo recomendarían / recomienda / recomendaríamos un cambio de director.
4 Creo que los profesores deberían / deben / debería hacer más para ayudar a los alumnos menos inteligentes.

Using the conditional tense

Gramática página 184

This is used to say what **would** happen or what someone **would** do.

Me gustaría tener un horario diferente.

I would like to have a different timetable.

Also revise adjectival agreement.

See page 143

Consejo

If you give an opinion, justify it without having to be asked.

Me gustaría cambiar la hora de comer, porque no tengo hambre a las doce.

5 You find a 'Rate-a-school' website in Spanish and decide to rate your own school according to the following score:

5 Sobresaliente 4 Notable 3 Bien 2 Bastante mal 1 Muy mal

The aspects that you must rate are:
El horario, Las instalaciones, El uniforme, La comida, Los profesores.

Justify the score you have given and suggest possible ways of improving each aspect.

Necesitamos		más	campos de deporte. laboratorios. profesores / vestuarios.
No tenemos		suficientes	
Empezamos Terminamos		demasiado / muy	temprano / tarde.
Sería	estupendo mejor buena idea fantástico perfecto	empezar a las nueve. tener un comedor nuevo. estudiar menos asignaturas. terminar a la una. prohibir los exámenes.	

kerboodle

School / college and future plans

Los días escolares de Carmen

Empecé a ir a la escuela primaria cuando tenía seis años y estaba muy contenta allí. Los profesores allí eran simpáticos y amables. La vida era fácil porque los estudios consistían en jugar con los amigos, bailar y escuchar historias.

El instituto

A los doce años empezó la enseñanza secundaria. No tenía miedo de ir al instituto porque mi hermano mayor ya era alumno allí, pero hay que admitir que tenía nervios. Un gran cambio era que tenía que coger el autobús en lugar de ir andando y por eso era necesario levantarme más temprano. Me acuerdo de mi primer día: todo pareció tan grande y los otros alumnos parecieron muy maduros y mayores.

Llevo ya casi cuatro años en el instituto y lo conozco muy bien. En realidad, no es tan grande como pensé – sólo tiene unos quinientos alumnos – y está en las afueras de la ciudad. Los profesores son bastante estrictos pero muy trabajadores y las reglas son justas. Lo que parece enfadar al director más que nada es el chicle ... ¡lo odia!

Las instalaciones son bastante buenas, sobre todo para deportes y ciencias, pero hay muy poco espacio para relajarse durante el recreo por ejemplo. Me gustaría tener una cafetería para comprar un bocadillo o algo para beber. Lo mejor son las actividades extraescolares porque hay un montón de clubs y excursiones. ¡Incluso hay un intercambio con un instituto en Inglaterra!

Ahora, tengo dieciséis años y estoy pensando en lo que quiero hacer en los dos próximos años. Me ha gustado mi tiempo aquí en el instituto y mis profesores dicen que voy a sacar buenas notas. Podría hacer el bachillerato en tecnología; se me dan bien estas asignaturas. ¿O sería mejor hacer la formación profesional? Pase lo que pase, no tengo la intención de buscar trabajo, hay muy pocos empleos para los jóvenes de mi edad y además, es posible que vaya a la universidad ...

1 Read Carmen's account and complete the following sentences with the correct option.

1 When Carmen started school, she was
a five b six c seven.

2 At primary school Carmen was
a timid b miserable c happy.

3 The teachers at primary school were
a nice b old c strict.

4 She found the primary school activities
a challenging b boring c easy.

5 Carmen started secondary school at the age of
a 10 b 11 c 12.

6 To go to her secondary school Carmen
a walked b got the bus c got a lift with her brother.

7 Carmen's secondary school is
a in the town centre b in the country c on the outskirts.

Study tip

It is a good idea to read through the questions before reading the text, as the questions direct you to the appropriate part of the text.

2 Answer the following questions in English.

1 Why didn't Carmen feel frightened on her first day at secondary school?
2 How many pupils are there at the school?
3 What does she think about the teachers?
4 What is the head teacher's pet hate?
5 Which subjects have the best facilities?
6 What aspect does Carmen criticize?
7 What school trip does Carmen mention?
8 What decision is Carmen trying to make?

3 Listen to Luis telling his brother what he will need when he starts school. Which six items from below are they going to buy?

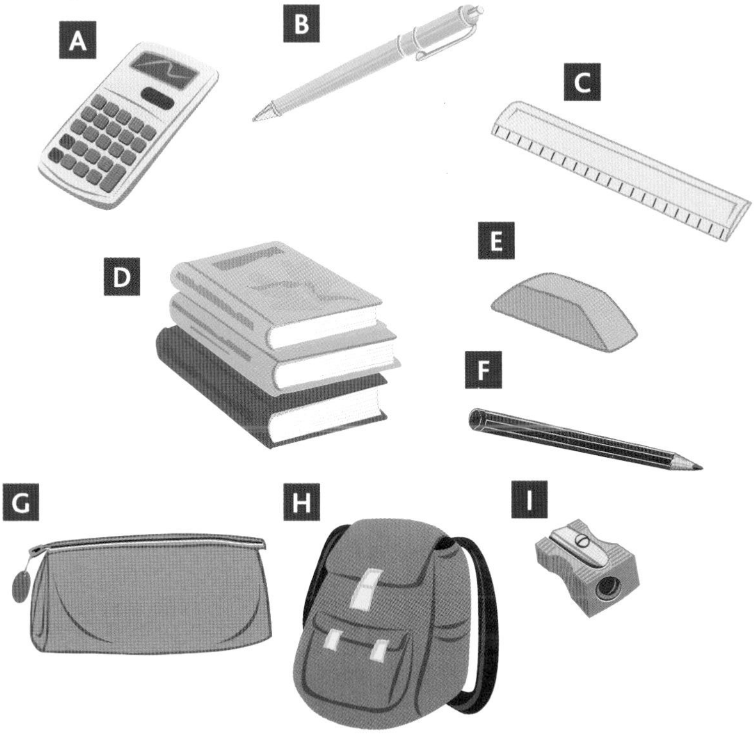

Imperfect and conditional tenses

Gramática *página 180*

Notice the use of the imperfect and conditional tenses in Carmen's account. She uses the imperfect tense to say what her primary school was (used to be) like (*era fácil; consistían en*). She uses the conditional to say what she could do or what something would be like (*podría; sería*).

Vocabulario

enfadar	to anger
la enseñanza secundaria	secondary education
un intercambio	exchange (visit)
maduro/a	mature

4 Listen to the head teacher explaining the school rules. Complete the following sentences with the correct option.

1 All pupils should …
  a arrive on time
  b treat others considerately
  c hand in work to teachers on time.
2 If you are ill you should …
  a phone school to say you won't be in
  b catch up with all work
  c bring a letter from home.
3 Smoking is allowed …
  a nowhere in the school
  b in specially marked areas
  c for teachers only.
4 In class you must …
  a listen and be quiet
  b make notes and listen
  c have all your books and equipment.
5 The fifth rule concerns …
  a procedure at break time
  b school uniform
  c bullying.

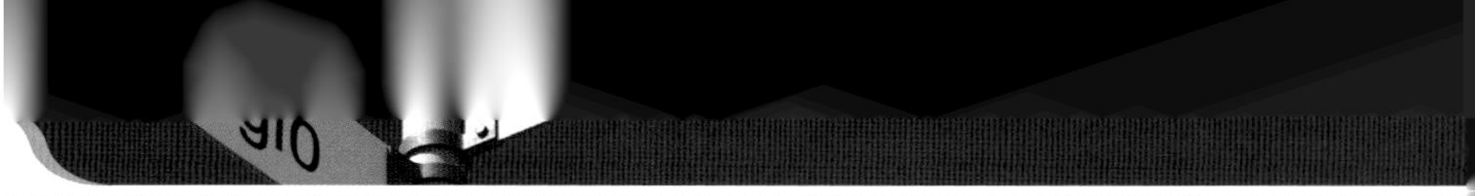

G School / college and future plans

1a Work in pairs. Take turns to buy things for school. Follow the examples given.

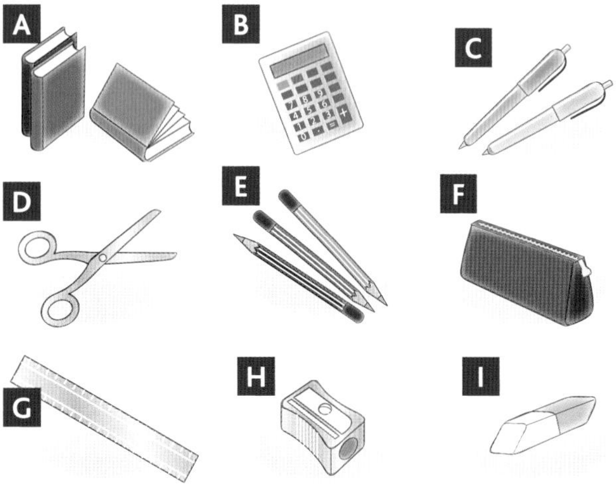

Demonstrative adjectives

Remember that demonstrative adjectives are the words for 'this', 'these', 'that' and 'those':

For 'this', use *este* before a masculine singular noun and *esta* before a feminine singular noun.

For 'these', use *estos* before a masculine plural noun and *estas* before a feminine plural noun.

For 'that', use *ese* before a masculine singular noun and *esa* before a feminine singular noun.

For 'those', use *esos* before a masculine plural noun and *esas* before a feminine plural noun.

este chico – this boy | *estas mesas* – these tables
esa mujer – that woman | *esos pósteres* - those posters

Gramática página 176

1b Translate the following words into Spanish. Use the nouns in the box below and check in a dictionary if you are unsure of the gender.

1 this exam
2 those classrooms
3 these bags
4 that word
5 this term
6 those teachers
7 that test
8 this uniform
9 these pupils
10 that vocabulary

uniforme aulas prueba alumnos mochilas profesores trimestre examen palabra vocabulario

2 Find a suitable expression (1–6) to match each of the following occasions.

a Your friend is going to a party.
b You are about to start lunch with your colleagues at a restaurant.
c Your father is leaving to go on a business trip.
d Your friend has an important interview.

1 ¡Que tengas buen viaje!
2 ¡Que todo vaya bien!
3 ¡Que lo pases bien!
4 ¡Que invites a Raúl!
5 ¡Que aproveche!
6 ¡Que duermas bien!

The present subjunctive in certain exclamatory phrases

You will sometimes see phrases which are formed by using *que* followed by the present subjunctive of the verb. In English they are often translated by 'I hope you …' or 'Let's …'.

¡Que llegues antes de las tres!
I hope you arrive before 3 o'clock.

Gramática página 184

3a ✎ Guillermo Sinamigos has to outdo what anyone says. What would he reply to the statements 1–10 below? Follow the example.

Ejemplo:
Las instalaciones son modernas.

Las instalaciones aquí son más modernas.

1 Los alumnos son inteligentes.
2 El director es bueno.
3 El gimnasio es grande.
4 Los recreos son largos.
5 Las aulas son cómodas.
6 La comida es deliciosa.
7 Los profesores son trabajadores.
8 Las actividades son interesantes.
9 Las notas son buenas.
10 El edificio es histórico.

3b Work in pairs. Take turns to compare the following things now with what they were like at primary school.

Ejemplo: las instalaciones: Las instalaciones son más variadas aquí.

a las matemáticas
b los profesores
c la comida
d las reglas
e el inglés
f los deberes
g el patio
h la educación física

3c ✎ Write a paragraph comparing your primary school with the school you are at now. Use *más* and *menos* to compare them. Write about the following things and anything else you would like to mention:

- los profesores
- las asignaturas
- el horario
- las instalaciones
- el edificio
- los deportes
- la comida

4 ✎ Copy the sentences and fill in the gaps with *a* if you think it is needed.

1 Busco ______ mi cuaderno.
2 ¿Has visto ______ Mónica?
3 Voy a terminar ______ mis deberes.
4 Manolo compró ______ un nuevo estuche.
5 Tuve que ver ______ la directora.

Comparative adjectives

Gramática página 175

In order to compare one thing with another, you will need to use one of two key words before an adjective (*más*, meaning 'more', or *menos*, meaning 'less').

Juan es más fuerte que Enrique.
Juan is stronger (literally 'more strong') than Enrique.

Manchester es menos grande que Londres.
Manchester is not as big (literally 'less big') as London.

There are two notable exceptions to this rule. *Mejor* means 'better', and *peor* means 'worse'.

The personal *a*

Gramática página 187

When the **object** of a verb is a person, you have to write ***a*** before that person, as in these examples:

*Vi **a** Elena en el patio.*
I saw Elena in the yard.

*Escuchamos **a** la profesora.*
We listened to the teacher.

V School / college and future plans

Bienvenidos al colegio ➡ *pages 132–133*

el	*alemán*	German
el / la	*alumno/a*	pupil
la	*asignatura*	subject
el	*aula (f)*	classroom
el	*bachillerato*	equivalent of an A-level course
la	*biología*	biology
el	*campo de deporte*	sports field
las	*ciencias*	science
las	*ciencias económicas*	economics
el	*colegio*	school
los	*conocimientos*	knowledge
el	*curso*	course / school year
los	*deberes*	homework
	difícil	difficult
el / la	*director(a)*	head teacher
	diseñar	to design
	divertido/a	fun
la	*educación física*	PE
la	*escuela*	school
el / la	*estudiante*	student
	estudiar	to study
los	*estudios*	studies
	fácil	easy
la	*física*	physics
el	*francés*	French
la	*geografía*	geography
la	*gimnasia*	gymnastics
el	*gimnasio*	gym
	hay	there is / there are
la	*historia*	history
el	*idioma*	language
la	*informática*	ICT
las	*instalaciones*	facilities
el	*instituto*	(secondary) school
el	*intercambio*	exchange (visit)
	interesante	interesting
el	*laboratorio*	laboratory
	maravilloso/a	marvellous
las	*matemáticas*	maths
	mejor	better / best
	mixto/a	mixed
	moderno/a	modern
	odiar	to hate
el / la	*profesor(a)*	teacher
la	*tecnología*	technology
	tener	to have
	terminar	to finish
los	*trabajos manuales*	craft subjects

Colegios británicos y españoles ➡ *pages 134–135*

los	*apuntes*	notes
	anoche	last night
el	*chicle*	chewing gum
	comenzar	to begin
el	*detalle*	detail
	disfrutar	to enjoy
	duro/a	hard
	empezar	to begin
la	*enseñanza*	education
el	*español*	Spanish
	estricto/a	strict
el	*examen*	exam
	fatal	awful
	incluso	even
de	*momento*	at the moment
	parecer	to seem
	pedir permiso	to ask for permission
el	*permiso*	permission
	ponerse a	to begin to
las	*prácticas laborales*	work experience
la	*pregunta*	question
	privado/a	private
la	*prueba*	test
	público/a	public ('state' when referring to schools)

el	*recreo*	break
la	*semana*	week
	severo/a	strict
	siempre	always
el	*silencio*	silence
	suspender	to fail
el	*trabajo*	work
el	*trimestre*	term
el / la	*tutor(a)*	tutor
el	*vocabulario*	vocabulary

¡Cuánto estrés! ➡ *pages 136–137*

el	*acoso escolar*	bullying
	a menudo	often
	apoyar	to support
el	*asunto*	matter / topic
	atacar	to attack
	aunque	although
	ausente	absent
la	*ayuda*	help
el	*bolígrafo*	pen
la	*calculadora*	calculator
la	*carpeta*	folder / file
	castigar	to punish
	charlar	to chat
el	*comportamiento*	behaviour
	comprender	to understand
la	*conducta*	behaviour
	divertirse	to have fun
	entender	to understand
el	*equilibrio*	balance
	estar a favor	to be in favour
	estar en contra	to be against
	estar harto de	to be fed up of
el	*estrés*	stress
el	*estuche*	pencil case
la	*evaluación*	assessment
el	*éxito*	success
	físico/a	physical
el	*fracaso*	failure
	generalmente	usually
	golpear	to hit
	insolente	insolent / cheeky
	insultar	to insult
	intimidar	to intimidate / threaten
la	*libertad*	freedom
	pasar	to spend (time)
la	*presión*	pressure
	prometer	to promise
	repasar	to revise
	respetar	to respect
la	*respuesta*	answer
el	*sondeo*	survey
la	*tarea*	task
el	*tema*	theme / topic
la	*víctima*	victim
	ya que	because

¿Qué piensas de tu colegio? ➡ *pages 138–139*

	alegrarse	to be pleased
	aprobar	to pass
la	*cantidad*	quantity
la	*cantina*	canteen
	comportarse	to behave
	conseguir	to get / achieve
	decepcionante	disappointing
	desobediente	disobedient
	faltar	to lack / be absent
	fastidiar	to annoy
	incómodo/a	uncomfortable
el	*inglés*	English
	mantener	to keep
la	*mayoría*	majority
	obligatorio/a	compulsory
	olvidar	to forget
la	*opción*	option
	optar	to choose / opt
	optativo/a	optional
	pensar	to think
	preferir	to prefer
el	*uniforme*	uniform
los	*vestuarios*	changing rooms

4.5 El trabajo a tiempo parcial

- Talking about part-time jobs and work experience
- Recognising the pluperfect tense
- Including different tenses in speaking and writing

This extract from a problem page in a teenage magazine concerns Elena's problems with her parents over her part-time job.

Consultorio de Rosario

Problema

Querida Rosario

Soy una alumna de dieciséis años y te escribo para pedirte consejo acerca de un problema que tengo con mis padres.

Siempre había pensado que era muy importante ganar dinero mientras estudiaba, y por eso hace un mes empecé a trabajar en un restaurante en mi barrio tres noches por semana. Mis padres me dan dinero cada semana y en el pasado ha sido bastante para comprar revistas y maquillaje. Sin embargo, ahora tengo novio y salimos a cafeterías o al cine y es bastante caro.

No quiero pedir más dinero a mis padres, porque a mi juicio no sería justo. Por otro lado, necesito más dinero para salir.

Ayer mi madre me dijo que no podía continuar con mi trabajo porque está afectan do mis notas en el colegio. No obstante, dejar el trabajo posiblemente sería el fin de la relación con mi novio, puesto que ya no podría salir con él.

¿Qué puedo hacer?

Elena

Respuesta

Querida Elena

Lo que está pasando contigo es común entre la gente de tu edad y no tienes que preocuparte. Tienes que encontrar un compromiso con tu madre y hablar también con tu padre, cuya opinión también será importante.

¿Por qué no sugieres a tus padres que trabajes una noche o dos noches solamente y que te den un poco más de dinero para que puedas seguir saliendo con tu novio? Estoy segura de que van a entender tu problema y ayudarte a disfrutar de tu tiempo libre y estudiar al mismo tiempo. Se puede hacer las dos cosas, pero tú tienes que ser responsable y no olvidar que el futuro dependerá de tus estudios.

Rosario

1a Copy the sentences and fill in the gaps with the correct word from the box.

más	cuatro	sale	optimista	17	16
padre	pesimista	ocho	llega	madre	menos

1. Elena tiene _______ años.
2. Trabaja en el restaurante desde hace aproximadamente _______ semanas.
3. Elena necesita más dinero porque _______ más.
4. Hasta ahora Elena no ha hablado con su _______.
5. En la opinión de Rosario, Elena debería trabajar _______.
6. Rosario tiene un punto de vista _______.

1b Answer the following questions in English.

1. What had Elena always thought that it was important to do?
2. What two things has Elena usually spent her money on?
3. Why has life become more expensive for Elena?
4. Why did her mother tell her that she could no longer work in the restaurant?
5. Why does Elena think that giving up her job would be a bad idea?
6. Why does Rosario think that Elena has no need to worry?
7. What two things does Rosario suggest that Elena should do?
8. How does Rosario tell Elena to behave and why?

2 Listen to three students talking about their work experience. For each one say:

a where they worked
b how long they stayed there
c what time they started
d what they thought of it.

3 **G** Copy the sentences, changing the infinitive in brackets into the correct part of the pluperfect tense. Those with a ! have an irregular past participle.

1 Yo siempre _______ (pensar) que era fácil trabajar en una tienda.
2 Marta _______ (dejar) su paraguas en la oficina y tuvo que volver a recogerlo.
3 Los chicos _______ (comer) demasiados caramelos y se sentían un poco enfermos.
4 Paula y yo _______ (volver !) muy tarde la noche anterior.
5 ¿Tú _______ (beber) sangría antes?
6 El Señor García, mi jefe, _______ (hacer !) planes para comprar una compañía en Madrid.

4a You want to find out your friends' thoughts about work experience. Plan and write a questionnaire in Spanish which will ask for people's opinions.

4b In groups of three or four ask the questions you have devised in Activity 4a and make notes in Spanish on the answers given. Report your findings to the class in Spanish.

Mis padres Mi madre	me	dijeron que dijo que	no podía trabajar. tendría que trabajar menos.
(No) Podría	salir		con mi novio/a.
	comprar		revistas.
Tienes que Hay que	ser		responsable. trabajador(a).
	encontrar		un compromiso.
	entender		el problema.

Gramática — página 183

Recognising the pluperfect tense

The pluperfect tense says what **had** happened or what someone **had** done. It is formed with the imperfect tense of *haber* and the past participle.

Habíamos salido cuando Marta llegó.
We had left when Marta arrived.

Also learn how to use *cuyo*.

See page 159

Estrategia

Including different tenses in speaking and writing

At higher tier, showing you can use the imperfect tense as well as the preterite and the future will help you to achieve higher grades:

¿Qué tenías que hacer todos los días?

¿Vas a hacer ese tipo de trabajo en el futuro?

Consejo

Remember, *a* is 'to' and *de* is 'from':

Voy a la oficina.

He recibido un correo electrónico de mi jefe.

4.6 Buscando trabajo

- Looking for and applying for jobs
- Asking questions using the preterite tense
- Using context to work out meaning

1 Ⓥ Write down as many Spanish words as you can think of which are associated with the following jobs:

cocinero/a   socorrista   camarero/a   recepcionista   guía

Ejemplo: cocinero/a – comida; cocina; plato, etc.

Nuevo complejo turístico en Mariroca.
Se necesitan personas para trabajar este verano.

A

Se busca cocinero para preparar platos regionales e internacionales. Experiencia esencial.

B

Buscamos a jóvenes para ayudar a cuidar niños en el club infantil. Organizarás juegos y excursiones. Conocimiento de primeros auxilios útil.

C

Se necesita socorrista para la seguridad en la playa. Ofrecemos formación.

D

Queremos camareros para los tres restaurantes. Imprescindible tener buenas relaciones con los clientes y buen aspecto personal.

E

Se busca recepcionista para el Hotel Solimar. El candidato ideal tendrá conocimientos de informática y hablará más de un idioma.

F

¿Quieres trabajar de guía? Este verano buscamos a alguien que acompañe a los veraneantes en sus excursiones en autobús. Conocimiento de la región sería útil.

2 These students are looking for work in Spain. Which job would suit each of them? Read the advertisements and write the correct letter for each person.

1 I'd really love to work here. I spent a year in this area as part of my Spanish degree so I know all the local beauty spots.

2 My main qualities are my extrovert personality and my ability to get on with people. I don't mind hard work and I'm often complimented on my smart appearance.

3 It would be great to work here to practise my Spanish, and I could probably use my German as well, as it's a popular area with tourists. Hopefully my IT skills will impress!

4 I'm looking for outdoor work hopefully. I haven't got any particular qualifications but I love sport and I'm very fit because I swim every day. I'm also prepared to learn!

3 Watch the video clip about summer jobs. Answer the questions in English.

1 a How many different shifts are available in the restaurant?
  b What bonus is offered to waiters?

2 a What does the restaurant specialise in?
  b What experience does Fátima have?

Estrategia

Using context to work out meaning

Use the **context** to work out the meaning of an unknown word. You read or hear the following:

Construimos nuevos apartamentos. Necesitamos trabajadores – electricistas, albañiles y carpinteros.

What do you think *albañil* means? It is someone needed to work on the new apartments. An *albañil* is a bricklayer.

4 G Work in pairs, changing the verbs in the infinitive into the *tú* form of the preterite tense. Answer each question with a sentence that includes a preterite verb in the first person. Take turns to ask and answer the questions.

1 ¿(Trabajar) el sábado?
2 ¿(Ganar) mucho dinero?
3 ¿Por qué (decidir) trabajar allí?

Gramática *página 186*

Asking questions using the preterite tense

To ask a person if they did something, simply tell them that they did it (using the preterite tense) and raise the pitch of your voice to sound like a question:

¿Fuiste a la oficina?
Did you go to the office? /
You went to the office?

Learn also how to use *usted / ustedes*. *See page 159*

5 Work in pairs. Your partner is preparing for an interview for one of the jobs advertised on page 148. Ask him / her questions like the ones below: note that these questions use the formal (*usted*) form of the verb in a formal situation. Then swap roles.

- ¿Por qué le interesa este trabajo?
- ¿Cuándo puede empezar?
- Su personalidad, ¿cómo va a ayudarle en el trabajo?
- ¿Cuántas horas puede trabajar por día / semana?
- Hábleme de su experiencia de trabajo.

Consejo

As you learn each new grammar point, try to write down an explanation of how it works for a potential learner of Spanish.

Se busca(n)	camarero/a / electrista.	
Se necesita(n)	cocineros / recepcionistas	
Creo que el trabajo	será	fascinante / emocionante / ideal.
	tendrá	muchas ventajas / buen sueldo.
Puedo / Quisiera	trabajar	todos los días / veinticinco horas a la semana / los fines de semana.
	empezar	en junio / en el verano / después de las vacaciones.
Soy una persona / Creo que soy	fiable / trabajador(a) / honesto/a / entusiasta.	
He	trabajado	en una panadería / como peluquera / con una empresa.
	ayudado	
¿Trabajaste	el sábado / la semana pasada?	
¿Fuiste	en autobús / con tus compañeros?	

4.7 Poniéndose en contacto

- Communicating in the workplace
- Using *quisiera*
- Using knowledge of grammatical categories

1 Write down in Spanish the item of work equipment that your teacher describes.

Memo

As the company focuses mainly on imports and exports between South America and the United Kingdom, the following information has been written in both English and Spanish. We hope you find this useful.

The Management.

Para llamar a otros departamentos dentro de la compañía, hay que marcar un cero antes del número del departamento.	To call other departments within the company, you should dial a five before the number of the department.
Cada oficina tiene una lista completa de las direcciones de correo electrónico de cada empleado.	A full list of email addresses for all employees can be found at reception.
La máquina de fax está situada en la planta baja.	The fax machine is situated on the first floor.
Todos los empleados deben ir a recepción una vez al día para recoger sus mensajes telefónicos.	All employees should go to reception once a day to collect deliveries.
Sólo las llamadas urgentes deben hacerse por la mañana. A veces es imposible hacer una llamada importante porque todas las líneas están comunicando.	Only non-urgent phone calls should be made in the morning. Sometimes it is impossible to make an important call because all lines are busy.

2 The memo above has been sent to all employees within a company. Unfortunately the English translation contains five errors. Find and correct them.

3 Copy and complete the sentences using the words below. Only one word will be suitable in each case, either grammatically or from a sense point of view.

1 Tengo que ______ una carta.
2 ¿Cómo se llama el ______?
3 ¿______ el fax al Señor Pizarro ayer?
4 Es un correo electrónico muy ______.
5 Tendrás que escribirlo ______.

rápidamente | enviarás | urgencia | jefe | largo
máquina | mandaste | enviar | cita | mando

Estrategia: Using knowledge of grammatical categories

If you can work out whether a word is a noun or a verb, you can take an educated guess at its meaning. The word in the gap must be a noun because *un* goes before: *Necesito un ______ inmediatemente*. But it has to be a verb in this example: *Tendrás que ______ mañana.*

4 🎧 Listen to the three telephone messages recorded at work. Write down the following details for each one.

- The caller's surname
- The caller's contact number or email address
- When to call or email back

5a Ⓖ Ask for the following items, using *quisiera*:

1 The phone number
2 A new fax machine
3 An appointment

5b Ⓖ Say that you would like to do these things, using *quisiera* followed by the infinitive:

1 Leave a message
2 Send an email
3 Phone the office

6 You are working for an English firm that does business with companies in Spain. How would you give the following information in Spanish?

- Say that you would like to speak to Señor Villa.
- Ask if they received your email.
- Say that you sent a fax last week.
- Ask what their email address is.
- Say that you need more information about the product.
- Ask how many copies they want.

Se debe Hay que	llamar	inmediatamente. a la directora.
	usar	la máquina antes de las nueve.
	enviar	un correo electrónico.
¿Puede	ir	a recepción? a la oficina?
	llamarme	pronto? antes de las seis?
Necesito	información sobre	el horario de trabajo. aquella compañía.
Quisiera	el número	del Señor Gómez.
	mandar	un fax. una carta.
¿Recibió usted	la carta?	
¿Cuál es	su número de teléfono? su dirección?	

Gramática *página 185*

Using *quisiera*

Quisiera can be used to say that you would like a particular item or to say that you would like to do a particular thing, in which case it is followed by the infinitive of the verb:

Quisiera un café.

Quisiera mandar un fax.

Revise possessive adjectives.

See page 176 ➡

Consejo

Use *que* to extend sentences in written and spoken language. Instead of using two sentences, you can use one longer sentence:

Recibí su correo electrónico. Lo leí esta mañana.

Leí su correo electrónico que recibí esta mañana.

4.8 Después de los exámenes

Objetivos

- Looking at opportunities for work and study post-16
- Using imperatives (commands)
- Finding different ways to say similar things

1 Work in pairs. You have five minutes to read the article and find the Spanish equivalent of the words below. Then close your book. Partner A reads out the English word and Partner B gives the Spanish equivalent. Then swap roles and see who has managed to find the most.

compulsory | to think | next year | advice | to earn | training | qualification | the world of work | electrician | to continue | university

Instituto San Jaime – ¿Qué vas a hacer el año que viene?

Tienes quince o dieciséis años y estás empezando el último curso obligatorio en el instituto. Este año es cuando tienes que empezar a pensar en las posibilidades para el futuro y tus planes para el año próximo.

Aquí, los profesores del Instituto San Jaime te ofrecemos algunos consejos …

Puedes **buscar trabajo**. La gran ventaja es comenzar a ganar un poco de dinero y a tener algo más de libertad. Si es posible, es mejor buscar trabajos que ofrezcan formación como parte del empleo. Muchos aprendizajes incluyen la oportunidad de obtener un certificado académico además de experiencia laboral.

Puedes hacer **formación profesional.** Aquí en el instituto ofrecemos cursos de uno o dos años en los que aprenderás todo lo que necesitas para entrar en el mundo laboral. Hay clases para los electricistas, los peluqueros y los mecánicos del futuro … ¡y muchas más!

Puedes hacer **el bachillerato.** Esta opción es ideal si te han gustado tus asignaturas en el instituto y simplemente quieres estudiar un poco más, o si estás pensando en seguir tus estudios en la universidad. Estudiarás una variedad de asignaturas comunes a todos pero también escogerás otras que correspondan con tus planes para el futuro.

2 Answer the following questions in English.

1. Who is this article written for?
2. What must the reader start to do this year?
3. Who has written the article?
4. According to the article, what are the two main advantages of getting a job?
5. Why are apprenticeships particularly recommended?
6. How long do vocational courses last?
7. What type of jobs could these courses lead to? Give two examples.
8. Give one reason why someone might opt to do the *bachillerato*.
9. Which of these statements is true:
   - a In the *bachillerato* you have a completely free choice of subjects.
   - b In the *bachillerato* there is a mixture of optional and compulsory subjects.

Consejo

Learn and revise vocabulary in small amounts, around 10 words at a time. Little and often is the best way.

3 Listen to the interview with Julia and choose the correct option to complete each sentence.

1 Of the three possible options, Julia immediately rejected:
   a getting a job
   b vocational training
   c continuing academic studies.
2 One disadvantage of continuing with her studies is:
   a it can be boring
   b she has no friends at school
   c she hasn't got much money.
3 The big advantage is that:
   a she likes what she is doing
   b she can be with her friends
   c she can work at weekends.
4 She criticizes her school for:
   a giving too much homework
   b not organizing work experience
   c not leaving her enough time for a Saturday job.
5 Julia does **not** express an interest in the work of:
   a a lawyer
   b a doctor
   c an accountant.
6 Julia thinks that university graduates:
   a get better job opportunities
   b earn more money
   c are less likely to be unemployed.

4 G You are giving advice to some of your friends about what not to do. Copy the sentences, changing the infinitive in brackets to the correct form of the imperative (*tú* form). Then make up more sentences giving advice to people on what not to do.

Ejemplo: ¡No (mencionar) ese incidente!
¡No menciones ese incidente!

1 ¡No (buscar) trabajo en esa región!
2 ¡No (ser) perezosa!
3 ¡No (escuchar) a Ramón!
4 ¡No (escribir) a esa empresa!

Gramática *página 184*

Using imperatives (commands)

Imperatives are used to give instructions to people on what to do or what not to do.

Negative commands always use the subjunctive of the verb:

¡No escribas eso! Don't write that.

Also learn about asking questions using prepositions.

See page 159 ➡

5 Write an email to your Spanish friend, Cristina, telling her about your plans for next year.

La ventaja	es que	ganas dinero.
		obtienes más calificaciones.
El aspecto negativo		hay que estudiar mucho más.
		las horas son largas.
Puedes	hacer	formación profesional.
		otras cosas.
	continuar	con tus estudios.
		estudiando lo que te gusta.
	empezar	a trabajar / a ser independiente.
Sería	fenomenal / útil	ir a la universidad / buscar trabajo.
	posible / perfecto	estudiar la química / tener más libertad.

Estrategia

Finding different ways to say similar things

Learn different ways of saying what you **would like to do** and remember that they all take the infinitive.

Me encantaría recorrer el mundo antes de ir a la universidad.

Tengo la intención de buscar trabajo en España.

Espero conseguir empleo como azafata.

kerboodle

4.9 Comparando empleos diferentes

- Talking about different jobs and careers
- Using irregular adverbs
- Checking grammar in written work

Luisa

Yo trabajo como contable para una gran empresa en la ciudad. Nunca pensé que trabajaría con números porque, de niña, no era muy buena en matemáticas. El trabajo puede ser aburrido, a veces, pero está muy bien pagado. Lo peor es que hay muchos exámenes al principio y hay que aprobarlos o perderás el empleo. Por eso, como te puedes imaginar, es muy estresante porque tengo que estudiar muchísimo. La empresa donde trabajo está en el centro de la ciudad, bastante cerca de mi piso – ¡menos mal!

Susana

Estoy muy contenta porque empecé mi nuevo trabajo el mes pasado y me encanta. Estoy haciendo un aprendizaje para ser peluquera y lo bueno es que es muy variado. Creo que siempre aprendes mejor cuando tienes la experiencia práctica del trabajo. También voy a un colegio un día a la semana para estudiar – es parte de la formación profesional. Las clases son muy interesantes porque son útiles en mi trabajo y puedo charlar con los otros alumnos para compartir ideas y hablar de problemas.

José

De momento, trabajo en una tienda de muebles en la ciudad. No está mal pero sólo tengo este trabajo hasta encontrar algo mejor. Mis padres tienen una granja y pensaban que yo iba a trabajar allí con ellos. Tuve que explicarles que no tenía ganas de quedarme en el campo y vivir la vida de un granjero. Trabajas muchas horas, el trabajo es sucio y te pagan peor que en la ciudad. Sé que el aire es puro, el trabajo es físico y te ayuda a mantenerte en forma, pero no es para mí. No me gusta la vida rural, la vida urbana es más divertida.

1 The people above have written about their jobs. Read the descriptions and select the correct person, Luisa (L), Susana (S) or José (J). Who:

1 ... doesn't have to study?
2 ... talks about the pressure of the job?
3 ... is going against parental wishes?
4 ... attends a training course once a week?
5 ... worries about losing their job?

Consejo

Learn and use a wide range of adjectives for giving opinions, so that everything is not simply *interesante* or *aburrido*. Check out the adjectives used in the main text as a starting point.

2 Read the three people's texts again and answer the following questions in English.

1 Who do you think is happiest in their job? Give a reason for your answer.
2 Who did not expect to be doing their current job? Give a reason for your answer.

3 Listen to the interview with a bullfighter, Emilio Gutiérrez. Copy the table and fill in the missing information in English.

a	**Location of first experience of 'bullfighting'.**
	Age at that time.
	Where he first got used to animals.
b	**Where he started to learn the job of a** *matador*.
	Two problems when he started to be a *matador*.
c	**What gave him his 'big break'.**
	The cost of a *traje de luces*.
	His overall view of the job of a *matador*.

4 Ⓖ Copy the following sentences and fill in the gaps with an appropriate irregular adverb from the list below.

1 Trabajo mucho, pero no me pagan bien porque lo hago ______.
2 Me gustaría ver una corrida, porque ______ he ido.
3 Se levanta temprano y por eso ______ es la primera en llegar a la oficina.
4 Sufría estrés y su médico le dijo que trabajaba ______.
5 Dicen que es muy perezoso porque trabaja ______.

mejor **siempre** **poco** **mal** **peor** **nunca** **demasiado**

Using irregular adverbs

Gramática página 177

Some of the most common adverbs are irregular:

bien – well *mal* – badly
mejor – better *peor* – worse

Éste es un trabajo muy bueno. This is a very good job.

Trabaja bien. He works well.

See also comparative and superlative adverbs.

See page 177 ➡

5 Make up a short description of a job, without mentioning the job itself. Read it out to the rest of the class to see whether they can guess what the job is.

6 Write an account of what would be your ideal job, giving a description of what it entails and why you would like it.

Estrategia

Check grammar carefully before handing in written work. Look especially at verb tenses and endings and at adjectival agreement.

Mi trabajo ideal ***serías*** *granjero porque me encantaría* ***trabajan el*** *aire libre. El campo es* ***tranquila****.*

The sentence should read: *Mi trabajo ideal* ***sería*** *granjero porque me encantaría* ***trabajar al*** *aire libre. El campo es* ***tranquilo****.*

El trabajo	está	bien pagado.
	es	malo.
		(muy / bastante) aburrido.
Tienes que	trabajar	demasiado / horas largas.
No te aburres	nunca / en absoluto.	
Tienes la oportunidad de	hacer formación profesional.	
	charlar con otra gente.	

Current and future jobs

Prepárate para el mundo laboral

1

A la hora de buscar trabajo, vale la pena estar preparado y tener todo listo para empezar. No es fácil encontrar el trabajo ideal y hay que poner mucho esfuerzo en el intento.

2

Primero, haz una lista de todos tus aspectos positivos, tus calificaciones y las experiencias de trabajo que has tenido con las fechas correspondientes.

3

Ahora, piensa bien el tipo de trabajo que quieres. Debe ser algo que corresponde con el nivel de tus estudios y tu formación. ¿Es apropiado para tus estudios y tu formación. ¿Es apropiado para tus ambiciones y tu personalidad? ¿Estarás contento trabajando en ese tipo de ambiente?

4

Luego, hay que buscar los mejores sitios para los anuncios de empleos – el periódico, por ejemplo, o una página web. También, si conoces a alguien que trabaja para una empresa que te interese, podrías preguntar si hay trabajos en su compañía. Vale la pena estudiar la página web de la empresa antes de ir para demostrar tu interés en la compañía.

5

Después, hay que rellenar la solicitud y es esencial hacer esto con mucho cuidado. Es importante destacar tus cualidades, hablar del trabajo con entusiasmo y explicar por qué serías ideal para el empleo.

6

El próximo paso es la entrevista. Es normal sentirte nervioso pero estarás más tranquilo si te preparas bien y llegas con tiempo. Es una buena idea escribir unas preguntas, por ejemplo sobre el horario, tus responsabilidades y el sueldo.

Ahora te toca a ti. ¡Buena suerte!

Busco a estudiantes ingleses para trabajar en hoteles durante el verano.

Se necesita:
- salud excelente
- al menos un idioma extranjero
- buenas referencias

Escribir con información detallada a:

Sra López
Hotel Miramar
Avenida Pablo Picasso
Málaga

Nos queda un puesto de carpintero … Pase, pase y tome asiento.

Study tip

You cannot expect to know every word all the time. Educated guesswork can be very valuable. Does the word remind you of a word in your own language? Does the rest of the sentence give you a clue?

1 Read the text *Prepárate para el mundo laboral* and put these headings into the order which matches the advice given in the text.

A Is it right for you?
B This could be hard work!
C Be calm, be prepared, be punctual.
D Get your facts ready.
E Where to look.
F Emphasise what makes you right for the job.

Enrique busca trabajo

Enrique está terminando sus estudios y va a buscar un trabajo. Hizo sus prácticas en una oficina y sabe que no quiere trabajar ni con ordenadores ni con teléfonos. Le gustaría un empleo más variado y bastante bien pagado. También prefiere el trabajo práctico y le gusta pasar tiempo al aire libre. Sabe que es un poco tímido así que decide evitar trabajos donde hay que tratar con la gente. Mira en el periódico y descubre que el ayuntamiento está buscando a nuevos jardineros. De repente, sabe que es exactamente lo que quiere hacer.

2 Read the text *Enrique busca trabajo* and decide if the following statements are true (T), false (F) or not mentioned in the text (?).

1 Enrique is about to start looking for work.
2 He likes the idea of working in an office.
3 He wants a job close to home.
4 Money is not important to him.
5 Ideally, he would like to work outside.
6 He is quite a confident person.
7 He can start work next week.
8 He finds the job advert on a website.
9 The hours look ideal.
10 He thinks the job is just what he is looking for.

3 Listen to the phone message for Enrique. Answer the following questions in English.

1 Who is the phone call from?
2 On which day does Enrique have an interview?
3 At what time is the interview?
4 What two ways are suggested for Enrique to reply to the message?
5 On which number can he contact Conchita Alonso?
6 What should he wear for the interview?

4 Listen to five people describing their jobs and match up each person with the correct job from the list below.

A Translator
B Police officer
C Firefighter
D Postal worker
E Flight attendant
F Vet
G Chef

Conjunctions of time

Look at the use of conjunctions of time such as *ahora, después, luego* and *entonces*. These are very useful to add variety to your written work and to clarify the sequence of events.

Gramática *página 187*

Vocabulario

a la hora de	when it comes to
el ambiente	environment
el anuncio	advert
el cielo	sky
destacar	to emphasise
la entrevista	interview
te toca a ti	it's up to you
traducir	to translate
vale la pena	it's worth

kerboodle

G Current and future jobs

1a The panel of interviewers is arguing over who to appoint for the job. Complete their arguments in the style of the example given.

Carlos contestó honestamente.
Isabel contestó más honestamente.
Pero Pablo contestó lo más honestamente.

1. Carlos respondió fácilmente …
2. Carlos se comportó tímidamente …
3. Carlos pensó profundamente …
4. Carlos escribió simplemente …
5. Carlos contestó seguramente …

Comparative and superlative adverbs

Gramática página 177

As with adjectives, use *más … que* and *menos … que* to form the comparative of adverbs.

To form the superlative, use *lo más / menos.*

Nosotros vamos al cine ***más*** *frecuentemente* ***que*** *vosotros.*

We go to the cinema **more** often **than** you.

Penélope trabaja ***lo más*** *rápidamente de todos.*

Penélope works the **quickest** of all.

1b Work in pairs. Have a competition with your partner to see how many adverbs you can each form in three minutes. Then check each other's lists to see if the adverbs have been formed correctly.

2a Fill in the gaps with the correct possessive adjective.

1. ¿Dónde está Martín? Voy a poner ______ cartas en la mesa.
2. Marta, he escrito ______ mensajes en el papel al lado del teléfono.
3. Buenas noticias. Vamos a tener nuevos ordenadores en ______ oficina.
4. Quiero hablar con el jefe para cambiar ______ horas de trabajo.
5. Chicas, me da mucho gusto decir que ______ sueldo va a subir.
6. David, no tienes que hacer eso. No es ______ responsabilidad.

mis **nuestra** **sus** **mi** **tu** **tus** **vuestro**

2b Work in pairs. Partner A makes up five questions. The questions must include one of the words *tu* or *tus*. Partner B must reply in a full sentence, using either *mi* or *mis*. Then swap roles.

Ejemplo: ¿Cómo se llama tu padre? – Mi padre se llama Mike.
¿Dónde están tus libros? – Mis libros están aquí.

Possessive adjectives

Gramática página 176

You learnt about possessive adjectives on page 33.

Remember that possessive adjectives are words that show a sense of belonging or ownership (**my** parents; **her** job). In Spanish these words have to agree with the noun which follows.

3 Translate these sentences into English.

1 ¿En qué consiste el trabajo?
2 ¿De quién es este libro?
3 ¿A quién vas a mandar la carta?
4 ¿Para cuándo tengo que terminar el trabajo?

Interrogatives with prepositions

When you ask a question which requires a preposition (*a, de, en, con, por, para, sin*, etc.) with the verb, the preposition will generally appear at the start of the sentence.

¿Con quién saliste anoche?
Who did you go out with last night? / With whom did you go out last night?

¿A qué ciudad vas?
Which town are you going to? / To which town are you going?

Gramática página 180

4a An interviewer gives feedback to someone who has recently been for an interview. Copy the following text, replacing the pictures with the correct verb from the box below. The verbs are in the preterite, in the *usted* form.

Durante la entrevista, usted (**a**) 

muy bien y siempre (**b**)  con atención. Sin duda, (**c**)  el anuncio y (**d**)  su solicitud con mucho cuidado.

Es evidente que (**e**)  antes de contestar y siempre me (**f**) 

si algo no era claro.

preguntó **escribió** **bailó** **habló**
pensó **vio** **escuchó** **leyó**

Usted and *ustedes*

When you are addressing someone as 'you', if you do not know them or if they are older than you are, you should address them as *usted*, or *ustedes* if you are speaking to more than one person. When using a verb, use the third person singular form for *usted* or the third person plural form for *ustedes*.

Gramática página 178

The relative adjective *cuyo*

Cuyo translates into English as 'whose' and must agree with the noun that follows it, as in these examples:

Éste es Manuel, ***cuya*** *hermana es mi mejor amiga.*

This is Manuel, whose sister is my best friend.

Es la mujer ***cuyas*** *fotos están en la pared.*

It's the woman whose photos are on the wall.

Gramática página 176

4b Choose the correct form of the verb to match the person to whom the question is addressed.

1 ¿Cuánto dinero tiene / tienes? (*your best friend*)
2 ¿Puedes / Puede decirme dónde están los servicios, por favor? (*an elderly lady at the station*)
3 ¿Eres / Es español? (*a boy of your age who you have just met*)
4 ¿Quieres / Quiere ir al cine? (*your sister*)
5 ¿Adónde fuiste / fue de vacaciones? (*a teacher from Spain who is with your exchange partner's school*)
6 ¿Enviaste / Envió el correo electrónico? (*your boss*)

5 Copy the sentences and fill in the gaps with *cuyo, cuya, cuyos* or *cuyas*.

1 Mi amigo, ______ padre es periodista, dice que hay oportunidades de trabajo con su periódico.
2 Éste es Esteban, ______ oficina está al lado de la mía.
3 Le voy a presentar a Ángela, ______ ideas siempre son interesantes.
4 Estarás trabajando con José, ______ hijos van a tu instituto.

Ⓥ Current and future jobs

El trabajo a tiempo parcial ➡ *pages 146–147*

el / la	*abogado/a*	lawyer
	ahora	now
	antiguo/a	old
	calificado/a	qualified
la	*compañía*	company
	común	common
el	*consejo*	advice
	cuyo/a	whose
el	*día festivo*	(bank) holiday
	encargado/a de	in charge of
	encargarse de	to be in charge of
la	*entrevista*	interview
	entusiasta	enthusiastic
	ganar	to earn
	hace un mes	a month ago
	hacer prácticas	to do work experience
	hasta	until
el	*horario de trabajo*	working hours
las	*horas de trabajo flexibles*	flexible working hours
la	*intención*	intention
al	*mismo tiempo*	at the same time
la	*participación*	participation
	por eso	therefore
	por otro lado	on the other hand
	probar	to have a go / try
	sin embargo	however
el	*taller*	workshop
a	*tiempo completo*	full time
a	*tiempo parcial*	part time
	trabajador(a)	hard-working
	ya no	no longer

Buscando trabajo ➡ *pages 148–149*

	adjuntar	to attach / enclose
el / la	*albañil*	bricklayer
el	*amo de casa*	house-husband
la	*ama de casa*	housewife
la	*ambición*	ambition
	aprender	to learn
el / la	*camarero/a*	waiter / waitress
el / la	*candidato/a*	candidate
	capaz	capable
el / la	*carnicero/a*	butcher
el / la	*carpintero/a*	joiner
la	*carrera*	profession
el / la	*cocinero/a*	chef
	competente	competent
las	*condiciones de trabajo*	working conditions
	contactar	to contact
	contratar	to take on / hire
el	*contrato*	contract
la	*desventaja*	disadvantage
el / la	*electricista*	electrician
	emocionante	exciting
la	*empresa*	company / firm
el	*entusiasmo*	enthusiasm
la	*experiencia laboral*	experience of work
la	*explicación*	explanation
	fascinante	fascinating
el	*idioma*	language
	llegar a ser	to become
	máximo/a	maximum
	mínimo/a	minimum
	ofrecer	to offer
el / la	*panadero/a*	baker
el / la	*peluquero/a*	hairdresser
el	*propósito*	aim
el / la	*recepcionista*	receptionist
	rellenar	to fill in
el	*salario*	salary
	sencillo/a	simple
	solicitar	to apply
la	*solicitud*	application
el	*sueldo*	salary
el	*título*	university degree
el / la	*trabajador(a)*	worker

	trabajar	to work
	útil	useful
la	*ventaja*	advantage

Poniéndose en contacto ➡ *pages 150–151*

la	*cita*	appointment
la	*copia*	copy
el	*correo*	mail
el	*correo electrónico*	email
la	*correspondencia*	mail / post
el / la	*empleado/a*	employee
el / la	*jefe/a*	boss
la	*línea*	line
la	*llamada*	call
	llamar (por teléfono)	to call
el	*mensaje*	message
el	*objetivo*	aim / objective
la	*oficina*	office
	pronto	soon

Después de los exámenes ➡ *pages 152–153*

el	*aprendizaje*	apprenticeship / learning
	así que	so
la	*calificación*	qualification
el / la	*contable*	accountant
los	*derechos*	rights
el	*empleo*	job
	encontrar	to find
el	*futuro*	future
el / la	*mecánico/a*	mechanic
	obtener	to obtain
la	*preocupación*	worry
	tomar un año libre / sabático	to have a gap year
la	*universidad*	university

Comparando empleos diferentes ➡ *pages 154–155*

el / la	*aprendiz*	apprentice
la	*azafata*	flight attendant
el / la	*bombero/a*	firefighter
el / la	*cajero/a*	cashier
el / la	*camionero/a*	lorry driver
la	*clínica*	clinic
el	*club taurino*	bullfighting club
el / la	*comerciante*	trader / shopkeeper
el	*comercio*	commerce / shop
el / la	*dentista*	dentist
el / la	*dependiente/a*	shop assistant
el / la	*ejecutivo/a*	executive
el	*ejército*	army
el / la	*enfermero/a*	nurse
el / la	*escritor(a)*	writer
	estar estresado/a	to be stressed
	estresante	stressful
	explicar	to explain
el / la	*granjero/a*	farmer
el	*hombre de negocios*	businessman
el / la	*ingeniero/a*	engineer
el / la	*intérprete*	interpreter
el / la	*jardinero/a*	gardener
el / la	*médico*	doctor
la	*mujer de negocios*	businesswoman
el / la	*obrero/a*	worker / labourer
	pagar	to pay
	pagar bien / mal	to pay well / badly
el	*periodismo*	journalism
el / la	*periodista*	journalist
el / la	*pintor(a)*	painter
el / la	*policía*	police officer
al	*principio*	at first
el / la	*soldado*	soldier
	soltar	to release
el / la	*traductor(a)*	translator
el	*triunfo*	triumph / success
	torear	to fight bulls
el	*traje de luces*	bullfighter's suit
	variado/a	varied
el / la	*veterinario/a*	vet
la	*vida rural*	country life

4 Las prácticas laborales

You are going to have a conversation with your teacher about work experience and your plans for next year. Your teacher will ask you the following:

1 If you think it is a good idea to do work experience and why (not)
2 Where you did your work experience
3 What you had to do there
4 What was your opinion of your work experience
5 What plans you have for your holidays after your work experience has finished
6 What you intend to do in September
7 **!** Remember you will have to respond to something that you have not yet prepared.

Study tips

Read through what is expected of you and begin to think about what you are going to say. The whole assignment lasts between four and six minutes, so it is important that you expand on your answers as much as you can.

You are allowed a maximum of 40 words of notes which you may consult during the test, but these must not include conjugated verbs (infinitives are allowed, however). Use six words per task.

You cannot use any symbols or codes or any visuals (drawings, etc) in addition to the 30–40 words.

1 If you think it is a good idea to do work experience and why (not).
- Say what you think is the best thing about doing work experience
- Say what you think is the worst thing
- Say how it can help you get to know what work is all about
- Say what your expectations of work experience are

Study tips

This task is in the present tense and is asking for your opinions about doing work experience and requires you to justify your opinions.

Choose the six words you will use as a plan, for example: *diferente, emocionante, difícil, nueva gente, repetitivo*.

2 Where you did your work experience.
- Mention what type of place it was (an office, a school, etc.)
- Say if it was near to or far from your house
- Say what the place was like
- Say how you got on with your work colleagues

Study tips

Say where you did your work experience, but go beyond merely saying such things as *Fui a una oficina en el centro*. Describe the place of work, say how you felt and so on.

Decide what your next six words will be, as you should do for each task.

3 What you had to do there.
- Say how your day began
- Say which jobs you had to do
- Say how well you could do those jobs and what you thought of them
- Say how it was different from your school routine

Study tips

You obviously need to mention the jobs you did, but you could also mention any differences in your daily routine and working hours compared to school.

You will be using past tenses here and you should use the imperfect tense to say what you did every day: ***Me levantaba*** *a las seis y media y* ***salía*** *de casa a las siete y cuarto*. See page 182.

4 What was your opinion of your work experience.

- Say what your first impressions were
- Say what you think makes a good boss
- Say how you felt when it was time to leave
- Say if it persuaded you to follow a similar career in the future

Study tips

Say what the work was like. Your opinion may have changed over the time you were there as you became more comfortable, so you could use expressions such as *al principio … pero más tarde … después de unos días*.

Again you will be using past tenses: *era* ('it was') will be a key word.

5 What plans you have for your holidays now that your work experience has finished.

- Say where you plan to go
- Say what you will do there
- Say why it is going to be good
- Say who you are going with

Study tips

A chance to use future tenses: *iré a / voy a* + infinitive. See page 183.

Again you should be developing your response, so if you will not be going away for the holidays either say what you will be doing at home, or make up a holiday you will go on (or both!).

6 What you intend to do in September.

- Say what options are available to you
- Say what you intend to do and why
- Say what your choice will lead to in the more distant future
- Say what sort of qualifications/training you might need

Study tips

Future tenses are needed again here, or you may use the conditional (*me gustaría* + infinitive). See page 184. Although you are not asked to give a reason for your choice of returning to school, going to a college or starting work, it is a good idea to do so.

7 ! At this point, you will be asked another question which you don't know in advance. However, you can try to guess what it might be and prepare various options:

- Would you like to do the same job as you did for work experience in the future? Why (not)?
- Do you prefer school or work experience? Why?
- Would you like to go to university? Why (not)?
- What is a positive thing about starting work?

Study tips

For this part of the task you will not have prepared an answer and **you will have to listen carefully to what your teacher asks and reply to the question.** Prepare answers for all the possibilities and in your plan write a few different points for each possibility.

You should now have completed your plan and prepared your answers. Give your plan to your teacher for feedback. Compare your answers to the online sample version – you might find some useful hints to make yours even better.

kerboodle

4 Mi colegio

Your Spanish friend, Blanca, has emailed you, asking for your views on your school. Reply to her email. You could include:

1 Details of what your school is like
2 What happens on a typical day at school
3 Your subjects and your opinions of them
4 The quality of food in the dining room
5 Extra-curricular activities you did last week
6 Homework – how much you get and your opinions
7 What you would like to change and why

Study tips

You could begin by saying what your school is called (*Mi instituto se llama …*) and where it is (*Está en …*).

1 Details of what your school is like.
- Mention how many pupils and teachers there are
- Say whether it is mixed or single sex, state or private, whether you have a uniform, etc.
- Mention the buildings and facilities – how modern they are
- Say what the atmosphere is like

Study tips

You are allowed to have a maximum of 40 words of notes in Spanish as a plan for the assignment, but they must not include conjugated verbs (although infinitives are allowed). Decide which words you will use, for example: *alumnos, profesores, mixto, aulas, campos, agradable*.

You will be using the present tense for this bullet point – give opinions as well as descriptions, and vary the words you use.

2 What happens on a typical day at school.
- Say how you get there
- Say at what time you arrive
- Mention the length of lessons and how many there are each day
- Say when you have breaks and what you do then

Study tips

Try to form longer sentences by using linking words. For instance, the first two tasks can be combined: *Voy al instituto en autobús que llega a las ocho y veinte*.

Think about your next six words for the plan for this task and for the rest.

3 Your subjects and your opinions of them.
- Say which subjects you study
- Say which you like and dislike and why
- Mention a subject or subjects that you chose not to opt for and why not
- Mention any plans you have for studying particular subjects next year

Study tips

The third bullet point requires you to use the preterite tense and the fourth one to use the future or conditional. Revise those tenses if you are not sure how to use them. See page 180.

You can give lots of different opinions here.

4 The quality of food in the dining room.
- Mention the type of food that you can buy
- Say what you think of it
- Give your opinions as to how healthy you think it is
- Say what you would prefer to be offered

Study tips

You may want to revise the Lifestyle topic at this point, when you discussed healthy eating.
Try to use phrases and structures that show off the grammar you have learnt. The words in your plan could include adjectives and ways to justify your opinions.

5 Extra-curricular activities you did last week.
- Begin by saying what extra-curricular activities are available
- Say what you did as extra-curricular activities last week
- Give your opinion of the activities you did
- Say how far you think extra-curricular activities are useful

Study tips

Even if you don't do any of the extra-curricular activities that are available at school, on this one occasion you need to pretend that you do. Otherwise you will be missing out on developing a task.
You will be using the present tense to say what is available, but then move on to the preterite to say what you did last week. Then you will return to the present tense for the final bullet point.

6 Homework – how much you get and your opinions.
- Say how much homework you usually do each night
- Give an example by saying what you did last night for homework
- Mention those subjects in which you get most and least homework
- Give your opinion of homework

Study tips

You can begin by either saying what 'I' or 'we' have to do (*Tengo / Tenemos que* + infinitive).
When giving your opinion of homework it is a good idea to give a balanced view: *Odio hacer los deberes, pero sé que son útiles*.

7 What you would like to change and why.
- Mention the things about school that you don't like
- Say why you don't like them
- Say what improvements you would make
- Mention anything about Spanish schools that you think is better than in your school

Study tips

When you say what changes you would like to make you could begin with *Si yo fuera director(a)* (If I were the head teacher). See pages 134–135 to revise using different tenses. Then you use the conditional tense in order to say what you would do. See page 184.

You should now have completed your plan and prepared your answers. Give your plan to your teacher for feedback. As this is a practice task, your teacher might choose to also give you feedback on your first draft. However, when it comes to a task that is part of your GCSE Spanish, you will get feedback on your plan but **not** on your first draft. Now compare your answers with the online sample version – you might find some useful hints to make yours even better.

kerboodle

Context summary

Resumen

1 Rearrange the following words to make a sentence.

muchas colegio impresionante de salón instalaciones En tenemos hay y deportivas un actos mi

2 What has happened in the following statement?

'¡Qué desastre! He perdido mis deberes de dibujo.'

3 Translate the following sentence into Spanish.

I am against wearing a uniform because it is very uncomfortable.

4 Correct the grammatical error in the second sentence.

Me molestan los exámenes. Creo que son muy difícil y causan mucho estrés.

5 Copy and complete the following sentence with the correct tense of the verb *estudiar*.

Este año estudio nueve asignaturas. Mañana ______ para un examen de historia.

6 Write a question for which the following would be a suitable reply.

Creo que voy a estudiar en otro colegio.

7 What would be a suitable answer to the following question?

¿Qué te fastidia más de tus prácticas laborales?

8 Translate this sentence into English.

He decidido que sería buena idea dejar el colegio.

9 Copy the following sentence and fill in the gap with an appropriate word.

La semana pasada Juan me dijo que ______ enviado el correo electrónico a la empresa.

10 What job is being described here?

A veces es un trabajo muy difícil, especialmente cuando llueve y tienes que llevar el saco pesado de casa en casa con todo el correo.

¿Lo sabes?

¿Sabías que en varias regiones de España (por ejemplo Cataluña, País Vasco, Galicia y Valencia) dan muchas clases en el idioma de esa región y no en español o, mejor dicho, en 'castellano'? Se habla catalán en Cataluña, vasco en el País Vasco y gallego en Galicia.

Frequently asked questions: Speaking

This general guidance is in the form of answers to 'frequently asked questions' (FAQs).

1 How many tasks do I have to complete for the speaking part of my GCSE Spanish?

There are two tasks, both of a similar kind. Your teacher will ask you the questions and listen to your answers. One of your tasks will be recorded as it may have to be submitted to the AQA Examination Board. Each task lasts between four and six minutes. The Speaking test counts for 30% of the whole GCSE Spanish so, each of the two speaking tasks is worth 15%.

2 When do the tasks have to be done?

There is no specified time for the completion of the tasks. When your teacher thinks that you have been taught the language you need and feels that you are ready, you will be given the task to prepare. It could be a task designed by the AQA Examination Board or a task designed by Spanish teachers in your school. Your teacher will decide how long you are allowed to prepare for the task (it cannot be more than six hours).

3 Who will mark my work?

Your teacher will mark your work. A Moderator (i.e. an examiner) will sample the work of your school and check that it has been marked correctly. A Team Leader will check the work of the Moderator. The Principal Moderator will check the work of the Team Leader. The Chief Examiner will check the work of the Principal Moderator. This complicated but secure system ensures that candidates are given the correct mark.

4 What am I allowed to write on my plan?

You are allowed to write a maximum of 40 words on your plan. Those words can be in Spanish or English. Choose them carefully so that your plan works well as an aide-mémoire. Remember that you are not allowed to use conjugated verbs (i.e. verbs with an ending other than the infinitive or the past participle) on your plan. Codes, letters or initialled words are not allowed.

5 What help is allowed from the moment I am given the task to prepare?

Your teacher is allowed to discuss the task in English with you, including the kind of language you may need and how to use your preparatory work. You can have access to a dictionary, your Spanish books and Internet resources. This is the stage when you will prepare your plan using the Task Planning Form. You will then give this form to your teacher who will give you feedback on how you have met the requirements of the task. When you actually perform the task, you will only have access to your plan and your teacher's comments (i.e. the Task Planning Form).

6 How can I prepare for the unpredictable element (the exclamation mark)?

Ask yourself: What question would logically follow the questions I have already answered? Practise guessing what the unpredictable bullet point might be about. You are likely to come up with two or three possibilities. Prepare answers to cover those possibilities. Practise your possible responses. When you are asked the question, focus on the meaning of the question itself to make sure you understand it and then give it your full answer.

7 How best can I practise for the test?

Treat each bullet point as a mini task. Practise your answer to one bullet point at a time. Say your answer aloud for what is illustrated by one word on your plan. Repeat the process for each word on your plan. Next, try to account for two words, then for three words, and so on. Time your answer for one whole bullet point. Repeat the process for each bullet point. Practise saying things aloud. Record yourself if possible.

8 Does it matter that my verbs are wrong as long as I can get myself understood?

Communication can break down because of poor grammatical accuracy. If that happens, you will lose marks in Communication and also in Accuracy. If you give the correct message but grammatical accuracy is poor, you will only lose marks in Accuracy. Communication is of primary importance, of course, but the quality of that communication matters too and is enhanced by grammatical accuracy.

9 How do I make sure I perform well in the Speaking test?

Make sure you:

- say a lot that is relevant to the question.
- have a good range of vocabulary.
- can include complex structures.
- can refer to present, past and future events.
- have a good Spanish accent.
- can speak fluently.
- can show initiative.
- can speak with grammatical accuracy.

10 How will my mark be affected if my Spanish accent is not very good?

You will receive a mark for Pronunciation. However, as long as your spoken Spanish is understandable, your Communication mark will not suffer.

11 What will I gain by giving long answers?

Consider the task as an opportunity for you to show off what you can do in Spanish. Offer long answers whenever possible, develop the points you are trying to make, give your opinion and justify that opinion as appropriate, etc. As a general rule, the more Spanish you speak, the more credit you will be given (provided that what you say is relevant and understandable).

12 What does speaking with fluency mean?

Fluency is your ability to speak without hesitation. Try and speak with fluency but not too fast. If you are likely to be nervous when performing the task, practise it and practise it again. Time your whole response. Make a point of slowing down if you feel that you are speaking too fast. Practise with your plan in front of you so that you know what you are going to say next and therefore do not hesitate when delivering your contribution to the dialogue.

13 What does showing initiative mean?

Showing initiative does not mean that you suddenly ask your teacher 'What about you, where did you go on holiday?' (although you could do that!). You are generally expected to answer questions. For instance, for a question like *¿Te gusta el fútbol?*, you would first answer it directly then try to develop your answer e.g. *Sí, me gusta el fútbol. A mí me gusta también la natación.*

Showing initiative means that you take the conversation elsewhere in a way that is connected to your answer and still relevant to the original question, e.g. *Normalmente los sábados jugamos al fútbol, pero a veces juego al baloncesto con mi hermano y sus amigos.* You were not asked about basketball. You decided to add it to your response. It is relevant, linked to what you were asked and follows your developed answer quite naturally. That is showing initiative. Use it to extend your answers and therefore show off extra knowledge of Spanish.

14 What about present, past and future events?

Make sure you use a variety of structures when you speak. In addition, try to include different time frames, reference to past and future events and a variety of verb tenses.

15 How many bullet points are there in each task?

There are typically between five and eight bullet points. One of the bullet points will be the unpredictable element and will appear on your task as an exclamation mark. All bullet points will be written in English.

16 Will I be asked questions which are not written in the task?

That is possible. Although you will have prepared the task thoroughly and will have a lot to say, your teacher may want you to expand or give further details on particular points you have made. **You must listen to your teacher's questions attentively as you will have to understand his / her questions in the first place.**

Frequently asked questions: Writing

This general guidance is in the form of answers to 'frequently asked questions' (FAQs).

1 How many writing tasks do I have to complete and what proportion of my Spanish GCSE is the writing test?

You have to complete two writing tasks. The tasks can be those provided by the AQA Examination Board, although your Spanish teachers have the option of devising their own tasks if they so wish. As in the Speaking, the two tasks count for 30% of your grade (15% for each writing task).

2 How much time do I have to complete the final version of a task?

You will be given 60 minutes to complete the final version of a task. It will be done under the direct supervision of your teacher. You will not be allowed to interact with others.

3 What resources will I be able to use on the day?

You can have access to a dictionary. You will also have the task itself, your plan and your teacher's feedback on your plan. These will be on the AQA Task Planning Form. That is all. You cannot use your exercise book, textbook or any drafts you may have written to help you practise.

4 What am I allowed to write on my plan?

Much the same as you are allowed in your plan for Speaking i.e. a maximum of 40 words, no conjugated verbs or codes. Your teacher will comment on your plan, using the AQA Task Planning Form. Make sure you take that information on board before you write the final version.

5 How many words am I expected to write for each task?

Students aiming at grades G–D should produce 200–350 words across the two tasks, i.e. 100–175 words per task.

Students aiming at grades C–A* should produce 400–600 words across the two tasks, i.e. 200–300 words per task.

6 Can I write a draft?

You may produce a draft but this is for your use only. Your teacher cannot comment on it and you cannot have access to any draft when you write the final version.

7 What do I have to do to perform well?

Make sure you:

- communicate a lot of relevant information clearly.
- can explain ideas and points of view.
- have a good range of vocabulary.
- can include complex structures.
- can write long sentences.
- can refer to past, present and future events.
- can write with grammatical accuracy.
- organise your ideas well.

You will have noticed that there are similarities between the ways Writing and Speaking are assessed. As most of the points above are discussed in the FAQs for Speaking, you are advised to read the answers again, before you embark on your first task.

8 When will I do the tasks?

When your teacher has taught you the necessary language for you to complete a task, you will be given the task to prepare. You may be asked to do a plan using the Task Planning Form. You will get some feedback on your plan from your teacher at that point on how you have met the requirements of the task. The final version will be done after that, under the direct supervision of your teacher.

9 Who will mark my work?

AQA Examiners will mark your work. A Team Leader will check the work of the Examiner. The Principal Examiner will check the work of the Team Leader. The Chief Examiner will check the work of the Principal Examiner – a complicated but secure system to ensure that candidates are given the correct mark for their work.

Mi vida

You are talking to your Spanish friend about your life at home.
He / She asks you the following:

1 Tell me about your house.
2 What are the facilities like for young people in your town?
3 What do you do in your free time?
4 Tell me what you did at school last week.
5 What do you think of work experience and why?
6 How are you going to spend your summer holidays?
7 !

! Remember, at this point, you will have to respond to something you have not yet prepared.
The dialogue will last between four and six minutes.

1 Tell me about your house.
- Talk about your house – its size, what rooms it has
- Describe the garden or what is around your house
- Give your opinion of your house
- Explain what your ideal house would be like

2 What are the facilities like for young people in your town?
- Describe your town
- Talk about what there is for young people
- Give your opinion of these facilities
- Explain what you would like to see in your town

3 What do you do in your free time?
- Say what you do in your free time
- Explain why you like to do those things
- Talk about what you did last week
- Mention other things that some of your friends do

4 Tell me what you did at school last week.
- Talk about your school day (start and finish times, etc.)
- Say how you got to school last week
- Mention some of the things you did – lessons, break, homework
- Give your opinion of the things you did

5 What do you think of work experience and why?
- Mention what you had to do or will have to do for work experience
- Say if you think it is a good idea or not
- Explain why you think that
- Talk about your ideal work experience

6 How are you going to spend your summer holidays?
- Say how you normally spend your summer holidays
- Talk about what you are going to do this year
- Mention what you think of these plans
- Explain the advantages and disadvantages of going abroad for your holidays

7 ! At this point, you will be asked another question which you don't know in advance. However, you can try to guess what it might be and prepare various options:
- What is there in your town for tourists?
  ¿Qué hay en tu ciudad para los turistas?
- What is your favourite type of film and why?
  ¿Qué tipo de película te gusta más y por qué?
- In general, do you like school and why (not)?
  En general, ¿te gusta el colegio? ¿Por qué (no)?
- What is your opinion of spending your summer holidays in your own country? Why?
  ¿Cuál es tu opinión de pasar las vacaciones de verano en tu propio país? ¿Por qué?

Now, compare your first draft with the online sample version – you might find some useful hints to make yours even better.

¡Los jóvenes no somos así!

You have seen a letter in a Spanish magazine from someone who is criticizing young people for being lazy and unconcerned about the well-being of others. You write a letter to the magazine to explain why this is not the case, by writing what you do.

You could write about the following things:

1. Your relationship with your family
2. How you helped at home last week
3. How you help the environment
4. What you do to maintain a healthy lifestyle
5. How you help other members of your community
6. Your part-time job
7. Your future plans

1 Your relationship with your family.
- Mention who the members of your family are
- Write what they are like
- Explain who you get on with best and why
- Mention why the relationship you have with your family is positive

2 How you helped at home last week.
- Write about what a good help you are at home
- Mention some things you did to help at home last week
- Explain how much this was appreciated by your family
- Say why you enjoyed doing the jobs

3 How you help the environment.
- Explain how important the environment is to you
- Write about what you do in the home to help the environment
- Mention other things that you do (walk to school, etc.)
- Explain what you think about young people who do nothing to help the environment

4 What you do to maintain a healthy lifestyle.
- Mention the healthy aspects of your diet
- Explain the positive effects of this diet
- Write about the physical exercise that you do
- Explain how this prevents you from becoming involved in anti-social activities

5 How you help other members of your community.
- Mention any people in your area who need help
- Explain why it is important to help these people
- Write about how you help them or how you intend to help them in the future
- Mention anything you do or have done for charity

6 Your part-time job.
- Write about where you work
- Mention the hours you work
- Explain how difficult the work is
- Write about the advantages of having a part-time job

7 Your future plans.
- Write about what you intend to do next year
- Explain how this is a good choice for you
- Mention the plans that your friends have
- Explain how this means that they aren't lazy

Now compare your first draft with the online sample version – you might find some useful hints to make yours even better.

G Gramática

Contents

Glossary of terms

Adjectives *los adjetivos*

Words that describe somebody or something:

pequeño	small
tímido	shy

Adverbs *los adverbios*

Words that complement (add meaning to) verbs, adjectives or other adverbs:

mal	badly
lentamente	slowly

Articles *los artículos*

Short words used to introduce nouns:

un / una	a, an
unos / unas	some, any
el / la / los / las	the

The infinitive *el infinitivo*

The verb form given in the dictionary:

ir	to go
tener	to have

Nouns *los nombres*

Words that identify a person, a place or a thing:

madre mother ***casa*** house

Prepositions *las preposiciones*

Words used in front of nouns to give information about when, how, where, etc.:

con	with
de	of, from
en	in

Pronouns *los pronombres*

Words used to replace nouns. For example, subject pronouns:

yo	I
tú	you
él	he
ella	she

Verbs *los verbos*

Words used to express an action or a state:

trabajo	I **work**
vive	he **lives**

A Nouns

Masculine and feminine nouns

All Spanish nouns are either masculine or feminine.

- In the singular, masculine nouns are introduced with *el* or *un*:

***el** padre*	**the** father
***un** libro*	**a** book

- Feminine singular nouns are introduced with *la* or *una*:

***la** madre*	**the** mother
***una** mesa*	**a** table

- Some nouns have two different forms, masculine and feminine:

un amigo	a male friend
una amiga	a female friend
un peluquero	a male hairdresser
una peluquera	a female hairdresser

- Some nouns stay the same for masculine and feminine:

el estudiante	the male student
la estudiante	the female student

Singular and plural forms

As in English, Spanish nouns can either be singular (one) or plural (more than one).

- Nouns ending in a vowel add *-s* for the plural.

*un perro > dos perro**s***	one dog > two dogs

- Nouns ending in a consonant add *-es* for the plural.

*un ordenador > dos ordenador**es***	one computer > two computers

- For nouns ending in *-z*, change the *z* to *c* and add *-es*:

*un lápiz > dos lápi**ces***	one pencil > two pencils

- If a noun ends in *-ión*, drop the accent and add *-es*:

*una invitación > dos invitaci**ones***	one invitation > two invitations

B Articles

Definite articles: *el, la, los, las* (the)

The word for 'the' depends on whether the noun it goes with is masculine, feminine, singular or plural.

masculine singular	feminine singular	masculine plural	feminine plural
el	*la*	*los*	*las*

***el** abuelo*	**the** grandfather
***la** fruta*	**the** fruit
***los** billetes*	**the** tickets
***las** palabras*	**the** words

Indefinite articles: *un, una, unos, unas* (a, an, some)

- The word for 'a / an' and 'some' also depends on whether the noun it goes with is masculine or feminine, singular or plural.

masculine singular	feminine singular	masculine plural	feminine plural
un	*una*	*unos*	*unas*

***un** autobús, **una** moto, **unos** coches*	**a** coach, **a** motorbike, (**some**) cars

- When talking about jobs, *un* and *una* are not used in Spanish where 'a' or 'an' is used in English.

Mi padre es electricista.	My father's an electrician.

The neuter article: *lo*

- Use *lo* with an adjective to mean 'the … thing.' The adjective after *lo* is always masculine and singular.

lo importante	the important thing

- Use it with an adjective + *es que*:

***Lo bueno es que** hay fruta fresca.*	The good thing is that there is fresh fruit.

- Use it with an adjective + *es* + an infinitive:

***Lo importante es comer** comida sana.*
The important thing is to eat healthy food.

C Adjectives

Feminine and masculine, singular and plural adjectives

In Spanish, adjectives have different endings depending on whether they describe masculine, feminine, singular or plural nouns:

– the masculine singular form usually ends in *-o*:

*El barco es blanc**o**.*	The boat is white.

– if the noun is feminine singular, the adjective will usually end in *-a*:

*Mi hermana es tímid**a**.*	My sister is shy.

– add *-s* to the masculine adjective if the noun is masculine plural:

*Los barcos son blanc**os**.*	The boats are white.

– add *-s* to the feminine adjective if the noun is feminine plural:

*Mis hermanas son tímid**as**.*	My sisters are shy.

– when an adjective describes a group of both masculine and feminine nouns, it has to be in the masculine plural form:

*Mis padres son alt**os**.*	My parents are tall.

- There are exceptions:

  – adjectives that already end in *-e* don't change in the feminine:

un chico inteligente	an intelligent boy
una chica inteligente	an intelligent girl

to form the plural, simply add an *-s*:

*unos chicos inteligente**s***	some intelligent boys
*unas chicas inteligente**s***	some intelligent girls

– adjectives that end in a consonant (except *r*) do not change in the feminine:

un bolígrafo azul	a blue pen
una regla azul	a blue ruler

to form the plural, add *-es*:

*unos bolígrafos azul**es***	some blue pens
*unas reglas azul**es***	some blue rulers

– adjectives of nationality often end in *-o* and follow the same rules as other adjectives ending in *-o*:

*un chico mexican**o***	a Mexican boy
*una chica mexican**a***	a Mexican girl
*unos chicos mexican**os***	some Mexican boys
*unas chicas mexican**as***	some Mexican girls

– for adjectives of nationality that end in a consonant, add *-a* for the feminine singular form, *-es* for the masculine plural form and *-as* for the feminine plural form:

un chico español	a Spanish boy
*una chica español**a***	a Spanish girl
*unos chicos español**es***	some Spanish boys
*unas chicas español**as***	some Spanish girls

– note that adjectives of nationality do not begin with a capital letter.

The position of adjectives

- Most adjectives follow the noun they describe:

una dieta sana	a healthy diet

- However, a few adjectives, such as *alguno, malo, ninguno, primero* and *tercero* come in front of the noun and lose their final *-o* when the following noun is masculine singular. Notice that an accent is sometimes needed the keep the stress on the correct syllable:

ningún dinero	no money
ninguna idea	no idea

Comparatives and superlatives

- To make comparisons, use:

  – *más ... que* — more ... than, ...er than

  *El alcohol es **más caro** en Inglaterra **que** en España.*
  Alcohol is **more expensive** in England **than** in Spain.

  – *menos ... que* — less... than

  *Mi hermano es **menos alto que** mi padre.*
  My brother is **less tall than** my father.

  – *tan* + adjective + *como* — as ... as

  *Los tomates son **tan sanos como** las naranjas.*
  Tomatoes are **as healthy as** oranges.

- For superlatives, use:

  – *el / la / los / las + más* — the most, the ...est

  *Esta casa es **la más vieja** de la región.*
  This house is **the oldest** in the area.

  – *el / la / los / las + menos* — the least

  *Este hotel es **el menos caro** de la región.*
  This hotel is **the least expensive** in the area.

- For 'as much ... as', use *tan* + adjective + *como*:

  *El alcohol es **tan peligroso como** el tabaco.*
  Alcohol is **as dangerous as** tobacco.

- For 'as many ... as', use *tantos(as)* + plural noun + *como*:

  *Las chicas practican **tantos** deportes **como** los chicos.*
  Girls take part in **as many** sports **as** boys.

- For 'better than', use *mejor que*:

  *Paga **mejor que** cultivar otros alimentos.*
  It pays **better than** growing other foods.

- For 'worse than', use *peor que*:

  *Te pagan **peor que** en la ciudad.*
  They pay **worse than** in the city.

- Note also two other irregular comparative adjectives:

  – *mayor* is a special comparative of *grande* used to refer to **older** brothers an d sisters

  – *menor* is a special comparative of *pequeño* used to refer to **younger** brothers and sisters

  Mi hermana ***mayor*** *es más tímida que mis hermanos* ***menores****.*
  My big sister is more shy than my little brothers.

Demonstrative adjectives: *este, esta, estos, estas; ese, esa, esos, esas; aquel, aquella, aquellos, aquellas* (this, that, these, those)

- Spanish has three groups of demonstrative adjectives: one group for 'this' and 'these' (*este, esta, estos, estas*), one for 'that' and 'those' (*ese, esa, esos, esas*), and one to indicate more distant things ('that / those over there' – *aquel, aquella, aquellos, aquellas*).

this		these	
este	*esta*	*estos*	*estas*
that (not very distant)		those (not very distant)	
ese	*esa*	*esos*	*esas*
that (more distant)		those (more distant)	
aquel	*aquella*	*aquellos*	*aquellas*

este *cine*	**this** cinema
esa *estrella*	**that** star
aquellas *películas*	**those** films

Indefinite adjectives: *cada, otro, todo, mismo, alguno*

- Although *cada* is an adjective, it never changes:

cada *sección*	each section
cada *resultado*	each result

- *Otro, todo* and *mismo* must agree with the noun they describe:

otra *ciudad*	**another** city
la ***misma*** *idea*	the **same** idea
todo *el mundo*	**all** the world (= everyone)
todas *las chicas*	**all** the girls
los ***mismos*** *libros*	*the* **same** books

- *Alguno* means 'some' and must agree with its noun. It drops the *-o* ending and gains an accent when it is placed before a masculine singular noun:

algunas *chicas*	**some** girls
algún *pan*	**some** bread
algunos *estudiantes*	**some** students

Relative adjective: *cuyo, cuya, cuyos, cuyas*

- *Cuyo* means 'whose' and agrees in number and gender with the noun that follows it.

  Ésta es Paulina ***cuya hermana*** *está casada desde hace seis meses.*
  This is Paulina **whose sister** has been married for six months.

Possessive adjectives, one 'owner'

mi / mis	my
tu / tus	your
su / sus	his / her / its

A possessive adjective must agree with the noun that follows it:

mi *padre*	**my** father
mi *madre*	**my** mother
mis *padres*	**my** parents
tu *padre*	**your** father
tu *madre*	**your** mother
tus *padres*	**your** parents
su *pie*	**his** / **her** / **its** foot
su *puerta*	**his** / **her** / **its** door
sus *ventanas*	**his** / **her** / **its** windows

Possessive adjectives, several 'owners'

nuestro / nuestra / nuestros / nuestras	our
vuestro / vuestra / vuestros / vuestras	your
su / sus	their

nuestro *padre*	**our** father
nuestra *madre*	**our** mother
nuestros *padres*	**our** parents
vuestro *padre*	**your** father
vuestra *madre*	**your** mother
vuestros *amigos*	**your** friends
su *hermano*	**their** brother
su *hermana*	**their** sister
sus *profesores*	**their** teachers

- Spanish doesn't have three different words for 'his', 'her' and 'its'. With a Spanish possessive adjective, what counts is whether the noun it describes is masculine, feminine, singular or plural. Like other adjectives, they agree with their noun.

- Possessive adjectives also have a 'long' form which is used just in certain expressions:

*hijo **mío***	my son
*Muy señora **mía***	Dear Madam (in a letter)

Interrogative adjectives: *qué, cuánto, cuántos, cuántas, cuál, cuáles*

- To ask 'what?', use *qué*:

¿Qué bebida quieres?	What drink would you like?

- To ask 'which?', use *cuál*. It must agree with the noun that follows it, but it does not change for the feminine, only for the plural:

¿Cuál coche prefieres?	Which car do you prefer?
¿Cuáles prefieres?	Which (ones) do you prefer?

- To ask 'how much?', use *cuánto*. It must agree with the noun that follows it: masculine / feminine, singular / plural.

*¿Cuánt**o** dinero tienes?*	How much money do you have?
*¿Cuánt**os** libros hay?*	How many books are there?
*¿Cuánt**as** hermanas tienes?*	How many sisters do you have?

- Remember that all interrogative adjectives must have an accent.

D Adverbs

Adverbs are used with a verb, an adjective or another adverb to express how, when, where, or to what extent something happens.

- Many Spanish adverbs are formed by adding *-mente* (the equivalent of '-ly' in English) to the feminine form of the adjective:

masculine adjective	feminine adjective	adverb
rápido	*rápida*	*rápidamente* – quickly

- Some common adverbs are completely irregular:

bien	well
*Habla **bien**.*	He / She speaks well.
mal	badly
*Come **mal**.*	He / She eats badly.

- As with adjectives, you can make some comparisons using *más / menos ... que*:

*Se puede comunicar **más fácilmente que** antes.*
It's possible to get in touch **more easily than** before.

*Como **menos rápidamente que** mi hermana.*
I eat **less quickly than** my sister.

- You can also use superlative adverbs. Use the definite article + *más* + adverb:

*El fútbol es **el** deporte que practico **más frecuentemente.***
Football is the sport I do **most often**.

Adverbs of time

hoy	today
mañana	tomorrow
ayer	yesterday
pasado mañana	the day after tomorrow
ahora	now
ya	already

Adverbs of frequency

a veces	sometimes
frecuentemente / a menudo	often
siempre	always
raramente	rarely, not very often

Adverbs of sequence

después	then, afterwards
luego	next
por último	finally

Adverbs of place

dentro de	inside
fuera de	outside
aquí	here
allí	(over) there
lejos	far

Quantifiers and intensifiers

- This group of adverbs (qualifying words) enables you to indicate intensity and quantity when you use an adjective or adverb:

bastante	enough
demasiado	too (much)
mucho	a lot
un poco	a little
muy	very

La gramática es ***un poco*** *complicada, pero es* ***bastante*** *interesante.*
Grammar is **a bit** complicated, but it's **quite** interesting.

Interrogative adverbs

Note that these words all have an accent when they are used as an interrogative.

¿cómo?	how?
¿cuándo?	when?
¿dónde?	where?

E Pronouns

Subject pronouns: *yo, tú, él, ella, usted, nosotros, vosotros, ellos, ellas, ustedes* (I, you, he, she, it, we, they)

In Spanish, subject pronouns are usually only used with the verb to emphasise who or what performs the action.

yo – I
tú – you
él – he / it
ella – she / it
usted – you (formal)

nosotros – we
vosotros – you
ellos – they (m)
ellas – they (f)
ustedes – you (formal pl)

Ella *es estudiante, pero* ***él*** *ha acabado de estudiar.*
She is a student, but **he** has finished studying.

- In Spanish there are two ways to translate 'you': *tú* (plural: *vosotros*) and *usted* (plural: *ustedes*).

  – Use *tú* when talking to someone (one person) of your own age or to someone in your family.

  – Use *vosotros* when talking to more than one person of your own age or to your relatives.

  – Use *usted* when talking to an adult not in your family (e.g. your teacher). *Usted* can be shortened to *Ud.* or *Vd.*

  – Use *ustedes* when talking to more than one adult not in your family. It can be shortened to *Uds.* or *Vds.*

Direct object pronouns: *me, te, lo / la, nos, os, los / las*

Direct object pronouns replace a noun that is not the subject of the verb.

singular	plural
me – me	*nos* – us
te – you	*os* – you
lo – him / it (masculine)	*los, las* – them
la – her / it (feminine)	

- These pronouns come in front of the verb, unlike in English:

  Los *compré en Barcelona.* I bought **them** in Barcelona.

Indirect object pronouns: *me, te, le, nos, os, les*

Indirect object pronouns are used to replace a noun which is not the direct object of the verb.

singular	plural
me – (to) me	*nos* – (to) us
te – (to) you	*os* – (to) you
le – (to) him / her / it	*les* – (to) them

Les *dio mil euros.* ***Le*** *escribieron para dar****le*** *las gracias.*
He gave **them** a thousand euros. They wrote **to him** to thank **him**.

- Note that when two pronouns are used together in the same sentence, the indirect object pronoun always comes before the direct object pronoun.

  Tengo un móvil. Mis padres ***me lo*** *regalaron por mi cumpleaños.*
  I have a mobile. My parents gave **it to me** for my birthday.

  me – indirect object pronoun, *lo* – direct object pronoun

Reflexive pronouns: *me, te, se, nos, os*

Reflexive pronouns are used in Spanish when the subject and object of the verb are the same. They come before the verb.

singular	plural
me – myself	*nos* – ourselves
te – yourself (informal)	*os* – yourselves (informal)
se – himself, herself, itself, yourself (formal)	*se* – themselves, yourselves (formal)

Me *lavo.* I am washing myself.

Disjunctive pronouns: *mí, ti, él, ella, usted, nosotros, vosotros, ellos, ellas, ustedes*

These are also called emphatic pronouns.

- Use them for emphasis:

  ***Para mí**, las vacaciones de invierno son las más divertidas.*
  For me, winter holidays are the most fun.

- Use them after a preposition:

  ***A mí**, no me gusta el pescado.* **Me**, I don't like fish.

- To say 'with me', 'with you (*tú*)' there is a special form:

conmigo	with me
contigo	with you
*Mi hermano viene **conmigo**.*	My brother is coming **with me**.

Possessive pronouns

A possessive pronoun is used to replace a possessive adjective and its noun.

*¿Ese es **su perro**? No, no es **el suyo**.*
Is that **their dog**? No, it isn't **theirs**.

masculine singular	feminine singular	masculine plural	feminine plural	
mío	*mía*	*míos*	*mías*	mine
tuyo	*tuya*	*tuyos*	*tuyas*	yours
suyo	*suya*	*suyos*	*suyas*	his / hers / its
nuestro	*nuestra*	*nuestros*	*nuestras*	ours
vuestro	*vuestra*	*vuestros*	*vuestras*	yours
suyo	*suya*	*suyos*	*suyas*	theirs

Use possessive pronouns with the definite article *el / la / los / las* and remember that they must agree with the noun they replace.

*Me gusta más la casa de Julia que la **mía**.*
I like Julia's house more than **mine**.

Relative pronouns: *que, quien, lo que*

Relative pronouns are used to link phrases together.

- *Que* is used as the subject of the relative clause. It can refer to people and things, and means 'who', 'that' or 'which':

  *el amigo **que** vive en Barcelona*
  the friend **who** lives in Barcelona

  – Remember that *que* is not optional. Although it is often not translated in English, you cannot leave it out in Spanish.

  *La película **que** veía era muy divertida.*
  The film **(that)** I was watching was very funny.

- *Quien* and its plural form *quienes* is only used to refer to people:

  *No sé **quién** dijo eso.*
  I don't know **who** said that.

- Use *lo que* to refer to a general idea:

  ***Lo que** me gusta de mi barrio es que hay un centro comercial.*
  What I like about my neighbourhood is that there is a shopping centre.

- The pronouns *el que, la que, los que, las que* (note the necessary agreement with singular, plural, masculine and feminine nouns) are used after prepositions, to refer to both people and things:

  *Mi hermana, **la que** es peluquera, vive en Madrid.*
  My sister, **the one who** is a hairdresser, lives in Madrid.

- *El cual, la cual, los cuales, las cuales* are relative pronouns that can be used in place of *el que, la que, los que* and *las que*. They are not used in everyday conversation and tend to be used more in formal written Spanish:

  *Me queda un poco de dinero, **el cual** no quiero gastar.*
  I have a little money left, **which** I don't want to spend.

Demonstrative pronouns: *éste, ésta, éstos, éstas; ése, ésa, ésos, ésas; aquél, aquélla, aquéllos, aquéllas*

- Demonstrative pronouns replace the noun, to avoid repeating it:

this one		these	
éste	*ésta*	*éstos*	*éstas*
that one		those	
ése	*ésa*	*ésos*	*ésas*
aquél	*aquélla*	*aquéllos*	*aquéllas*

*¿Te gusta **ese** vestido?*	Do you like **that** dress?
*Prefiero **ése**.*	I prefer **that one**.

- Each demonstrative pronoun also has a neuter form: *esto, eso* and *aquello*. These do not agree in number or gender with a noun because they represent an idea rather than a person or a thing:

  ***Eso** es cierto.* **That**'s true.

  *Martina es demasiado habladora. No me gusta **eso**.*
  Martina is too talkative. I don't like **that**.

Indefinite pronouns: *algo, alguien*

- The Spanish for 'something' is *algo*:

¿Quieres ***algo*** *de comer?*	Do you want **something** to eat?

- The Spanish for 'someone' is *alguien*:

Busco a ***alguien****.*	I'm looking for **someone**.

Interrogative pronouns: *cuál, cuáles; qué; quién, quiénes* (which one; what; who)

- As in English, interrogative pronouns usually come at the beginning of a sentence:

  *¿****Cuál*** *de estas preguntas es más difícil?*
  Which one of these questions is harder?

*¿****Cuáles*** *prefieres?*	**Which** ones do you prefer?
*¿****Qué*** *quieres?*	**What** do you want?
*¿****Quién*** *habla?*	**Who** is speaking?
*¿****Quiénes*** *son?*	**Who** are they?

However, if a preposition is used with the interrogative, it is the preposition which comes first:

*¿****Con quién*** *vas a la fiesta?*	**Who** are you going to the party **with**?
*¿****Por qué*** *estás triste?*	***Why*** *are you sad?*

F Verbs

- Spanish verbs have different endings depending on who is doing the action and whether the action takes place in the past, the present or the future. The verb tables on pages 190–193 set out the patterns of endings for some useful verbs.
- When using a name or a singular noun instead of a pronoun, use the same form of the verb as for *él / ella*:

Jamie ***habla*** *español.*	Jamie **speaks** Spanish.

- When using two names or a plural noun, use the same form of the verb as for *ellos / ellas*:

Laura y Javier ***viven*** *en Sevilla.*	Laura and Javier **live** in Seville.

- When referring to yourself and someone else, use the same form of the verb as for *nosotros*:

Laura y yo ***vamos*** *a Madrid.*	Laura and I **are going** to Madrid.

The infinitive

The infinitive is the form of the verb you find in a dictionary, e.g. *hablar, comer, vivir*. It never changes.

- When two verbs follow each other, the second one is always in the infinitive. That is what happens in the following sentences:

Me gusta dormir bien.	I like to sleep well.
Prefiero salir con mis amigos.	I prefer to go out with my friends.

  – *Ir a* + infinitive is a useful expression meaning 'to be going to do something' in the immediate future. The verb *ir* is conjugated, but the second verb will remain in the infinitive. The preposition *a* is always used:

  Voy a *visitar España.*
  I am going to visit Spain.

  – *Volver a* + infinitive means to do something again.

Volveré a leer *ese libro.*	**I will read** that book **again**.

  – *Acabar de* + infinitive means to have just done something very recently. Note that the preposition *de* is needed in this expression.

  Acabas de *invitar a muchos amigos.*
  You **have just** invited many friends.

G Verb tenses

The present indicative

- Use the present tense to describe:
  – something that is taking place now:

Como *una manzana.*	**I am eating** an apple.

  – something that happens regularly:

Voy *mucho al cine.*	**I go** to the cinema a lot.

- Verb endings change depending on who is doing the action:

Mi amigo ***habla*** *español.*	My friend **speaks** Spanish.
Hablamos *inglés.*	We **speak** English.

- Most verbs follow a regular pattern, as in the paradigms (lists) shown here. See the verb tables on pages 190–193 for irregular verb forms.

	-ar verbs	*-er* verbs	*-ir* verbs
	hablar – to speak	*comer* – to eat	*vivir* – to live
(yo)	*hablo*	*como*	*vivo*
(tú)	*hablas*	*comes*	*vives*
(él / ella)	*habla*	*come*	*vive*
(nosotros)	*hablamos*	*comemos*	*vivimos*
(vosotros)	*habláis*	*coméis*	*vivís*
(ellos / ellas)	*hablan*	*comen*	*viven*

Other *-ar* verbs:

aceptar	to accept
ganar	to win
invitar	to invite
tocar	to play

Other *-er* verbs:

deber	to owe
proteger	to protect

Other *-ir* verbs:

producir	to produce
salir	to go out

A few common verbs have an irregular first person in the present tense:

dar > *doy*

decir > *digo*

estar > *estoy*

hacer > *hago*

oír > *oigo*

poner > *pongo*

saber > *sé*

salir > *salgo*

ser > *soy*

tener > *tengo*

venir > *vengo*

Radical-changing verbs

- The biggest group of Spanish irregular verbs is called radical-changing, or stem-changing verbs.

The first part of the verb changes when stressed:

In one type, *u* changes to *ue*

jugar – to play

***jue**go*	*jugamos*
***jue**gas*	*jugáis*
***jue**ga*	***jue**gan*

In another type, *o* changes to *ue*

poder – to be able to

***pue**do*	*podemos*
***pue**des*	*podéis*
***pue**de*	***pue**den*

In another type, *e* changes to *ie*

preferir – to prefer

*pref**ie**ro*	*preferimos*
*pref**ie**res*	*preferís*
*pref**ie**re*	*pref**ie**ren*

The changes do not happen in the *nosotros* and *vosotros* parts of the verb, because the stress is not on the stem.

The gerund

- The gerund (or present participle) is formed by replacing the infinitive verb ending *-ar* with *-ando,* and the *-er and -ir* verb endings with *-iendo:*

  – *hablar* > *habl**ando***

Estoy hablando.	I am talking.

  – *comer* > *com**iendo***

¿Qué estás comiendo?	What are you eating?

  – *salir* > *sal**iendo***

Ana está saliendo.	Ana is going out.

- Some irregular gerunds are:

  dormir > *durmiendo*

  leer > *leyendo*

  oír > *oyendo*

  preferir > *prefiriendo*

  sentir > *sintiendo*

  vestir > *vistiendo*

  Note that where in English we often use the gerund of a verb in sentences like:
  I love swimming. My brother prefers going on bike rides.
  Spanish uses the infinitive.
  *Me gusta **nadar**. Mi hermano prefiere **dar** paseos en bici.*

The present continuous

- The present continuous tense is the Spanish equivalent of the English form 'I am …ing, you are …ing' etc. It indicates something that is happening at the time of speaking. It is formed by adding the gerund to the present tense of *estar*:

*¿Qué **estás leyendo**?*	What **are you reading**?

  ***Estoy leyendo** un libro estupendo.*
  I'm reading a fantastic book.

The preterite

- Use the preterite tense to talk about a single, completed event in the past.

  *Por la tarde **recibí** un mensaje de mi amiga.*
  In the afternoon **I got** a message from my friend.

- Regular verbs:

  – To form the preterite tense, remove the infinitive endings, *-ar*, *-er* or *-ir* to leave the stem, then add the following endings:

	-ar verbs	*-er* verbs	*-ir* verbs
	hablar – to speak	*comer* – to eat	*vivir* – to live
(yo)	*hablé*	*comí*	*viví*
(tú)	*hablaste*	*comiste*	*viviste*
(él / ella)	*habló*	*comió*	*vivió*
(nosotros)	*hablamos*	*comimos*	*vivimos*
(vosotros)	*hablasteis*	*comisteis*	*vivisteis*
(ellos / ellas)	*hablaron*	*comieron*	*vivieron*

Note that the endings for *-er* and *-ir* verbs are the same.

– Some regular verbs have spelling changes in the first person in the preterite tense. These changes are there in order to keep the consonant sounds the same:

empezar	to begin
empecé	I began
jugar	to play
jugué	I played
sacar	to take
saqué	I took out
tocar	to play (instrument)
toqué	I played

- Irregular verbs:

  – Some common Spanish verbs are irregular in the preterite tense: *ser* and *estar, hacer, ir, poner, tener* and *ver*. The verb tables on pages 190–193 set out the patterns for these. The verbs *ser* (to be) and *ir* (to go) are the same in the preterite and you have to use the context to work out which verb is being used:

fui	I was / went
fuiste	you were / went
fue	he, she, it, you was / were / went
fuimos	we were / went
fuisteis	you were / went
fueron	they, you were /went

Por la mañana ***fuimos*** *al partido.*
We went to the match in the morning.

El ambiente en el estadio ***fue*** *fantástico.*
The atmosphere in the stadium **was** fantastic.

The perfect

- Use the perfect tense to say what you **have** done recently:

  He comprado *un móvil.* **I've bought** a mobile phone.

- The perfect tense is formed with the present tense of *haber* (to have) plus the past participle:

  – *haber* to have

  he
  has
  ha
  hemos
  habéis
  han

  – to form the past participle add *-ado* to the stem of *-ar* verbs and *-ido* to the stem of *-er* and *-ir* verbs.

hablar	to speak	> *hablado*	spoken
comer	to eat	> *comido*	eaten
vivir	to live	> *vivido*	lived

Este marzo ***he ido*** *a Valencia a ver la fiesta.*
This March **I went** to Valencia to see the fiesta.

– some Spanish verbs have irregular past participles. Here are some common ones:

decir	to say	> *dicho*	said
hacer	to make	> *hecho*	made
volver	to come back	> *vuelto*	came back
poner	to put	> *puesto*	put
ver	to see	> *visto*	saw / seen

Ya hemos visto esta película. We have already seen this film.

The imperfect

- Use the imperfect tense:

  – to describe what something or someone was like in the past:

  Cuando ***era*** *pequeño las fiestas de Navidad* ***eran*** *las mejores del año.*
  When **I was** young, the Christmas festivities **were** the best of the year.

  – to say what was happening at a certain time in the past:

  Trabajaba *entonces en Madrid.*
  At that time **I was working** in Madrid.

  – to describe something that used to happen regularly in the past:

Iba al cine todos los sábados.
I used to go to the cinema every Saturday.

- To form the imperfect tense of regular verbs, add the following endings to the stem of the verb:

	-ar verbs	*-er* verbs	*-ir* verbs
	hablar – to speak	*comer* – to eat	*vivir* – to live
(yo)	*hablaba*	*comía*	*vivía*
(tú)	*hablabas*	*comías*	*vivías*
(él / ella)	*hablaba*	*comía*	*vivía*
(nosotros)	*hablábamos*	*comíamos*	*vivíamos*
(vosotros)	*hablabais*	*comíais*	*vivíais*
(ellos / ellas)	*hablaban*	*comían*	*vivían*

Para los cumpleaños siempre ***preparábamos*** *una cena especial.*
We always **used to prepare** a special meal for birthdays.

- Three common Spanish verbs are irregular in the imperfect tense: *ser, ir* and *ver*:

	ser – to be	*ir* – to go	*ver* – to see
(yo)	*era*	*iba*	*veía*
(tú)	*eras*	*ibas*	*veías*
(él / ella)	*era*	*iba*	*veía*
(nosotros)	*éramos*	*íbamos*	*veíamos*
(vosotros)	*erais*	*ibais*	*veíais*
(ellos / ellas)	*eran*	*iban*	*veían*

Después de la cena ***íbamos*** *a la iglesia a celebrar le Misa de Gallo a medianoche.*
After the meal we **used to go** to church to celebrate Midnight Mass.

- You need the imperfect tense of *hacer* and *estar* to describe the weather in the past:

No ***hacía*** *frío pero* ***estaba*** *nublado.*
It **was**n't cold but it **was** cloudy.

The imperfect continuous

- The imperfect continuous tense is used to describe an ongoing action more vividly. It is formed using the imperfect of *estar* and the gerund:

Estaba comiendo *cuando llegó mi hermano.*
I was eating when my brother arrived.

Preterite or imperfect?

- To help you decide between the preterite and the imperfect:

– remember that the following time expressions describe a single, completed action and should be used with the preterite:

ayer	yesterday
el otro día	the other day
la semana pasada	last week
hace tres años	three years ago

– these time expressions indicate a repeated action and are used with the imperfect:

siempre	always
frecuentemente	frequently
a veces	sometimes
todos los días	every day

The pluperfect

- This tense is used to refer to something further back in the past than the perfect or the imperfect, to say what someone had done or had been doing. You use the imperfect tense of *haber* and the past participle:

Ya ***habíamos visto*** *aquella película.*
We had already **seen** that film.

The immediate future

- Use the present tense of *ir* + *a* followed by an infinitive to say what you are going to do or what is going to happen:

Hasta los 65 años ***voy a continuar*** *trabajando.*
I'm going to carry on working until the age of 65.

The future

- The future tense expresses what will happen or will be happening in the future:

Si no reducimos las emisiones de CO_2*, la situación* ***será*** *irreversible.*
If we don't reduce carbon emissions, the situation **will be** irreversible.

Las especies en peligro de extinción ***desaparecerán*** *por completo.*
Endangered species **will disappear** completely.

- To form the future tense, add the correct ending to the infinitive of the verb:

	-ar verbs	*-er* verbs	*-ir* verbs
	hablar – to speak	*comer* – to eat	*vivir* – to live
(yo)	*hablaré*	*comeré*	*viviré*
(tú)	*hablarás*	*comerás*	*vivirás*
(él / ella)	*hablará*	*comerá*	*vivirá*
(nosotros)	*hablaremos*	*comeremos*	*viviremos*
(vosotros)	*hablaréis*	*comeréis*	*viviréis*
(ellos / ellas)	*hablarán*	*comerán*	*vivirán*

- A few verbs have an irregular stem in the future (see the verb tables on pages 190–193), but all have the same future endings:

hacer – to do	*haré, harás, hará, haremos, haréis, harán*
poder – to be able	*podré*, etc.
poner – to put	*pondré*, etc.
tener – to have	*tendré, tendrás, tendrá, tendremos, tendréis, tendrán*
haber (hay) there is / are	*habrá*

The conditional

- You use the conditional in Spanish when 'would' is used in English:

  ***Me gustaría** ir a Perú.* — **I would like** to go to Peru.

  ***Sería** una oportunidad fantástica.*
  It would be a fantastic opportunity.

- The conditional has the same stem as the future tense and the same endings as the imperfect tense of *-er* and *-ir* verbs:

	-ar verbs	*-er* verbs	*-ir* verbs
	hablar – to speak	*comer* – to eat	*vivir* – to live
(yo)	*hablaría*	*comería*	*viviría*
(tú)	*hablarías*	*comerías*	*vivirías*
(él / ella)	*hablaría*	*comería*	*viviría*
(nosotros)	*hablaríamos*	*comeríamos*	*viviríamos*
(vosotros)	*hablaríais*	*comeríais*	*viviríais*
(ellos / ellas)	*hablarían*	*comerían*	*vivirían*

As the conditional tense uses the same stem as the future tense, the irregular stems are exactly the same as the future tense irregulars.

The imperative

- Use the imperative to give advice or instructions. Commands are either positive (**do** something) or negative (**don't** do something). They are also either informal (*tú / vosotros)* or formal (*usted / ustedes)*.
- To form positive commands:

  – For *tú*, simply use the *tú* form of the verb, but without the final *-s*:

  ***Come** muchas frutas.* — **Eat** a lot of fruit.
  ***Compra** aquel vestido.* — **Buy** that dress.

  – For the *vosotros* form, remove the *-r* from the end of the infinitive and replace it with *-d*:

  ***Escuchad** con atención.* — **Listen** carefully.
  ***Escribid** la carta.* — **Write** the letter.

  – *Usted* and *ustedes* use the third person of the present subjunctive:

  ***Hable** inglés.* — **Speak** English.
  ***Coman** las patatas fritas.* — **Eat** the chips.

- To form negative commands, always use the negative word plus the present subjunctive:

	tú	*vosotros*	*usted*	*ustedes*
hablar	*no hables*	*no habléis*	*no hable*	*no hablen*
comer	*no comas*	*no comáis*	*no coma*	*no coman*
vivir	*no vivas*	*no viváis*	*no viva*	*no vivan*

***No escuches** a Nuria.* — **Don't listen** to Nuria.

The subjunctive

- The subjunctive is a form of the verb that is used when there is an element of wishing or doubt. It is used in certain set expressions of surprise or exclamation:

  ¡Viva la Reina! — Long live the Queen!
  ¡Que aproveche! — Cheers!

- Some verbal expressions are followed by the subjunctive:

  – wishes, advice and requests such as *querer que, pedir que, decir que*

  *Mi madre no quiere que **salga** con eso chico.*
  My mother doesn't want me to **go out** with that boy.

  – emotional reactions: joy, hope, sorrow, anger, fear such as *me gusta que, lo siento que*:

  *Tengo miedo que me **estén buscando**.*
  I'm afraid that they **are looking for** me.

– doubt, uncertainty, possibility such as *es posible que, es probable que, no es cierto que*:

No es posible que ***vengan*** *ahora.*
It's not possible that **they will come** now.

– expressions of purpose: *para que, a menos que, a condición que*:

Te prestaré dinero para que ***puedas*** *ir de vacaciones.*
I'll lend you some money so **you can** go on holiday.

– conjunctions of time - *cuando, hasta que* – when they refer to the future:

Cuando ***vengáis*** *vamos a hacer la fiesta.*
When **you come** we'll have a party.

- To form the present subjunctive, take the *yo* form of the present tense of the verb and replace the *-o* ending with the following endings:

	-ar verbs	*-er* verbs	*-ir* verbs
	hablar -- to speak	*comer* – to eat	*vivir* – to live
(yo)	*hable*	*coma*	*viva*
(tú)	*hables*	*comas*	*vivas*
(él / ella)	*hable*	*coma*	*viva*
(nosotros)	*hablemos*	*comamos*	*vivamos*
(vosotros)	*habléis*	*comáis*	*viváis*
(ellos / ellas)	*hablen*	*coman*	*vivan*

- The imperfect subjunctive is used in the same expressions as the present subjunctive, but in past tense sentences. It has two forms: one ending in *-ra* and one ending in *-se*. Either can be used, but the *-ra* form is more common than the *-se* form. The stem is always taken from the third person singular of the preterite form:

hablar		*comer*		*vivir*	
-ra form	*-se* form	*-ra* form	*-se* form	*-ra* form	*-se* form
hablara	*hablase*	*comiera*	*comiese*	*viviera*	*viviese*
hablaras	*hablases*	*comieras*	*comieses*	*vivieras*	*vivieses*
hablara	*hablase*	*comiera*	*comiese*	*viviera*	*viviese*
habláramos	*hablásemos*	*comiéramos*	*comiésemos*	*viviéramos*	*viviésemos*
hablarais	*hablaseis*	*comierais*	*comieseis*	*vivierais*	*vivieseis*
hablaran	*hablasen*	*comieran*	*comiesen*	*vivieran*	*viviesen*

- The imperfect subjunctive form of *querer* (*quisiera*) is used to say what someone would like:

Quisiera *llamar a su amigo.* **He'd like** to call his friend.
Quisiera *un café.* **I'd like** a coffee.

H Reflexive verbs

- Reflexive verbs have a reflexive pronoun in front of the verb:

(yo)	***me*** *quejo*	**I** complain
(tú)	***te*** *quejas*	**you** complain
(él / ella)	***se*** *queja*	**he** / **she** complains
(usted)	***se*** *queja*	**you** (formal) complain
(nosotros)	***nos*** *quejamos*	**we** complain
(vosotros)	***os*** *quejáis*	**you** complain
(ellos / ellas)	***se*** *quejan*	**they** complain
(ustedes)	***se*** *quejan*	**you** (formal plural) complain

- Common impersonal expressions using reflexive phrases are:

– *se puede* + infinitive you can

Se puede *cambiar las actitudes racistas.*
You can change racist attitudes.

– *se debe* + infinitive you must

Se debe *leer más para comprender mejor la situación.*
You must read more in order to understand the situation better.

– *se habla de* + noun people talk about

Se habla de *la violencia.*
People talk about violence.

Se habla *español.* Spanish **spoken.**

– *se necesita* + noun … is needed

Se necesita *un programa de acción.*
An action programme **is needed**.

– *se dice que*	it is said that

Se dice que *hay mucho racismo contra los inmigrantes.*
It is said that there is a lot of racism towards immigrants.

I Negatives

- To make a sentence negative, you normally put *no* before the verb:

No tengo dinero.	I haven't any money.

- Other common negative expressions: *nunca, nadie, nada, ni … ni*; never, no one, nothing, neither … nor.

There are two ways of using *nunca, nadie, nada*. They can go at the start of the sentence or *no* can go before the verb with *nunca, nadie, nada* after the verb.

– *nunca / jamás*	never

No voy nunca a Madrid. / Nunca voy a Madrid.
I never go to Madrid.

– *nadie*	no one

No habla nadie. / Nadie habla.
No one talks.

– *nada*	nothing

No me preocupa nada. / Nada me preocupa.
I am not worried about anything.

– *ni …ni*	neither … nor

No soy ni guapo ni feo.
I'm neither good-looking nor ugly.

– *no ningún(o/a)*	no / not any

No tengo ningún problema.
I don't have a problem.

J Questions (Interrogatives)

- Forming questions in Spanish is easy. You can turn statements into questions by adding an inverted question mark at the beginning and a question mark at the end:

Nati habla español.	Nati speaks Spanish.
¿Nati habla español?	**Does** Nati speak Spanish?

- These are common question words – note that they all have an accent:

¿Adónde?	Where (to)?
¿Dónde?	Where?
¿Cómo?	How?
¿Cuál(es)?	What? (Which?)
¿Cuándo?	When?
¿Cuánto?	How much?
¿Qué?	What?
¿Quién(es)?	Who?
¿Por qué?	Why?

K The passive

- The passive is used to say what is done to someone or something. It is formed from *ser* and a past participle:

active form:	*Los habitantes construyeron el castillo.* The inhabitants built the castle.
passive form:	*El castillo* ***fue construido****.* The castle **was built**.

- The passive is quite rare in Spanish – it is very formal. To avoid using the passive, Spanish speakers often use the pronoun *se* and the third person of the verb:

Se venden *caramelos aquí.*	Sweets **are sold** here.

L Impersonal verbs

- The most common impersonal verbs in Spanish are *gustar* (to like) and *encantar* (to love).

  Me gusta esta isla.

This sentence means 'I like this island.' Its literal translation, however, is 'This island pleases me.'

Note that you need to include the indirect object pronoun to show who is doing the liking:

*¿**Te** gusta esta isla? Sí, **me** encanta.*
Do **you** like this island? Yes, **I** love it.

M Verbs + infinitive constructions

- There are many common verbs in Spanish that can be used with a second verb which appears in the infinitive. For example:
  Quiero pasar el verano en España.
  I want to spend the summer in Spain.

The following are ones you are most likely to use: *poder* (to be able to), *querer* (to want to), *soler* (to 'usually' do something), *necesitar* (to need), *deber* and *tener que* (both mean 'to have to').

N Expressions with *tener*

- *Tener* is a useful verb in Spanish. As well as its basic meaning 'to have', it is used in a range of expressions:

tener que	to have to

tener sed / hambre / sueño / miedo / frío / calor / suerte
to be thirsty / hungry / tired / afraid / cold / hot / lucky

tener prisa	to be in a hurry
tener éxito	to be successful

O Uses of *ser* and *estar*

- *Ser* and *estar* both mean 'to be'.

  – *Ser* describes who someone is, or what something is.

***Es** mi hermana.*	She **is** my sister.
***Es** una revista.*	It **is** a magazine.

It describes something that is unlikely to change.

*Madrid **es** grande.*	Madrid **is** big.
*Mi madre **es** habladora.*	My mother **is** chatty.

– *Estar* describes the location of someone or something.

*Mis padres **están** en Barcelona.*
My parents **are** in Barcelona.

It is used with the past participle to describe a condition that might change. In such expressions the past participle works like an adjective, agreeing with its noun.

***Estamos** preocupad**os**.*	**We are** worried.

P Prepositions

- Prepositions of place, with *estar*

  Because *estar* is the verb for 'to be' when you want to state where something is, the following prepositions are often seen after *estar.*

arriba	upstairs, above
debajo de	under
delante de	in front of
detrás de	behind
encima de	on top of
enfrente de	opposite
a la derecha de	to the right of
a la izquierda de	to the left of
al lado de	next to

personal *a*

- When the object of a verb is a person, you need to include personal *a* before that person:

*Vi **a** María en el cine.*	I saw Maria in the cinema.

por, para

- *Por* and *para* both mean 'for'.

  – *Por* means 'per', 'because of', 'through', 'along':

*30 kilómetros **por** hora*	30 kilometres **per** hour
***por** exceso de ruido*	**because of** too much noise
***por** el parque, **por** el camino*	**through** the park, **along** the road

– *Para* means 'in order to', 'for the purpose of', 'intended for':

***para** reducir la contaminación*
to reduce pollution

*Esta carta es **para** ti.*	This letter is **for** you.

Q Expressions of time

desde hace and *desde hacía*

- To say how long you **have been doing** something which you are still doing, use the present tense with *desde hace*:

  *Vivo en Madrid **desde hace** diez años.*
  I have been living in Madrid **for** ten years.

- To say how long you **had** been doing something in the past, use the imperfect tense with *desde hacía*:

  *Vivía en Madrid **desde hacía** ocho años.*
  I had been living in Madrid **for** eight years.

R Conjunctions

The following words are used to link parts of sentences together:

y	and	*María **y** su hermana*	Maria **and** her sister
pero	but	*Hace frío **pero** no me importa.*	It's cold **but** I don't mind.
o	or	*el veinte de agosto **o** el seis de junio*	the 20th August **or** the 6th June
porque	because	*Estoy viendo la tele **porque** está nevando.*	I'm watching television **because** it's snowing.
como	as	***Como** soy atleta, bebo mucha agua.*	**As** I'm an athlete, I drink a lot of water.
cuando	when	*Empecé a ir a la escuela primaria **cuando** tenía seis años.*	I started primary school **when** I was six years old.

S Numbers, dates and time

1	*uno*	11	*once*	21	*veintiuno*
2	*dos*	12	*doce*	22	*veintidós*
3	*tres*	13	*trece*	23	*veintitrés*
4	*cuatro*	14	*catorce*	24	*veinticuatro*
5	*cinco*	15	*quince*	25	*veinticinco*
6	*seis*	16	*dieciséis*	26	*veintiséis*
7	*siete*	17	*diecisiete*	27	*veintisiete*
8	*ocho*	18	*dieciocho*	28	*veintiocho*
9	*nueve*	19	*diecinueve*	29	*veintinueve*
10	*diez*	20	*veinte*	30	*treinta*

31	*treinta y uno*	82	*ochenta y dos*
32	*treinta y dos*	90	*noventa*
40	*cuarenta*	91	*noventa y uno*
41	*cuarenta y uno*	92	*noventa y dos*
50	*cincuenta*	100	*cien*
51	*cincuenta y uno*	101	*ciento uno*
52	*cincuenta y dos*	102	*ciento dos*
60	*sesenta*	200	*doscientos*
61	*sesenta y uno*	201	*doscientos uno*
62	*sesenta y dos*	300	*trescientos*
70	*setenta*	301	*trescientos uno*
71	*setenta y uno*	1000	*mil*
72	*setenta y dos*	1001	*mil uno*
80	*ochenta*	1002	*mil dos*
81	*ochenta y uno*	2000	*dos mil*

Ordinal numbers: *primero, segundo*, etc.

- The Spanish for 'first' is *primero* in the masculine and *primera* in the feminine:

  – use *primer* before a masculine singular noun:

  *mi **primer** niño* — my **first** child
- To say 'second', 'third', etc:

segundo	second
tercero	third
cuarto	fourth
quinto	fifth
sexto	sixth
séptimo	seventh
octavo	eighth
noveno	ninth
décimo	tenth

Days and dates

lunes	Monday
martes	Tuesday
miércoles	Wednesday
jueves	Thursday
viernes	Friday
sábado	Saturday
domingo	Sunday

enero	January
febrero	February
marzo	March
abril	April
mayo	May
junio	June
julio	July
agosto	August
septiembre	September
octubre	October
noviembre	November
diciembre	December

- Use normal numbers for dates:

  *Mi cumpleaños es **el 27 de diciembre.***
  My birthday is **on the 27th of December**.

  But *el primero* can be used, as well as *el uno* for 'the 1st': *El primero de mayo tenemos una fiesta.*
  On the 1st of May we have a party.
- Days of the week and months do not start with a capital letter in Spanish (unless they are at the beginning of a sentence):

  *El cumpleaños de mi madre es el 13 de **abril.***
  My mother's birthday is on the 13th of **April**.
- Use *el + lunes / martes*, etc. to say '**on** Monday / Tuesday', etc.:

  ***El domingo** un amigo me regaló dos entradas para un partido entre Villareal y Valencia.*

  On Sunday a friend gave me two tickets for the match between Villareal and Valencia.
- Use *los + lunes / martes*, etc. to say '**on** Monday**s** / Tuesday**s**' etc.:

  *Normalmente **los sábados** voy a una clase de música.*

  On Saturdays I normally go to a music lesson.

Time

- The 12-hour clock goes as follows:

Es la una.	It's one o'clock.
Son las dos.	It's two o'clock.
Es la una y cinco.	It's five past one.
Son las dos y diez.	It's ten past two.
Son las dos y cuarto.	It's a quarter past two.
Son las dos y media.	It's half past two.
Son las tres menos veinte.	It's twenty to three.
Son las tres menos cuarto.	It's a quarter to three.
A mediodía.	At midday.
A medianoche.	At midnight.

- As in English, when using the 24-hour clock, use numbers such as *trece*, *dieciocho,* etc:

a las ***veinte*** *diez*	at 20.10

- To ask the time:

¿Qué hora es?	What time is it? / What's the time?

Verb tables

Regular *-ar* verbs

infinitive	present	preterite	imperfect	future
hablar **to speak**	*hablo*	*hablé*	*hablaba*	*hablaré*
	hablas	*hablaste*	*hablabas*	*hablarás*
	habla	*habló*	*hablaba*	*hablará*
	hablamos	*hablamos*	*hablábamos*	*hablaremos*
	habláis	*hablasteis*	*hablabais*	*hablaréis*
	hablan	*hablaron*	*hablaban*	*hablarán*

Regular *-er* verbs

comer **to eat**	*como*	*comí*	*comía*	*comeré*
	comes	*comiste*	*comías*	*comerás*
	come	*comió*	*comía*	*comerá*
	comemos	*comimos*	*comíamos*	*comeremos*
	coméis	*comisteis*	*comíais*	*comeréis*
	comen	*comieron*	*comían*	*comerán*

Regular *-ir* verbs

vivir **to live**	*vivo*	*viví*	*vivía*	*viviré*
	vives	*viviste*	*vivías*	*vivirás*
	vive	*vivió*	*vivía*	*vivirá*
	vivimos	*vivimos*	*vivíaimos*	*viviremos*
	vivís	*vivisteis*	*vivíais*	*viviréis*
	viven	*vivieron*	*vivían*	*vivirán*

Irregular verbs

infinitive	present	preterite	imperfect	future
dar **to give**	*doy*	*di*	*daba*	*daré*
	das	*diste*	*dabas*	*darás*
	da	*dio*	*daba*	*dará*
	damos	*dimos*	*dábamos*	*daremos*
	dais	*disteis*	*dabais*	*daréis*
	dan	*dieron*	*daban*	*darán*
decir **to say**	*digo*	*dije*	*decía*	*diré*
	dices	*dijiste*	*decías*	*dirás*
	dice	*dijo*	*decía*	*dirá*
	decimos	*dijimos*	*decíamos*	*diremos*
	decís	*dijisteis*	*decíais*	*diréis*
	dicen	*dijeron*	*decían*	*dirán*
estar **to be**	*estoy*	*estuve*	*estaba*	*estaré*
	estás	*estuviste*	*estabas*	*estarás*
	está	*estuvo*	*estaba*	*estará*
	estamos	*estuvimos*	*estábamos*	*estaremos*
	estáis	*estuvisteis*	*estabais*	*estaréis*
	están	*estuvieron*	*estaban*	*estarán*
haber **to have**	*he*	*hube*	*había*	*habré*
	has	*hubiste*	*habías*	*habrás*
	ha	*hubo*	*había*	*habrá*
	hemos	*hubimos*	*habíamos*	*habremos*
	habéis	*hubisteis*	*habíais*	*habréis*
	han	*hubieron*	*habían*	*habrán*
hacer **to make**	*hago*	*hice*	*hacía*	*haré*
	haces	*hiciste*	*hacías*	*harás*
	hace	*hizo*	*hacía*	*hará*
	hacemos	*hicimos*	*hacíamos*	*haremos*
	hacéis	*hicisteis*	*hacíais*	*haréis*
	hacen	*hicieron*	*hacían*	*harán*

infinitive	present	preterite	imperfect	future
ir to go	*voy* *vas* *va* *vamos* *vais* *van*	*fui* *fuiste* *fue* *fuimos* *fuisteis* *fueron*	*iba* *ibas* *iba* *íbamos* *ibais* *iban*	*iré* *irás* *irá* *iremos* *iréis* *irán*
jugar to play	*juego* *juegas* *juega* *jugamos* *jugáis* *juegan*	*jugué* *jugaste* *jugó* *jugamos* *jugasteis* *jugaron*	*jugaba* *jugabas* *jugaba* *jugábamos* *jugabais* *jugaban*	*jugaré* *jugarás* *jugará* *jugaremos* *jugaréis* *jugarán*
poder to be able to	*puedo* *puedes* *puede* *podemos* *podéis* *pueden*	*pude* *pudiste* *pudo* *pudimos* *pudisteis* *pudieron*	*podía* *podías* *podía* *podíamos* *podíais* *podían*	*podré* *podrás* *podrá* *podremos* *podréis* *podrán*
poner to put	*pongo* *pones* *pone* *ponemos* *ponéis* *ponen*	*puse* *pusiste* *puso* *pusimos* *pusisteis* *pusieron*	*ponía* *ponías* *ponía* *poníamos* *poníais* *ponían*	*pondré* *pondrás* *pondrá* *pondremos* *pondréis* *pondrán*
querer to want	*quiero* *quieres* *quiere* *queremos* *queréis* *quieren*	*quise* *quisiste* *quiso* *quisimos* *quisisteis* *quisieron*	*quería* *querías* *quería* *queríamos* *queríais* *querían*	*querré* *querrás* *querrá* *querremos* *querréis* *querrán*

infinitive	present	preterite	imperfect	future
saber **to know**	*sé*	*supe*	*sabía*	*sabré*
	sabes	*supiste*	*sabías*	*sabrás*
	sabe	*supo*	*sabía*	*sabrá*
	sabemos	*supimos*	*sabíamos*	*sabremos*
	sabéis	*supisteis*	*sabíais*	*sabréis*
	saben	*supieron*	*sabían*	*sabrán*
ser **to be**	*soy*	*fui*	*era*	*seré*
	eres	*fuiste*	*eras*	*serás*
	es	*fue*	*era*	*será*
	somos	*fuimos*	*éramos*	*seremos*
	sois	*fuisteis*	*erais*	*seréis*
	son	*fueron*	*eran*	*serán*
tener **to have**	*tengo*	*tuve*	*tenía*	*tendré*
	tienes	*tuviste*	*tenías*	*tendrás*
	tiene	*tuvo*	*tenía*	*tendrá*
	tenemos	*tuvimos*	*teníamos*	*tendremos*
	tenéis	*tuvisteis*	*teníais*	*tendréis*
	tienen	*tuvieron*	*tenían*	*tendrán*
venir **to come**	*vengo*	*vine*	*venía*	*vendré*
	vienes	*viniste*	*venías*	*vendrás*
	viene	*vino*	*venía*	*vendrá*
	venimos	*vinimos*	*veníamos*	*vendremos*
	venís	*vinisteis*	*veníais*	*vendréis*
	vienen	*vinieron*	*venían*	*vendrán*
ver **to see**	*veo*	*vi*	*veía*	*veré*
	ves	*viste*	*veías*	*verás*
	ve	*vio*	*veía*	*verá*
	vemos	*vimos*	*veíamos*	*veremos*
	veis	*visteis*	*veíais*	*veréis*
	ven	*vieron*	*veían*	*verá*

Spanish pronunciation

It is not hard to produce the correct sounds for a good Spanish accent.

The most important thing to remember is that all Spanish vowels are short:

a	as in *casa*	*o*	as in *como*
e	as in *tengo*	*u*	as in ***su***
i	as in ***si***		

Then there are some patterns of letters which make these sounds:

ca *co* *cu*	hard 'c' (before 'a', 'o' or 'u') sounds like the English 'k' e.g. *caro, costumbre, cultivar*
ce *ci* *z*	soft 'c' (before 'e' or 'i') and the letter 'z' sound like 'th' e.g. *doce* (do**th**eh); *cinco* (**th**inkoh); *diez* (die**th**)
NB In Latin America these are pronounced like an 's'.	
ch	sounds like English 'ch' in 'chop' e.g. ***ch**ica*
ga *go* *gu*	hard 'g' (before 'a'. 'o' or 'u') sounds like English 'g' in 'got' e.g. ***ga**to, **go**rdo, **gu**sto*
ge *gi* *j*	soft 'g' (before 'e' or 'i') and the letter 'j' sound like an 'h' produced from the back of the throat e.g. ***ge**ografía, **gi**mnasia, **j**amón*
h	the letter 'h' is always silent in Spanish e.g. *¡Hola!*
ll	the double consonant 'll' sounds like 'y' e.g. *me **ll**amo (meh yamo)*
ñ	accented 'ñ' sounds like 'ny' e.g. *Espa**ñ**a*
qu	always sounds like 'k' and never like 'kw' in Spanish e.g. *¿**Qué** tal?*
r	within a word always pronounced more strongly than in English, try to 'roll' or 'growl' it slightly e.g. *enero*
r	at the beginning of a word, *rr* within a word should be rolled quite strongly if you can e.g. ***R**oberto, pe**rr**o*
v	at the beginning of a word sounds like 'b' e.g. ***v**einte*

Now try saying these well-known Spanish-speaking places with the correct accent:

Barcelona **Argentina** **Lanzarote** **Venezuela** **Mallorca**

The alphabet sounds

A	ah	*B*	beh	*C*	theh
CH	cheh	*D*	deh	*E*	eh
F	efeh	*G*	jeh (back of your throat)	*H*	atcheh
I	ee	*J*	jota	*K*	kah
L	eleh	*LL*	eyeh	*M*	emeh
N	eneh	*Ñ*	enyeh	*O*	oh
P	peh	*Q*	koo	*R*	erreh
RR	erreh dobleh	*S*	eseh	*T*	teh
U	oo	*V*	ooveh	*W*	ooveh dobleh
X	ehkees	*Y*	eh greeyega	*Z*	thetah

Typing Spanish accents and punctuation

When typing in Spanish make sure you change the language by clicking on:

Tools > Language > Set language > Spanish (Spain – Traditional Sort)

The punctuation for ¿ and ¡ should then appear automatically.

The easiest way to get the accents on vowels is by pressing the Ctrl and @ keys at the same time, then remove your fingers from the keys and press the letter you want: *á; é; í; ó; ú*. To get the *ñ* you have to click on: Insert > symbol > then find *ñ*.

Alternatively, to type accents you can hold down the ALT key and type the appropriate number on the number pad. Make sure that the Number Lock is on. You can't do this on laptops.

160 = *á*	130 = *é*	161 = *í*	162 = *ó*
163 = *ú*	164 = *ñ*	168 = *¿*	173 = *¡*

Using a dictionary

Stress

Stress when pronouncing a language does not have the same meaning as 'being stressed out'. Stress is where you put the emphasis on a word, e.g. in English we say 'com**pu**ter' not '**com**puter'.

In Spanish the stress rules are:

- if a word ends in a vowel, an *n* or *s*: stress the second to last syllable.

  e.g. Bar / ce / **lo** / na   ex / **am** / en   **chi** / cos
- for words ending in the other consonants: stress the last syllable.

  e.g. pa / **pel**   pro / fe / **sor**   co / **mer**
- **BUT** some words don't follow these rules, so there is an accent to show you where to put the emphasis.

  e.g. ma / te / **má** / ti / cas   es / ta / **ción**
  jó / ven / es (but *joven* – no accent needed)

Note that all words ending in *-ón* and *-ión* need an accent on the *o*.

Using a dictionary

Spanish > English

- Make sure that you find the meaning that makes sense for the particular sentence you are translating. Many Spanish words have more than one meaning, e.g. *el tiempo* = time **and** weather. Some words mean different things in different Spanish-speaking countries as well.
- If you are trying to work out the meaning of a verb, you will have to find the infinitive in the dictionary (ending in *-ar*, *-er* or *-ir*) and then look at the verb ending to work out the person and tense of the verb.

  e.g. *grabaron* > *grabar* = to record

English > Spanish

- Make sure you know whether the word you need is a noun (a person, place or thing), a verb (usually an action) or an adjective (describes a noun).
- Sometimes the word in English can be the same.

Example of dictionary layout

Ignore the words in [ ]. They are to show Spanish speakers how to pronounce the English word.

light [laÎt] n. *luz* f.

English word | n. = noun | the Spanish noun 'light' | f. = feminine (you will need *la luz* for 'the light' and *una luz* for 'a light')

light [laÎt] adj. *ligero* (not heavy); *claro* (colour)

adj. = adjective | the Spanish adjectives for 'light' (two meanings)

light [laÎt] vt. *encender*

vt. / vi. = verb | the Spanish verb 'to light' (i.e. 'to light a candle')

- It is very important to understand that a dictionary will help you to find individual words but you have to use your knowledge of how the Spanish language works in order to put a sentence together. Very often the way a phrase is said is completely different from the English, e.g. *Me gusta el chocolate* literally means 'the chocolate pleases me', but we would say 'I like chocolate'.
- The most common mistake people make when using a dictionary is thinking that they can translate something literally word for word, without realising if the Spanish they have looked up is a noun, verb or adjective. The result can be quite funny for an English speaker who knows Spanish, but a Spanish speaker won't understand anything.

See if you can work out what the student wanted to say, then try to produce the correct version:

Yo lata la obra de teatro fútbol.

- *Yo* ('I') – not usually used with the verb
- *lata* ('can') – noun, e.g. a can of drink
- *la obra de teatro* ('play') – noun, e.g. a play at the theatre
- *fútbol* (football) – noun

Correct version: *puedo jugar al fútbol*.
puedo ('I can' – irregular verb, present tense); *jugar* (infinitive of verb 'to play'); *al fútbol* (*al* needed after *jugar* with a sport).

Glosario

A

abandonar to leave / abandon
abiertamente openly
el / la *abogado/a* lawyer
la *abuela* grandmother
el *abuelo* grandfather
aburrido/a boring
acabar to finish
el *acceso* access
el *accidente* accident
la *acción política* political action
el *acento* accent
acoger to welcome
el *acoso escolar* bullying
acostarse to go to bed
acostumbrado/a a accustomed to / used to
la *actitud* attitude
la *actividad* activity
me *acuesto* I go to bed
además also
adictivo/a addictive
el / la *adicto/a* addict
adjuntar to attach / enclose
el / la *adolescente* teenager
el / la *adulto* adult
el *aeropuerto* airport
afectar to affect
las *afueras* suburbs / outskirts
agradable pleasant
el *agua (f) corriente* running water
el *agua (f) mineral* mineral water
aguantar to tolerate / put up with
ahora now
ahorrar to save
el *aire* air
el *aire acondicionado* air conditioning
el *aire libre* open air
el *albañil* bricklayer
el *albergue juvenil* youth hostel
la *alcantarilla* drain
alcohólico/a alcoholic
el *alcoholismo* alcoholism
alegrarse to be pleased
alegre happy / cheerful
el *alemán* German (language)
Alemania Germany
la *alfombra* rug
algo something
alguno/a some
la *alimentación* food
el *alimento* food
allá over there
allí there
el *almuerzo* lunch
alojarse to stay
alquilar to hire
el *alquiler* hire
alrededor around
alto/a tall
el / la *alumno/a* pupil
amable nice / pleasant
el / la *amante* lover
la *ambición* ambition
el *ambiente* atmosphere / environment
el / la *amo/a de casa* house-husband / housewife
el *amor* love
el *andén* platform
animado/a lively
anoche last night
antes before
antiguo/a old
antipático/a unpleasant
el *anuncio* advert
apagar to turn off
el *aparcamiento* parking
el *apellido* surname
apoyar to support
el *apoyo* support
aprender to learn
el / la *aprendiz* apprentice
el *aprendizaje* apprenticeship / learning
aprobar to pass
aprovechar to make the most of
apuntarse to sign up
los *apuntes* notes
el *árbol* tree
la *arena* sand
el *armario* wardrobe
arreglar to tidy
me *arreglo* I get myself ready
arriba up
arroba @
el *arroz* rice
arruinar to ruin
el *arte dramático* drama
el *artículo* article
el *ascensor* lift
asegurar to ensure
el *aseo* toilet
así que so
el *asiento* seat
la *asignatura* subject
la *asistenta* maid
asqueroso/a awful
el *asunto* matter / topic
atacar to attack
el *atletismo* athletics
atrás back
el *aula (f)* classroom
aumentar to increase
aunque although
ausente absent
el *autocar* coach
la *autopista* motorway
la *aventura* adventure
el *avión* plane
la *ayuda* help
el *ayuntamiento* town hall
la *azafata* air stewardess
el *azúcar* sugar

B

el *bachillerato* equivalent of an A-level course
bailar to dance
el *baile* dance
bajar to drop / go down
bajo/a short (not tall)

el balcón balcony
el baloncesto basketball
bañarse to swim
la banda ancha broadband
la bañera bathtub
barato/a cheap
la barba beard
el barco boat
la barra slash
la barrera generacional generation gap
el barrio district / area / neighbourhood
bastante quite
bastar to be enough
la basura rubbish
la batería drums
beber to drink
la bebida drink
bebo I drink
el beneficio benefit
la biblioteca library
bien well
el bigote moustache
el billete ticket
la biología biology
el bistec steak
la blusa blouse
el bocadillo sandwich
el bolígrafo pen
la bolsa de plástico plastic bag
el / la bombero/a firefighter
bonito/a pretty
borracho/a drunk
el bosque forest
las botas boots
el botellón binge drinking
broncearse to sunbathe
lo bueno the good thing
buscar to look for
la butaca armchair
el buzón postbox / mailbox

C

el caballo horse
la cabeza head
cada every
el café coffee
el / la cajero/a cashier
los calcetines socks
la calculadora calculator
la calefacción heating
el calentamiento global global warming
la calidad quality
de buena calidad good quality
caliente warm
la calificación qualification
calificado/a qualified
callado/a quiet
callarse to be quiet
la calle street
caluroso/a hot
calvo/a bald
la cama de matrimonio double bed
la cámara digital digital camera
el / la camarero/a waiter / waitress
cambiar to change
el cambio climático climate change
a cambio de in exchange for
el / la camionero/a lorry driver
la camisa shirt
la camiseta t-shirt
el campamento camp
el campeonato championship
el campo field / countryside
el campo de deporte sports field
el canabis cannabis
el cáncer cancer
la cancha (de baloncesto) (basketball) court
la canción song
el / la candidato/a candidate
cansado/a tired
la cantidad quantity
la cantina canteen
canto I sing
capaz capable
el caramelo sweet
la cárcel prison
cargar to load
cariñoso/a affectionate
la carne meat
el carné joven student card
el carnet de conducir driving licence
el carnet / documento de identidad (DNI) ID
el / la carnicero/a butcher
caro/a expensive
la carpeta folder / file
el carpintero joiner
la carrera profession / race
la carretera road
la carta letter
el/ la cartero/a postman/ postwoman
el cartón cardboard
la casa house
una casa adosada semi-detached / terraced house
casado/a married
casarse to get married
casi almost
castaño/a brown
castigar to punish
el castigo punishment
el castillo castle
la catástrofe natural natural disaster
catorce fourteen
causar to cause
el CD (el disco compacto) CD (compact disc)
celebrar to celebrate
celoso/a jealous
la cena evening meal
el centro the centre
el centro comercial shopping centre
cerca (de) close (to)
cercano/a near
los cereales cereal
cero zero
el césped lawn
un chalé / chalet detached house
la chaqueta jacket
charlar to chat
chatear to chat (online)
el cheque de viaje traveller's cheque
la chica girl
el chicle chewing gum
el chico boy
la chimenea fireplace / chimney

el chiringuito refreshment stand
el chocolate chocolate
el chorizo Spanish sausage
el ciclismo cycling
el cielo sky
cien, ciento one hundred
la ciencia ficción science fiction
las ciencias science
las ciencias económicas economics
ciento uno (ciento una) one hundred and one
por cierto certainly
el cigarrillo cigarette
cinco five
cinco mil five thousand
cincuenta fifty
el cine cinema
el cinturón belt
la cita appointment
la clase class
el clima climate
la clínica clinic
el club de jóvenes youth club
el club taurino bullfighting club
el / la cobarde coward
la cobaya guinea pig
la cocaína cocaine
el coche car
(la) cocina kitchen / food technology
la cocina (de gas / eléctrica) (gas / electric) cooker
el / la cocinero/a chef
coger to pick / take
el colegio school
el collar necklace
el combustible fuel
la comedia comedy
el comedor dining room
el comentario comment
comenzar to begin
comer to eat
el / la comerciante trader / shopkeeper
el comercio commerce / shop / business studies
cometer to commit
cómico/a funny
la comida food
la comida basura junk food
la comida rápida fast food
la comisaría police station
como I eat
la comodidad comfort
cómodo/a comfortable
el / la compañero/a companion / friend
la compañía company
comparar to compare
compartir to share
competente competent
el comportamiento behaviour
comportarse to behave
comprar to buy
ir de compras to go shopping
comprender to understand
la comprensión understanding
comprensivo/a understanding
el compromiso commitment
común common
comunicando engaged (phone)
la comunidad community
las comunidades indígenas indigenous communities
el concierto concert
la condición condition
las condiciones de trabajo working conditions
conducir to drive
la conducta behaviour
el/ la conductor(a) driver
conectarse to connect
el conejo rabbit
confesar to confess
la confianza trust
conocer to meet / get to know
los conocimientos knowledge
la consecuencia consequence
conseguir to get / achieve
el consejo advice
considerar to consider
la consigna left-luggage office
una construcción nueva new development (housing)
construir to build
consumir to consume
el consumo consumption
el / la contable accountant
contactar to contact
la contaminación pollution
el contenedor container
contener to contain
contento/a happy
contestar to answer
contratar to take on / hire
el contrato contract
contribuir to contribute
convencer to convince
conversar to talk
la copa cup / trophy
la copia copy
el corazón heart
la corbata tie
el correo mail
el correo basura junk mail
el correo electrónico email
correr to run
la correspondencia mail / post
la corrida de toros bullfight
corro I run
las cortinas curtains
corto/a short (hair)
la cosa thing
la costa the coast
costar to cost
la costumbre custom / tradition
crecer to grow
el crimen crime
el cristal glass
criticar to criticize
el cruce junction / crossroad
el cuaderno exercise book
en cuanto sea posible as soon as possible
cuarenta forty
el cuarto de baño bathroom
el cuarto de huéspedes guest room
cuatro four
cuatrocientos four hundred

el *cubo de la basura* rubbish bin
cubrir to cover
la *cuchara* spoon
el *cuchillo* knife
el *cuero* leather
el *cuerpo* body
cuidar to look after
cultivar to grow
el *cumpleaños* birthday
el *curso* course / school year
cuyo whose

D

dañar to damage / spoil
el *daño* damage / harm
dar a to have a view of
los *deberes* homework
debido a because of / owing to
decepcionante disappointing
los *dedos* fingers / toes
dejar de (fumar) to stop (smoking)
delgado/a thin
delicioso/a delicious
demasiado/a too much / too many
democrático/a democratic
demostrar to show / demonstrate
el / la *dentista* dentist
por *dentro* inside
la *denuncia* complaint
el / la *dependiente/a* shop assistant
el *deporte* sport
los *deportes de invierno* winter sports
deportista sporty
los *derechos* rights
desaparecer to disappear
el *desarrollo* development
desastroso/a disastrous
el *desayuno* breakfast
descansar to rest
el *descanso* break / half-time / interval
descargar to download
el *descuento* discount
desde … a … from … to …
la *desigualdad* inequality
desobediente disobedient
el *despacho* office
despejado/a clear
me *despierto* I wake up
después after(wards)
destacar to emphasise
el *destino* destination
destruir to destroy
el *desván* loft
la *desventaja* disadvantage
el *detalle* detail
detestar to hate
la *deuda* debt
devolver to give back
el *día festivo* holiday / bank holiday
la *diarrea* diarrhoea
dibujar to draw
el *dibujo* art
los *dibujos animados* cartoons
el *diccionario* dictionary
diecinueve nineteen
dieciocho eighteen
dieciséis sixteen
diecisiete seventeen
la *dieta* diet
diez ten
diez mil ten thousand
la *diferencia* difference
difícil difficult
la *dificultad* difficulty
el *dinero* money
el / la *director(a)* head teacher
la *discriminación* discrimination
la *discusión* argument
diseñar to design
disfrutar to enjoy
disponer de to have available
la *distancia* distance
distinto/a different
la *diversión* entertainment
divertido/a fun
divertirse to have fun
divorciado/a divorced
doce twelve
dormir to sleep
el *dormitorio* bedroom
dos two
doscientos (doscientas) two hundred
dos mil two thousand
dos millones two million
la *droga* drug
el *drogadicto* drug addict
las *drogas blandas* soft drugs
las *drogas duras* hard drugs
la *ducha* shower
ducharse to have a shower
me *ducho* I shower
me *duermo* I go to sleep
el *dulce* sweet
durante during
durar to last
duro/a hard

E

la *economía* economy
la *edad* age
el *edificio* building
el *edredón nórdico* quilt
la *educación* education
la *educación física* PE
educar to educate
en *efectivo* in cash
el *efecto invernadero* greenhouse effect
egoísta selfish
el *ejecutivo* executive
el *ejercicio* exercise
el *ejército* army
la *electricidad* electricity
el / la *electricista* electrician
el *electrodoméstico* household appliance
embarazada pregnant
emborracharse to get drunk
las *emisiones* emissions
emocionante exciting
empezar to begin
el / la *empleado/a* employee
el *empleo* job
empotrado/a fitted
la *empresa* company / firm
enamorado/a in love

me *encanta(n)* I love
encargado/a de in charge of
encargarse de to be in charge of
encontrar to find / meet
la *encuesta* survey
la *energía* energy
enfadar to anger
enfadarse to get angry
la *enfermedad* illness / disease
la *enfermedad cardíaca* heart disease
el / la *enfermero/a* nurse
la *ensalada* salad
la *enseñanza* education
la *enseñanza secundaria* secondary education
enseñar to learn / teach
entender to understand
la *entrada* ticket / entry
la *entrada gratis* free entry
entrar to come in / enter
entregar to hand in
entretenido/a entertaining
la *entrevista* interview
el *entusiasmo* enthusiasm
entusiasta enthusiastic
el *envase* container
equilibrado/a balanced
el *equilibrio* balance
el *equipaje* luggage
el *equipo* team
el *equipo de música* music system
es is
la *escalera* stairs
la *escasez* scarcity
Escocia Scotland
escoger to choose
escribir to write
el / la *escritor(a)* writer
el *escritorio* desk
escuchar to listen (to)
escuchar música to listen to music
la *escuela* school
el *esfuerzo* effort
el *espacio* space
el *español* Spanish (language)
especial special
la *especialidad* speciality
el *espectáculo* performance / show
el *espectáculo de flamenco* flamenco show
el *espejo* mirror
la *esperanza* hope
esperar to wait
espiar to spy
la *esposa* wife
el *esposo* husband
estable stable
la *estación* station
la *estación de autobuses / trenes* bus / railway station
la *estación de esquí* ski resort
el *estadio* stadium
el *estado civil* marital status
los *Estados Unidos* the United States
las *estanterías* shelves
estar a favor to be in favour
estar cerrado/a to be closed
estar de acuerdo to agree
estar de moda to be fashionable
estar en contra to be against
estar en forma to be fit
estar en huelga to be on strike
estar estresado/a to be stressed
estar harto de to be fed up of
estar ocupado/a to be occupied
estar pintado/a to be painted
el *estereotipo* stereotype
estrecho/a narrow
el *estrés* stress
estresante stressful
estricto/a strict
el *estuche* pencil case
el / la *estudiante* student
estudiar to study
los *estudios* studies
estupendo/a great
la *evaluación* assessment
evitar to avoid
el *examen* exam
el *éxito* success
las *expectativas* expectations
la *experiencia laboral* experience of work
la *explicación* explanation
explicar to explain
el *éxtasis* ecstasy
la *extinción* extinction
extrañamente strangely
el *extranjero* foreigner / abroad
extrovertido/a extrovert / outgoing

F

la *fábrica* factory
fácil easy
la *falda* skirt
faltar to lack / be absent
fantástico/a fantastic
fascinante fascinating
fascinar to fascinate
me *fastidia* it annoys me
fastidiar to annoy
fatal awful
favorito/a favourite
la *fecha* date
feliz happy
femenino/a girls'
fenomenal great
feo/a ugly
fiable trustworthy
la *ficha* form
la *ficha de trabajo* worksheet
la *fiesta* party / festival
el *fin de semana* weekend
el *finde* weekend (colloquial)
la *física* physics
físico/a physical
la *flor* flower
la *formación* training
formal polite
fracasar to fail

el *fracaso* failure
el *francés* French (language)
el *fregadero* sink
fregar to wash (dishes)
fresco/a fresh
el / la *friolero/a* person who feels the cold
la *fruta* fruit
el *fuego artificial* firework
fuera away / outside
fumador smoking
el / la *fumador(a)* smoker
fumar to smoke
el *fumar pasivo* passive smoking
funcionar to work
el *futuro* the future

G

las *gafas* glasses
la *galleta* biscuit
ganar to earn
la *gaseosa* fizzy drink
la *gasolina* petrol
gastar to spend
los *gastos* expenses
el *gato* cat
el / la *gemelo/a* twin
generalmente usually
la *gente* people
la *geografía* geography
el *gerente* manager
la *gimnasia* gymnastics
el *gimnasio* gym
el / la *gitano/a* gypsy
glotón / glotona greedy
el *gobierno* government
golpear to hit
la *goma* eraser
gordo/a fat
la *gorra* cap / hat
gracioso/a funny
el *grado* degree
el *Gran Hermano* Big Brother
los *grandes almacenes* department stores
la *granja* farm
el / la *granjero/a* farmer
la *grasa* fat
grave serious
Grecia Greece
grueso/a thick
los *guantes* gloves
guapo/a good-looking
guardar to keep / save
el *guía* guide
la *guía* guidebook
el *guión bajo* underscore
la *guitarra* guitar
me *gusta(n)* I like

H

la *habitación* room
el / la *habitante* inhabitant
el *hábito* habit
hablador(a) chatty / talkative
hablo I talk
hace (un mes) (one month) ago
hace (dos semanas) (two weeks) ago
hacer to do
hacer falta to need / be needed
hacer la cama to make the bed
hacer la compra to do the shopping
hacer los deberes to do homework
hacer prácticas to do work experience
hacia towards
el *hambre* hunger
la *hamburguesa* hamburger
la *hamburguesería* hamburger joint
hasta up to / until
hay there is / there are
hay que you have to
hecho de made from
la *heladería* ice-cream parlour
el *helado* ice cream
la *herida* injury
la *hermana* sister
los *hermanastros* step-brothers and sisters
el *hermano* brother
la *heroína* heroin
el *hielo* ice
el *hígado* liver
la *hija* daughter
el *hijo* son
los *hijos* children
la *historia* history
el *hogar* home
la *hoja de papel* sheet of paper
el *hombre de negocios* businessman
honesto/a honest
honrado/a honest / honourable
a la *hora de* when it comes to
el *horario de trabajo* working hours
las *horas de trabajo flexibles* flexible working hours
horroroso/a horrific
el *huevo* egg
el *huracán* hurricane

I

el *idioma* language
la *iglesia* church
igual same
la *igualdad* equality
la *imagen* image
imitar to imitate
impaciente impatient
impedir to impede / prevent
impresionante impressive
el *impuesto* tax
el *incendio* fire
incluso even
incómodo/a uncomfortable
increíble incredible
independiente independent
industria industry
la *influencia* influence
la *información* information
la *informática* ICT
el / la *ingeniero/a* engineer
el *inglés* English (language)
la *injusticia* injustice
injusto/a unfair
el / la *inmigrante* immigrant
la *insolación* sunstroke

insolente insolent / cheeky
la *instalación* facility
las *instalaciones* facilities
el *instituto* school
insultar to insult
la *integración* integration
la *intención* intention
el *intercambio* exchange
interesante interesting
el / la *intérprete* interpreter
intimidar to intimidate / threaten
la *inundación* flood
el *invierno* winter
el / la *invitado/a* guest
invitar to invite
la *inyección* injection
ir to go
ir de camping to go camping
ir de compras to go shopping
ir de excursión to go on a trip
Irlanda Ireland
el / la *irlandés / irlandesa* Irishman/woman
irreversible irreversible
irse bien to fit / suit (of clothes, etc.)
la *isla* island
el *IVA* VAT

J

el *jamón* ham
el / la *jardinero/a* gardener
el / la *jefe/a* boss
joven young
los *jóvenes* young people
jubilado/a retired
jubilarse to retire
el *juego* game
el *jugador juvenil* youth team player
jugar to play
jugar a las cartas to play cards
el *juguete* toy
a mi *juicio* in my opinion

L

el *laboratorio* laboratory
el *ladrillo* brick
el *lago* lake
la *lámpara* lamp
la *lana* wool
los *lápices de colores* coloured pencils
el *lápiz* pencil
largo/a long
el *lavabo* handbasin
el *lavaplatos* dishwasher
me *lavo los dientes* I brush my teeth
la *lección* lesson
la *leche* milk
leer to read
las *legumbres* vegetables
lejos (de) far (from)
la *lengua* language
lentamente slowly
lento/a slow
la *letra* letter
levantar la mano to put your hand up
me *levanto* I get up
la *ley* law
la *libertad* freedom
libre free
la *librería* bookshop
el *libro* book
el *libro de guía* guidebook
el / la *líder* leader
ligero/a light
limitado/a limited
limpiar el cuarto de baño to clean the bathroom
limpio/a clean
la *línea* line
liso/a straight
la *literatura* literature
la *llamada* call
llamar (por teléfono) to call / telephone
la *llegada* arrival
llegar to arrive / get to
llegar a ser to become
lleno/a full
llevar to wear
llevar una vida (sana) to lead a (healthy) life
llevarse bien / mal con to get on (well / badly) with
loco/a mad
luchar to fight
luego then
el *lugar* place
en *lugar de* instead of
la *luz* light

M

la *madre* mother
la *madre soltera* single mother
maduro/a mature
mal badly
mal diseñado/a badly designed
maleducado/a rude
la *maleta* suitcase
lo *malo* the bad thing
maltratar to abuse
mandar to send
la *manera* way
las *manos* hands
mantener to keep
mantenerse en forma to keep fit
el *mapa* map
la *máquina* machine
maravillosamente wonderfully
maravilloso/a marvellous
la *marca (la ropa de marca)* make (designer clothes)
marcar un número to dial a number
el *marido* husband
los *mariscos* seafood
más more
más de more than
masculino boys
matar to kill
las *matemáticas* maths
el *matrimonio* marriage
máximo/a maximum
mayor older
la *mayoría* the majority
el / la *mecánico/a* mechanic

la medianoche midnight
media pensión half board
las medias stockings / tights
el / la médico/a doctor
la medida measure
el medio ambiente environment
en medio de in the middle of
por medio through the middle
el / la mejor the best
lo mejor the best
mejor better
mejorar to improve
menos less
el mensaje message
el mensajero instantáneo Instant Messenger
a menudo often
el mercado market
el metro underground train system
la mezquita mosque
el microondas microwave (oven)
mientras while
mientras que while
mil thousand
mil dos one thousand and two
el militar soldier
un millón million
mínimo/a minimum
mirar to look at / watch
al mismo tiempo at the same time
mixto/a mixed
la mochila rucksack / school bag
la moda fashion
moderno/a modern
mojarse to get wet
me molesta it bothers me
molestar to annoy
de momento at the moment
la montaña mountain
la montaña rusa roller coaster (theme park ride)
montar to ride / go on a ride (at a theme park)
montar a caballo to go horse riding
montar en bici to ride a bike
la moqueta fitted carpet
moreno/a (dark) brown
morir to die
mostrar to show
motivar to motivate
una moto(cicleta) motorbike
el móvil (teléfono móvil) mobile (mobile phone)
el mueble furniture
la muerte death
muerto/a dead
la mujer woman
la multa fine
el mundo world
el mundo laboral the world of work
el museo museum
la música music
muy very

N

el nacimiento birth
la nacionalidad nationality
nadar to swim
nadie no one
la naranja orange
la nariz nose
la natación swimming
la naturaleza nature
navegar la red to surf the internet
navegar por Internet to surf the internet
la Navidad Christmas
necesario/a necessary
necesitar to need
el negocio business
la nevera / el frigorífico fridge
la nieta granddaughter
el nieto grandson
la nieve snow
la niñera nanny
el / la niño/a child
el nivel level
el nivel del mar sea level
la Nochebuena Christmas Eve
la Nochevieja New Year's Eve
nocivo/a harmful
no fumador no smoking
no hacer nada to do nothing
el nombre (first) name
la nota mark
notable very good
las notas marks
las noticias news
novecientos nine hundred
noventa ninety
la novia girlfriend
el novio boyfriend
el nuestro / la nuestra ours
nueve nine
nuevo/a new
numeroso/a large / numerous
nunca never

O

el objetivo aim / objective
obligatorio/a compulsory
las obras building work
el /la obrero/a worker
observar to observe
obtener to get / obtain
ochenta eighty
ocho eight
ochocientos eight hundred
el ocio leisure
odiar to hate
ofender to offend
la oferta (especial) (special) offer
la oficina office
ofrecer to offer
los ojos eyes
el olor smell
olvidar to forget
olvidarse to forget
once eleven
la ONG (Organización No Gubernamental) NGO (non-governmental organisation)
la opción option
la oportunidad opportunity / chance
optar to choose / opt

optativo/a optional
el *ordenador* computer
el *ordenador portátil (el portátil)* laptop computer (laptop)
las *orejas* ears
la *organización benéfica* charity
orgulloso/a proud
el *otoño* autumn
el *oxígeno* oxygen

P

paciente patient
el *padrastro* stepfather
el *padre* father
la *paga* pocket money
pagar to pay
pagar bien to pay well
pagar mal to pay badly
la *página* page
el *país* country
el *pájaro* bird
la *palabra* word
las *palomitas* popcorn
el / la *panadero/a* baker
los *pantalones* trousers
Papá Noel Father Christmas
el *paquete* parcel / packet
la *parada* stop
el *parador* state-run hotel
el *paraguas* umbrella
parecer to seem
parecido/a similar
la *pared* wall
la *pareja* couple
los *parientes* relatives
el *paro* unemployment
en el *paro* unemployed
el *parque infantil* playground
el *parque temático* theme park
la *participación* participation
participar to participate
el *partido* game / match
el *pasaporte* passport
pasar to spend (time)
pasar la aspiradora to hoover
pasar lista to take the register
pasarlo bien / mal to have a good / bad time
el *pasatiempo* hobby
pasearse to walk / stroll
el *pasillo* hallway
el *pastel* cake
las *patatas fritas* chips / crisps
las *pecas* freckles
pedir to ask for
pedir permiso to ask for permission
pelearse to fight
la *película* film
la *película de acción* action film / thriller
la *película de horror* horror film
la *película romántica* romantic film
el *peligro* danger
peligroso/a dangerous
pelirrojo/a red-haired
el *pelo* hair
la *peluquería* hairdresser's
el / la *peluquero/a* hairdresser
los *pendientes* earrings
pensar to think
pensión completa full board
peor worse / worst
el *periodismo* journalism
el / la *periodista* journalist
el *periquito* parakeet
el *permiso* permission
el *permiso de conducir* driving licence
se *permite (fumar)* (smoking) is allowed
pero but
el *perrito caliente* hot dog
la *persiana* blind
la *pesadilla* nightmare
el *pescado* fish
pesimista pessimistic
el *petróleo* oil
picante spicy
a *pie* on foot
la *piedra* stone
los *pies* feet
el *ping-pong* table tennis
el / la *pintor(a)* painter
el *piso* flat (housing)
la *pista* ski slope / runway
la *pizarra* board
las *placas solares* solar panels
planchar to do the ironing
los *planes* plans
el *planeta* planet
la *planta* floor / storey
el *plátano* banana
el *plato* dish
la *plaza* square
la *plaza de toros* bullring
la *población* population
pobre poor
los *pobres* poor people
la *pobreza* poverty
un *poco* a little
poco/a little / few
el / la *policía* police officer
el / la *político/a* politician
el *pollo* chicken
el *polo norte* north pole
poner de los nervios to get on one's nerves
ponerse to put on (clothes)
ponerse a to begin to
ponerse de pie to stand up
por eso therefore
por lo tanto therefore
por otro lado on the other hand
porque because
el *porro* joint / hash
la *postal* postcard
practicar to do
practicar deporte to play sport
practicar la pesca to go fishing
las *prácticas laborales* work experience
el *precio* price
precioso/a beautiful
preferir to prefer

la *pregunta* question
preguntar to ask
el *prejuicio* prejudice
la *preocupación* worry
preocupado/a worried
preocupante worrying
preocupar(se) to worry
preparar to prepare
la *presentación (oral)* (oral) presentation
presente present
la *presión* pressure
el *préstamo* lending
la *prima* female cousin
primario/a primary
la *primavera* spring
primera clase first class
los *primeros auxilios* first aid
el *primo* male cousin
al *principio* at first
privado/a private
probar to have a go / try
probarse to try on
el *problema* problem
producir to produce
el *producto* product
el / la *profesor(a)* teacher
el *programa* programme
la *prohibición* ban
prohibido/a banned
prometer to promise
pronto soon / ready
la *propina* tip
proporcionar to provide
el *propósito* aim
proteger to protect
la *proteína* protein
provocar to cause / provoke
la *prueba* test
la *publicidad* advertising
público/a public ('state' when referring to schools)
el *puerto* port
los *pulmones* lungs
punto dot
puntocom .com
el *punto de vista* point of view
puro/a pure / clean

Q

quedarse to stay
la *queja* complaint
quejarse to complain
quemar to burn
querer decir to mean
el *queso* cheese
quiero I want
la *química* chemistry
quince fifteen
quinientos five hundred

R

el *racismo* racism
racista racist
rápidamente quickly
raro/a strange
el *rato / un rato* (short) time / a little while
la *reacción* reaction
realista realistic
el / la *recepcionista* receptionist
recibir to receive
reciclable recyclable
reciclar to recycle
reconocer to recognise
el *recreo* break (time)
el *recuerdo* memory
el *recurso* resource
reducir to reduce
regalar to give (as a present)
el *regalo* present
la *regla* ruler / rule
regresar to return
la *rehabilitación* rehabilitation
reír to laugh
relacionarse to relate to / get to know
relajarse to relax
la *religión* religion
rellenar to fill in
RENFE State railway in Spain
renovable renewable
repartir to share / give out
repasar to revise
la *residencia para ancianos* retirement home
el *residuo* waste
los *residuos químicos* chemical waste
respetar to respect
el *respeto* respect
respirar to breathe
respiratorio/a breathing / respiratory
la *responsabilidad* responsibility
responsable responsible
la *respuesta* reply / answer
el *resultado* result
el *resumen* summary
el *retraso* delay
reutilizar to reuse
la *revista* magazine
rico/a tasty / rich
riguroso/a strict / tough
rizado/a curly
las *rodillas* knees
la *ropa* clothes
rubio/a blond
el *ruido* noise
ruidosamente noisily
la *rutina* routine

S

saber to know
el *sacapuntas* pencil sharpener
sacar la basura take out the rubbish
sacar buenas notas to get good marks
sacar malas notas to get bad marks
el *saco de dormir* sleeping bag
la *sala de espera* waiting room
la *sala de profesores* staff room
el *salario* salary
salgo I leave / go out
la *salida* exit
salir to go out
salir con los amigos to go out with friends
el *salón* lounge

el *salón de actos* assembly hall
la *salud* health
saludable healthy
sanitario/a sanitary / health
sano/a healthy
el *santo* saint's day
el / la *secretario/a* secretary
secundario/a secondary
según according to
de *segunda mano* second hand
la *seguridad* safety
seguro/a safe / secure / sure
el *seguro (del coche)* (car) insurance
seis six
seiscientos (seiscientas) six hundred
el *sello* stamp
la *selva* jungle
las *selvas tropicales* tropical forests
los *semáforos* traffic lights
la *semana* week
la *Semana Santa* Easter Holidays / Holy Week
sencillo/a simple
la *sensación* sensation
sensible sensitive
el *sentimiento* feeling
separado/a separated
separar to separate
la *sequía* drought
la *serie policíaca* crime series
seropositivo/a HIV positive
sesenta sixty
setecientos (setecientas) seven hundred
setenta seventy
severo/a strict
la *sidra* cider
siempre always
la *sierra* mountain range
siete seven
el *silencio* silence
simpático/a nice
sin duda without a doubt
sin embargo nevertheless / however
sin techo homeless
el *sitio* place
la *situación* situation
el *sobre* envelope
la *sobrepoblación* overpopulation
sobresaliente excellent
la *sociedad* society
el / la *socorrista* lifeguard
solamente only
el *soldado* soldier
solicitar to apply
la *solicitud* application
solo/a alone
sólo only
soltar to release
soltero/a single
la *solución* solution
solucionar to solve
la *sombrilla* sunshade
son are
el *sondeo* survey
la *sopa* soup
el *sótano* cellar / basement
suave gentle
subir to go up / rise
la *suciedad* dirt
el *sueldo* salary
el *suelo* the floor
el *sueño* sleep / dream
sufrir to suffer
la *sugerencia* suggestion
el *supermercado* supermarket
el *suplemento* supplement
suspender to fail

T

el *tabaco* smoking / tobacco
la *talla* size (clothes, shoes, etc.)
el *taller* workshop
los *talones* heels
tal vez perhaps
el *tamaño* size
también also
tampoco nor
(ni) *tampoco* neither
tan so
tanto/a so much
las *tapas* snacks
la *taquilla* ticket office
tardar to take (time)
tarde late
la *tarea* task
la *tarjeta* card
la *tarjeta de crédito* credit card
la *tarta* cake / tart
la *tasa* rate
el *teatro* theatre
el *techo* roof
la *tecnología* technology
la *telenovela* soap opera
el *teletrabajo* working from home
la *televisión plana* flatscreen television
el *tema* theme / topic
temprano early
el *tenedor* fork
tener to have
tener derecho a to have the right to
tener dolor de (cabeza) to have a (head)ache
tener hambre to be hungry
tener miedo to be afraid
tener nervios to be nervous
tener que to have to
tener razón to be right
tener sed to be thirsty
tener sueño to be tired
tengo I have
el *tenis* tennis
terminar to finish
la *terraza* terrace
el *terreno* land
el *terrorismo* terrorism
el *texto* text
la *tía* aunt
a *tiempo completo* full time
el *tiempo libre* free time
a *tiempo parcial* part time
la *tienda* tent / shop
la *tienda de ropa* clothes shop
las *tijeras* scissors

tímido/a shy
el *tío* uncle
típico/a typical
el *tipo* type
tirar to throw / throw away
el *título* university degree
el *tobillo* ankle
te *toca a ti* it's up to you / it's your turn
tocar to play (a musical instrument)
todavía still
la *tolerancia* tolerance
tomar to have (breakfast / food / drink) / to take
tomar el sol to sunbathe
tomar un año libre / sabático to have a gap year
torear to fight bulls
torpe clumsy
una *torre / un bloque* tower block
la *tortilla* omelette
la *tortuga* tortoise
la *tostada* toast
tóxico/a poisonous / toxic
el / la *trabajador(a)* worker
trabajador(a) hard-working
trabajar to work
el *trabajo* work
los *trabajos manuales* craft subjects
traducir to translate
el / la *traductor(a)* translator
el *tráfico* traffic
el *traje* costume / outfit
el *traje de luces* bullfighter's suit
tranquilo/a quiet / calm
el *transporte público* public transport
el *tratamiento* treatment
tratar to treat
travieso/a naughty
trece thirteen
treinta thirty
treinta y uno (treinta y una) thirty-one
el *tren* train
el *tren de cercanías* local train
tres three
trescientos (trescientas) three hundred
el *trimestre* term
triste sad
el *triunfo* triumph / success
el / la *tutor(a)* tutor

U

único/a only
el *uniforme* uniform
la *universidad* university
uno one
usar to use
útil useful
utilizar to use
la *uva* grape

V

vago/a lazy
vale la pena it's worth
valer to be worth
los *vaqueros* jeans
variado/a varied
a *veces* sometimes
el / la *vecino/a* neighbour
vegetariano/a vegetarian
veinte twenty
veintiuno (veintiuna) twenty-one
la *velocidad* speed
la *ventaja* advantage
la *ventana* window
ver to see / watch (a film / television)
veranear to spend your summer holidays
el *verano* summer
las *verduras* green vegetables
el *vertedero* rubbish tip
el *vertido* spillage
el *vestido* dress
los *vestuarios* changing rooms
el / la *veterinario/a* vet
de *vez en cuando* from time to time
la *vía* track
viajar to travel
la *víctima* victim
la *vida* life
la *vida campesina* country life
la *vida familiar* family life
la *videoconsola* video console
el *videojuego* video game
el *vidrio* glass
viejo/a old
el *vino* wine
la *violencia* violence
la *violencia doméstica* domestic violence
la *vista* view
me *visto* I get dressed
la *vitamina* vitamin
la *viuda* widow
el *viudo* widower
en *vivo* live (music)
el *vocabulario* vocabulary
volver to return
el *voto* vote
la *voz* voice
el *vuelo* flight
vuelvo I return

Y

y and
ya no no longer
ya que because
el *yogur* yogurt

Z

la *zapatería* shoe shop
las *zapatillas de deporte* trainers
los *zapatos* shoes
una *zona céntrica* central area
el *zumo (de naranja)* (orange) juice

Acknowledgements

Illustrations:
Kathy Baxendale pp9, 10, 13, 16, 19, 25, 26, 35, 63, 66, 70, 83, 94, 97, 100, 121, 135, 142, 149, 151, 156; Rafa Ramos p68; Mark Draisey pp58, 81, 112; Dylan Gibson pp12, 14, 28, 41, 99, 106; Celia Hart pp11, 12, 17, 57, 79, 85, 105, 141, 142, 149, 159

Photographs courtesy of:
p9 © Creatista. Image from BigStockPhoto.com, © iStockphoto.com / francisblack, © matka_Wariatka / Shutterstock, Inc, © Juriah. Image from BigStockPhoto.com, © Olga Sapegina / 123rf.com, © Rui Vale De Sousa / 123rf.com; p15 © iStockphoto.com / Vera-g; p18 © iStockphoto.com / Stockphoto4u, © ejwhite. Image from BigStockPhoto.com, © i love images / Alamy, © Agencja FREE / Alamy; p20 © iStockphoto.com / beckyrockwood, © Mandy Godbehear / 123rf.com, © Beth Van Trees – Fotolia.com; p22 © iStockphoto.com / Juanmonino, © iStockphoto.com / pink_cotton_candy, © iStockphoto.com / aabejon; p24 © phildate. Image from BigStockPhoto.com, © 123rf.com; p26 © iStockphoto.com / juanestey, © Mandy Godbehear / 123rf.com; p27 © iStockphoto.com / eyecrave, © iStockphoto.com / Juanmonino, © Raisa Kanareva – Fotolia.com, © iStockphoto.com / kevinruss; p32 © Fotowerner – Fotolia.com, © iStockphoto.com / chrisboy2004, © iStockphoto.com / TriggerPhoto, © Paha_L. Image from BigStockPhoto.com, © Yuri Arcurs – Fotolia.com, © iStockphoto.com / jordanchez; p34 © andres. Image from BigStockPhoto.com, © Jon Feingersh / zefa / Corbis, © iStockphoto.com / jgroup, © Cathy Yeulet / 123rf.com, © iStockphoto.com / Juanmonino, © andres. Image from BigStockPhoto.com; p36 © John Birdsall / Alamy, © Design Pics Inc. / Alamy, © iStockphoto.com / digitalskillet; p38 © Cathy Yeulet / 123rf.com, © Moodboard / 123rf.com, © drx – Fotolia.com; p40 © andres. Image from BigStockPhoto.com, © nruboc. Image from BigStockPhoto.com, © sokolovsky – Fotolia.com; p42 © iStockphoto.com / follow777, © Thomas Cockrem / Alamy, © Jacques Jangoux / Alamy; p44 © PondShots – Fotolia.com; p54 © Creatista / Shutterstock, Inc; p55 © iStockphoto.com / matthewleesdixon; p58 © iStockphoto.com / LeggNet; p60 © Christopher Nolan – Fotolia.com, © iStockphoto.com / dwphotos, © Rui Araújo – Fotolia.com, © Kevin Dodge / Corbis, © iStockphoto.com / barsik, © Ingolf Pompe 54 / Alamy, © Frances Roberts / Alamy, © Trutta – Fotolia.com; p61 © Dndavis / 123rf.com, © loutocky – Fotolia.com, © Iriza. Image from BigStockPhoto.com, © iStockphoto.com / davidf; p62 © Monkey Business – Fotolia.com, © Media Minds / Alamy; p64 © iStockphoto.com / hidesy, © Rui Vale de Sousa – Fotolia.com, © iStockphoto.com / jhorrocks, © Geo Martinez / 123rf.com; p66 © Ken Hurst – Fotolia.com, © lenm. Image from BigStockPhoto.com, © iStockphoto.com / Quirex; p74 © Greg Balfour Evans / Alamy, © Denis Babenko – Fotolia.com, © PhotoAlto / Ale Ventura / Getty Images, © Sergey Mostovoy – Fotolia.com; p76 © Walter Luger – Fotolia.com, © Melissa Schalke / 123rf.com, © iStockphoto.com / Dancer01, © iStockphoto.com / podgorsek; p78 © Lola. Image from BigStockPhoto.com, © korgan75 – Fotolia.com, © Endos / Alamy, © Oliver Gerhard / Alamy; p80 © Life File Photo Library Ltd / Alamy, © Atlanpic / Alamy; p82 © iStockphoto.com / dimol, © iStockphoto.com / dyana_by, © Charles O. Cecil / Alamy, © Graça Victoria – Fotolia.com, © iStockphoto.com / jeffwang; p94 © iStockphoto.com / vgajic p93 © Freefly – Fotolia.com; p96 © iStockphoto.com / Juanmonino; p98 © iStockphoto.com / sleddogtwo, © iStockphoto.com / grekoff, © iStockphoto.com / cunfek, © AFP / Getty Images, © xmasbaby. Image from BigStockPhoto.com; p101 © iStockphoto.com / filo, © iStockphoto.com / buzbuzzer, © iStockphoto.com / THEPALMER, © hmproudlove. Image from BigStockPhoto.com; p102 © mpworks / Alamy, © iStockphoto.com / infospeed; p104 © Tilio & Paolo – Fotolia.com, © Charlene. Image from BigStockPhoto.com; p112 © Eva Madrazo / 123rf.com; p114 © Byron Moore – Fotolia.com, © iStockphoto.com / Snowleopard1; p118 © Milanka Petkova – Fotolia.com, © Erkki Tamsalu – Fotolia.com; p128 © babenkodenis. Image from BigStockPhoto.com; p129 © iStockphoto.com / Anton Seleznev; p130 © iStockphoto.com / aldomurillo; p131 © John Cole / Alamy, © David R. Frazier Photolibrary, Inc. / Alamy; p132 © JonnyB – Fotolia.com; p134 © picsfive – Fotolia.com; p136 © iStockphoto.com / track5; p137 © Jan Will – Fotolia.com; p138 © Petro Feketa. Image from BigStockPhoto.com, © Ablestock Premium / 123rf.com; p140 © Moodboard / 123rf.com; p143 © iStockphoto.com / hidesy; p146 © erwinova – Fotolia.com; p148 © Radovan Kraker – Fotolia.com, © Cathy Yeulet / 123rf.com, © monkeybusinessimages. Image from BigStockPhoto.com, © robertpinna – Fotolia.com, © iStockphoto.com / izusek; p150 © iStockphoto.com / Pinopic; p152 © debbiesuniques – Fotolia.com; p154 © Jake Hellbach / 123rf.com, © iStockphoto.com / erierika, © andres. Image from BigStockPhoto.com; p155 © iStockphoto.com / miguelinus; p157 © Mika / zefa / Corbis; p158 © AVAVA – Fotolia.com; p166 © Peter Horree / Alamy

Every effort has been made to contact the copyright holders and we apologise if any have been overlooked and would be happy to rectify any errors or omissions at the first opportunity.